HOME REPAIR AND IMPROVEMENT

BATHROOMS

TIME®
LIFE
BOOKS

Other Publications
VOICES OF THE CIVIL WAR
THE TIME-LIFE COMPLETE GARDENER
JOURNEY THROUGH THE MIND AND BODY
WEIGHT WATCHERS® SMART CHOICE RECIPE COLLECTION
TRUE CRIME
THE AMERICAN INDIANS
THE ART OF WOODWORKING
LOST CIVILIZATIONS
ECHOES OF GLORY
THE NEW FACE OF WAR
HOW THINGS WORK
WINGS OF WAR
CREATIVE EVERYDAY COOKING
COLLECTOR'S LIBRARY OF THE UNKNOWN
CLASSICS OF WORLD WAR II
TIME-LIFE LIBRARY OF CURIOUS AND UNUSUAL FACTS
AMERICAN COUNTRY
VOYAGE THROUGH THE UNIVERSE
THE THIRD REICH
MYSTERIES OF THE UNKNOWN
TIME FRAME
FIX IT YOURSELF
FITNESS, HEALTH AND NUTRITION
SUCCESSFUL PARENTING
HEALTHY HOME COOKING
UNDERSTANDING COMPUTERS
LIBRARY OF NATIONS
THE ENCHANTED WORLD
THE KODAK LIBRARY OF CREATIVE PHOTOGRAPHY
GREAT MEALS IN MINUTES
THE CIVIL WAR
PLANET EARTH
COLLECTOR'S LIBRARY OF THE CIVIL WAR
THE EPIC OF FLIGHT
THE GOOD COOK
WORLD WAR II
THE OLD WEST

For information on and a full description of any of the Time-Life Books series listed above, please call 1-800-621-7026 or write:
Reader Information
Time-Life Customer Service
P.O. Box C-32068
Richmond, Virginia 23261-2068

HOME REPAIR AND IMPROVEMENT

BATHROOMS

BY THE EDITORS OF TIME-LIFE BOOKS, ALEXANDRIA, VIRGINIA

The Consultants

Jeff Palumbo is a registered journeyman carpenter who has a home-building and remodeling business in northern Virginia. His interest in carpentry was sparked by his grandfather, a master carpenter with more than 50 years' experience. Mr. Palumbo teaches in the Fairfax County Adult Education Program.

Mark M. Steele is a professional home inspector in the Washington, D.C., area. He has developed and conducted training programs in home-ownership skills for first-time homeowners. He appears frequently on television and radio as an expert in home repair and other consumer topics.

John E. Shreve is a past secretary, treasurer, vice president, and president of the Virginia Association of Plumbing, Heating, and Cooling Contractors. He is president of Shreve/McGonegal Inc., Falls Church, Virginia, which is a parent firm for several companies in the plumbing, remodeling, and related fields.

CONTENTS

1 Common Bathroom Repairs

With surprisingly little time and effort, you can apply the methods described in the following pages to end drips, clogs, and other bathroom annoyances—and to replace worn-out fittings with attractive new ones. Keeping up with repairs not only makes your bathroom more comfortable, it also may prevent small problems from turning into big ones, as when an uncorrected leak damages the floor or walls.

Drain assembly—with pop-up plug—for a bathroom washbasin →

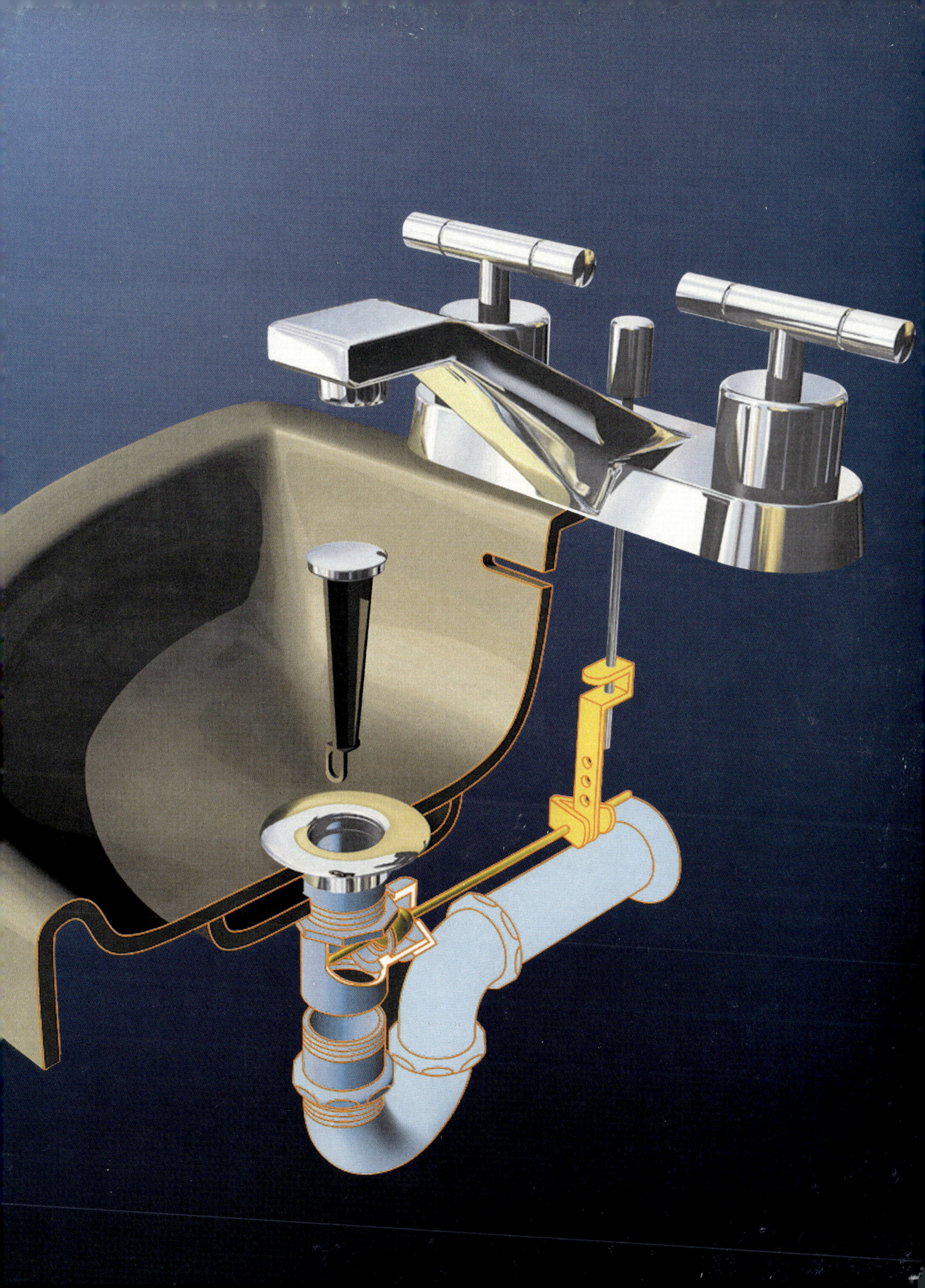

Replacing a Broken Accessory

Towel bars or a soap dish can be a handy addition to a tiled bathroom wall, but an accessory can be an eyesore if it breaks or is damaged. As shown below and at right, you can often replace the damaged item with no harm to the wall. Work carefully to avoid cracking nearby tiles, and keep them from loosening by laying strips of masking tape from one tile to the next.

A Variety of Accessories: Flush-set accessories, such as the soap dish below, are attached directly to the same backing that the tiles are mounted on. To avoid exposing the backing, replace a flush-set accessory with one of the same dimensions or slightly larger. Other accessories, such as the towel bar at right, are mounted to the tile surface. Replace a surface-mounted accessory with another that will attach to the same tiles; in the case of a towel bar, the new bar should be the same length as the one it replaces, so that its brackets rest on the same pair of tiles.

Some older bathrooms have recessed accessories, which are sunk into the tiled wall. You can often unscrew a recessed toilet-paper holder from its mounting bracket and install a new one, but a recessed soap dish or other sort of shelf cannot be replaced without extensive retiling.

TOOLS

- Cold chisel
- Ball-peen hammer
- Putty knife
- Grout saw
- Punch
- Electric drill with carbide-tipped masonry bit
- Screwdriver
- Hex wrench

SAFETY TIPS

Wear goggles as you free the accessory with hammer and chisel and whenever you drill into tile.

SETTING A SOAP DISH INTO A TILE WALL

1. Removing the old soap dish.

◆ Protect the tile at the edge of the soap dish with masking tape. Hold down the nearby tiles with more tape.

◆ Remove any caulk or grout around the soap dish, then position a cold chisel at its edge. Tap with a ball-peen hammer *(above)* until the dish comes free.

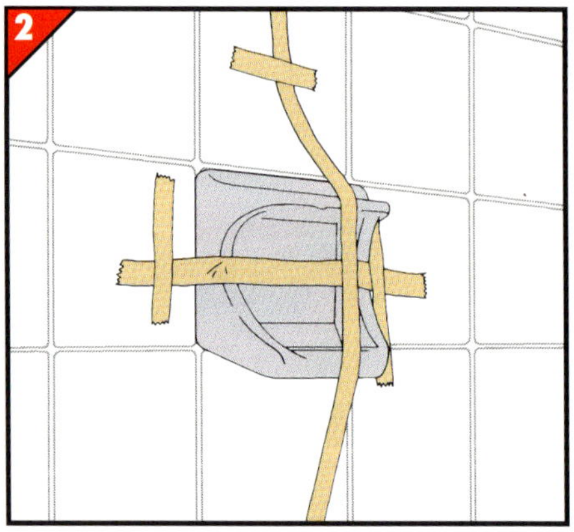

2. Positioning the new soap dish.

◆ Remove the tape and clean the exposed area with a putty knife.

◆ Apply silicone tile adhesive to the new soap dish, press it into place, and secure it with masking tape *(above)*.

◆ After 24 hours, take off the tape and grout the joints around the soap dish.

A SURFACE-MOUNTED TOWEL BAR

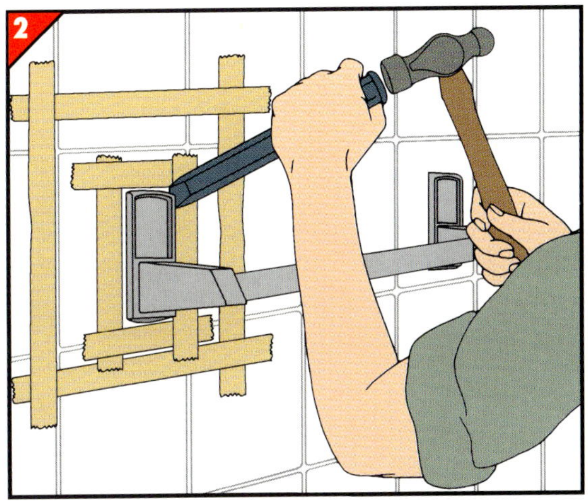

1. Preparing the surface.

◆ With a grout saw, cut out the grout around each tile to which the towel bar is attached *(above)*; this will help minimize any movement of the adjacent tiles as you work.

◆ Lay strips of masking tape around the edges of the towel bar's mounting brackets. For each bracket, add a square of masking tape over the nearby tiles.

2. Removing the old towel bar.

If you can, remove the old towel bar from its mounting brackets and unscrew the brackets. For brackets secured not with screws but with adhesive, place a cold chisel against each bracket and tap with a ball-peen hammer *(above)* to free it. Clean the exposed area and make sure any marred surface will be covered by the mounting brackets of the new towel bar you select.

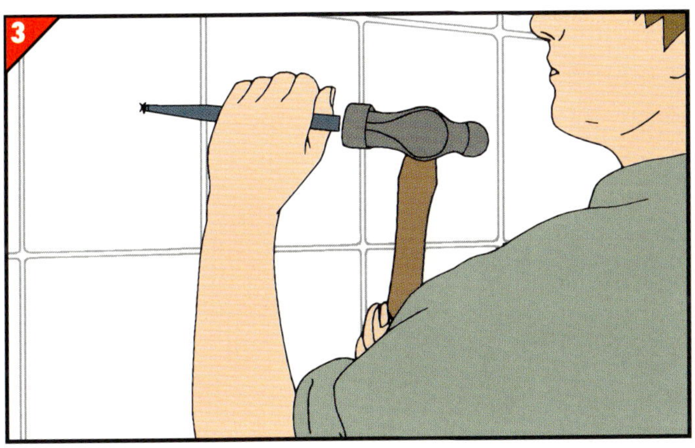

3. Preparing the wall for drilling.

For screw-mounted brackets, check whether you can reuse the old screw holes; otherwise, drill new holes large enough for hollow-wall anchors.

◆ Hold a bracket in place; if it has tapered edges, position them at top and bottom. Mark the screw hole. Position the second bracket with a level and mark that hole as well. With a punch, make an indentation on each mark *(left)*.

◆ Fit an electric drill with a carbide-tipped masonry bit; keeping the drill speed as low as possible, make a hole at each indentation.

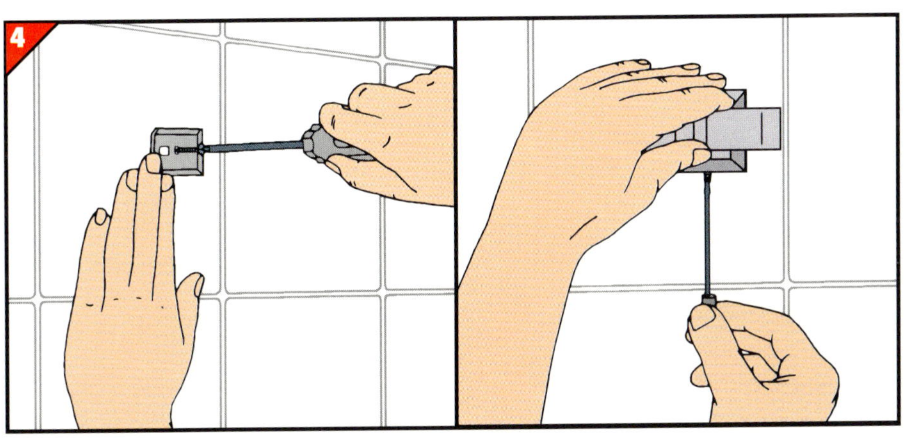

4. Installing the towel bar.

◆ For brackets without screw holes, apply tile adhesive, press the brackets into place, and allow to dry. For screw-mounted brackets, seat hollow-wall anchors in the drilled holes, then screw the brackets into place *(far left)*.

◆ Slip the towel bar onto the mounting brackets; secure a metal towel bar by tightening setscrews with a hex wrench or screwdriver *(near left)*.

◆ Regrout the tile joints that you cut out in Step 1, above.

Drips and Leaks in Four Kinds of Faucets

Often a bathroom faucet with a dripping spout or leaking handles can be fixed with a small investment of time and some spare parts. Although they come in many sizes and shapes, for repair purposes most faucets are grouped into four types: stem, cartridge, disk, and ball.

Stem, or compression, faucets, depicted here and on pages 12 and 13, employ hard-rubber seat washers to provide a tight seal. When stem faucets drip, check for worn washers. You may also need to replace the stem and the seat, metal parts that come in contact with the washers. For a leaking handle, tighten the packing nut *(below)* or replace the packing washer.

Cartridge, disk, and ball faucets, all of which usually have single handles, develop drips and leaks less often. When they do, repair methods differ from one type to another, as shown on pages 14 to 17. In each case, the trick is to know how to disassemble the faucet.

Before You Begin: As with any plumbing job, locate the main shutoff valve in your house ahead of time in case of emergency. Turn off the shutoff valves below the basin and drain the faucet. If the valves will not close, turn off the main valve; drain the system by opening the faucets at the highest point in the house and working down to the lowest point. This prevents a vacuum from forming.

Plug the drain so parts cannot fall in, and protect the sink with a towel. As you work, set parts aside in the exact order you remove them to allow for easier reassembly.

TOOLS

Utility knife
Screwdriver
Adjustable wrench
Long-nose pliers
Vise
Flashlight
Seat wrench
Hex wrench

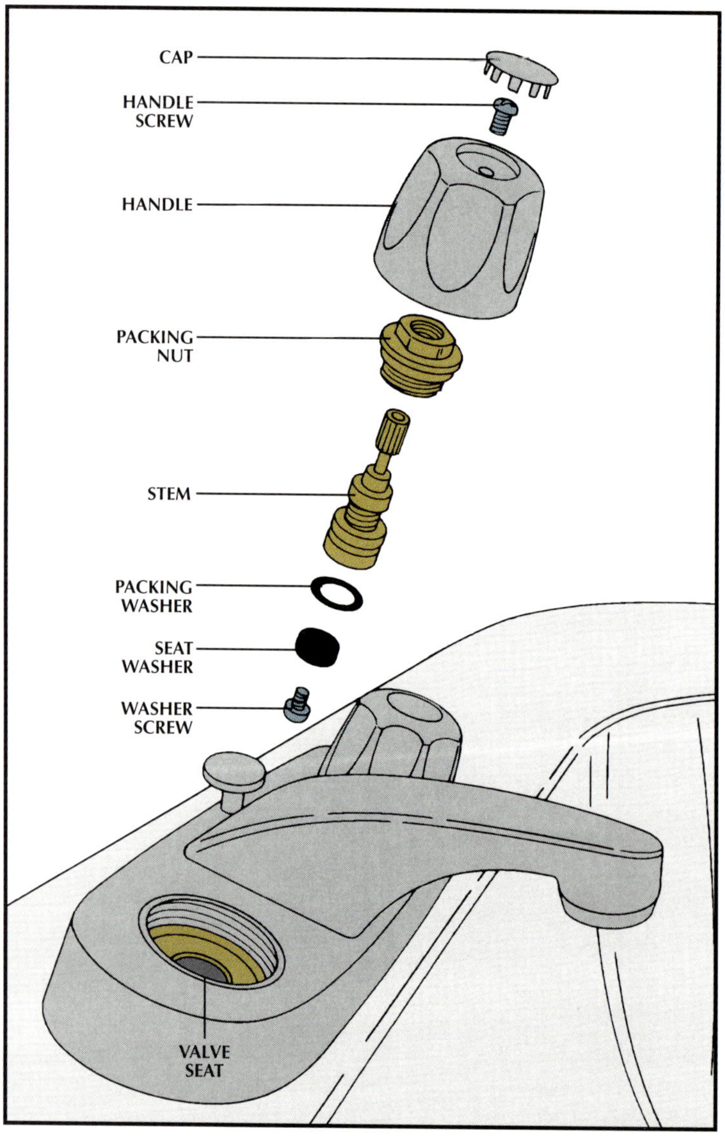

The inner anatomy of a stem faucet.
Although they vary in design, most stem faucets include the basic components shown at left. Each of the two handles is secured by a screw, often concealed under a decorative cap. The screw attaches the handle to the packing nut located at the top of the stem. Under the stem and packing washer, the seat washer closes against the valve seat to cut off the flow of water to the spout.

STEM FAUCETS

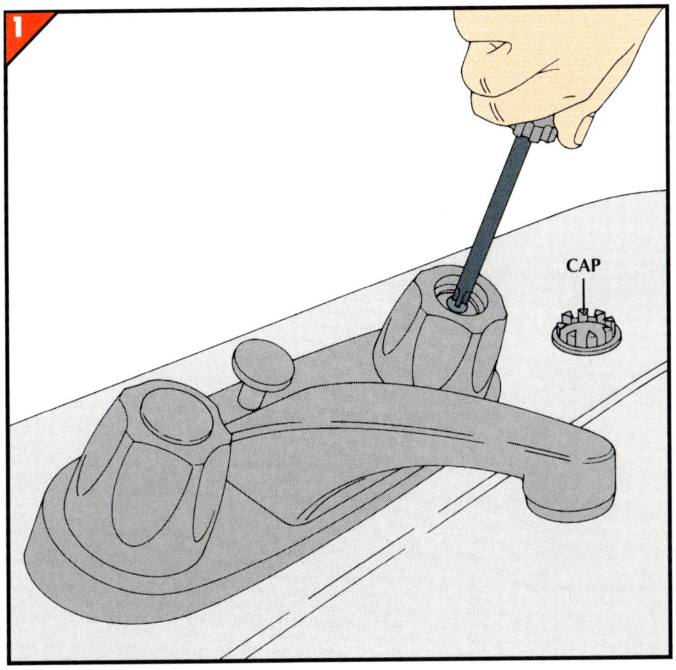

1. Removing a stem-faucet handle.

When a stem faucet drips, repair both hot and cold faucet assemblies. Do one at a time.

◆ Pry out the cap on one handle with a utility knife.

◆ Remove the screw and pull the handle straight up. If it is wedged on tight, protect the basin or base plate underneath with a towel and pry the handle off with a screwdriver. If it is very resistant, use a faucet-handle puller *(below)*.

TRICKS OF THE TRADE

Freeing a Handle

A stubborn handle can be freed with a faucet-handle puller without marring the finish. Insert the center shaft into the hole on the handle, and fit the puller arms under it. Turn the puller handle clockwise to lift the faucet handle off.

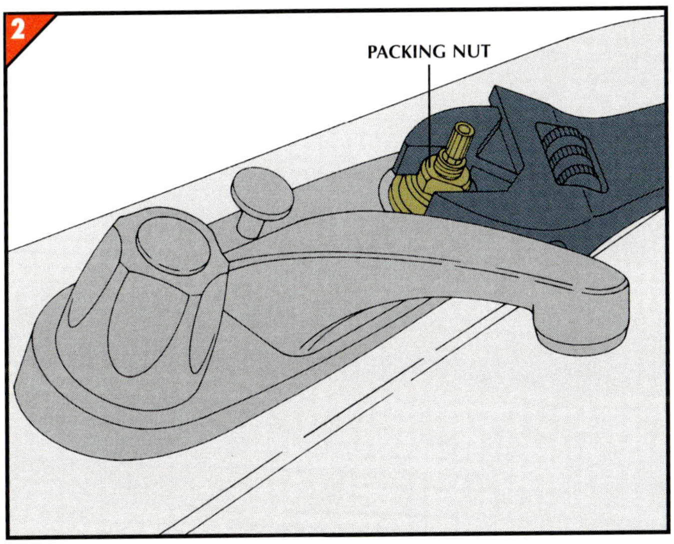

2. Removing the packing nut.

Unscrew the packing nut with an adjustable wrench *(above)*. The stem below may come out with the nut; to separate them, protect the stem with electrician's tape, clamp it in a vise, and remove the nut with the wrench.

3. Taking out the stem.

◆ Try to unscrew the stem by hand *(right)*.

◆ Should that fail, set the handle on the stem and turn it in the same direction that you would to turn on the water; this will remove most stems.

◆ If the stem does not unscrew, the faucet may be a diaphragm or a cartridge type; remove the stem as described on page 12.

REPLACING WASHERS

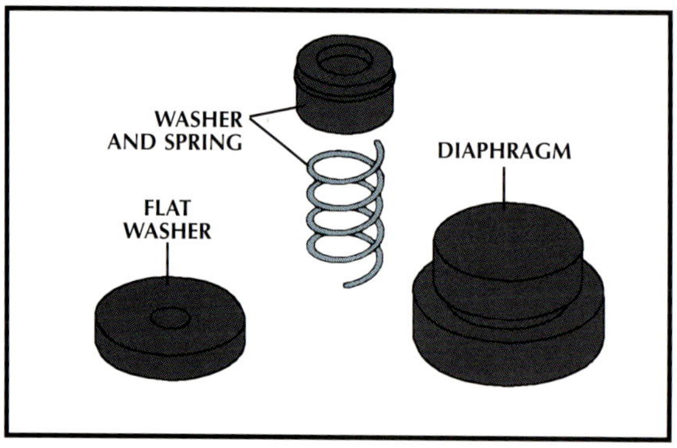

A variety of seat washers.
Different stem faucets require their own type of seat washer. Standard stem faucets use flat washers with holes for washer screws; cartridge-type stem faucets may have washers and springs. In a diaphragm stem faucet, caps called diaphragms do the work of washers, covering the bottom end of each stem. If you are not certain which washers fit your faucet, remove a valve seat *(opposite, below)* and take it to a plumbing-supply store.

Making repairs to a diaphragm stem faucet.
Suction between the diaphragm and the valve seat may make the stem difficult to remove.

◆ Wrap the top of the stem with cloth and pull out the stem with pliers.
◆ If the old diaphragm sticks, pry it out with the tip of a screwdriver.
◆ Using a flashlight, make sure that there are no pieces of the old diaphragm remaining inside; otherwise, the new one will not seat properly.
◆ Fit the new diaphragm over the bottom of the stem *(above)*, making sure the diaphragm is snug all around.
◆ Replace the stem, the packing nut, and the handle.

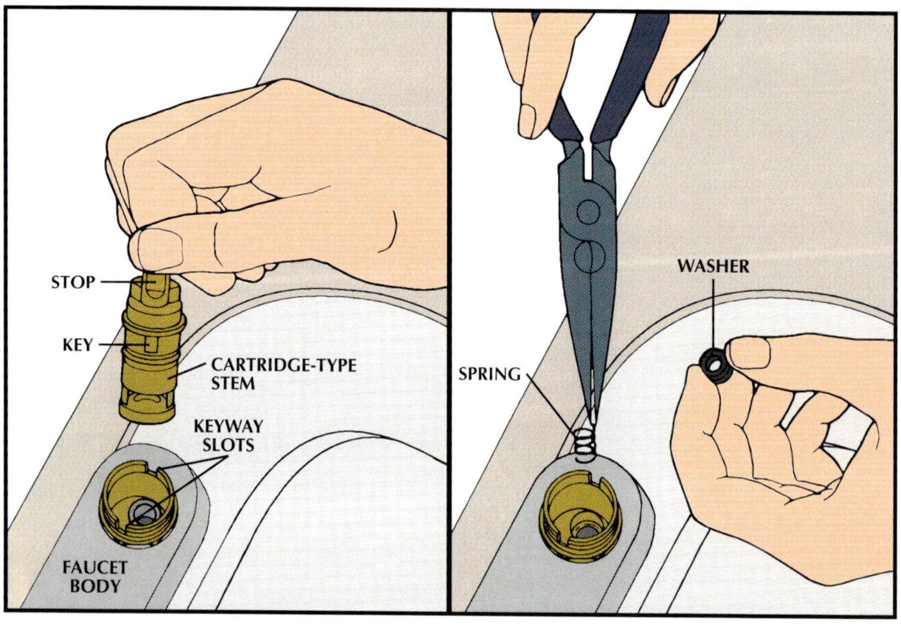

Servicing a cartridge-type stem faucet.
◆ Lift the cartridge out of the faucet *(far left)*, making sure as you do so to observe the alignment of the stop on the top of the cartridge and the keys on its side. The latter fit into two keyway slots on the faucet body.
◆ With long-nose pliers, pull the washer and spring out of the faucet body *(near left)*.
◆ Push the new spring and washer firmly into place with a finger. Insert the cartridge in the same orientation as before and attach the handle. If the spout still drips, replace the cartridge.

SERVICING A VALVE SEAT

1. Inspecting the valve seat.
If the spout of a stem faucet continues to drip after you have replaced the washers, check the valve seats for signs of wear—scratches, pits, or an uneven surface. Use a flashlight to look inside the faucet body, then run a fingertip around the edge of the valve seat *(left)*. If necessary, install a new seat as shown below.

2. Installing a new seat.
◆ With a seat wrench, turn the valve seat counterclockwise and lift it out *(near right)*. Take it to a plumbing-supply store to get an exact duplicate.
◆ Lubricate the outside of the replacement with a pipe-joint compound, push it onto the wrench, and screw it into the faucet body *(far right)*.

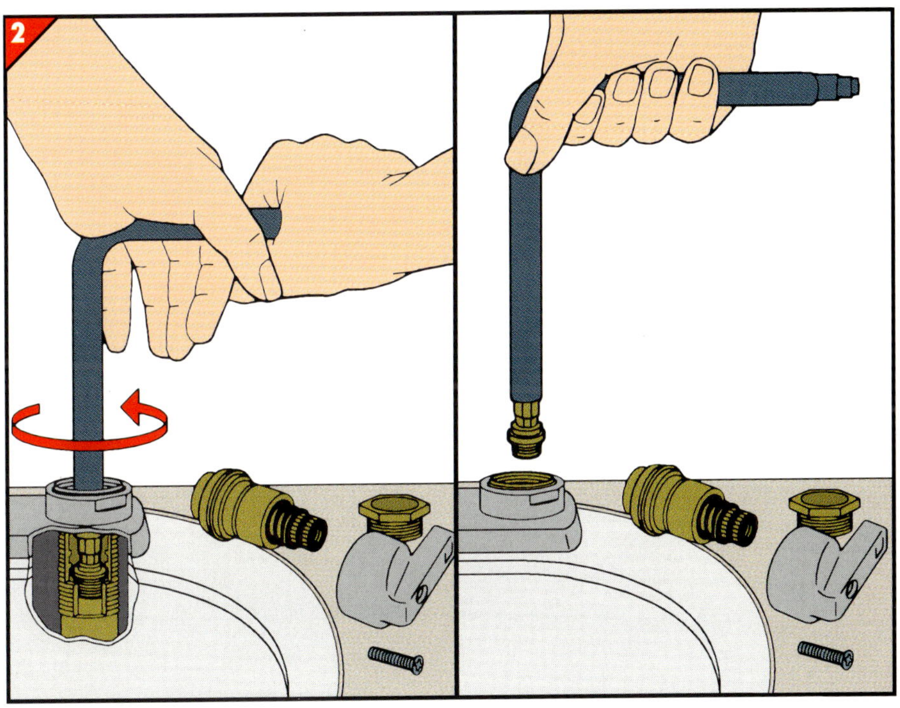

SINGLE-LEVER CARTRIDGE FAUCETS

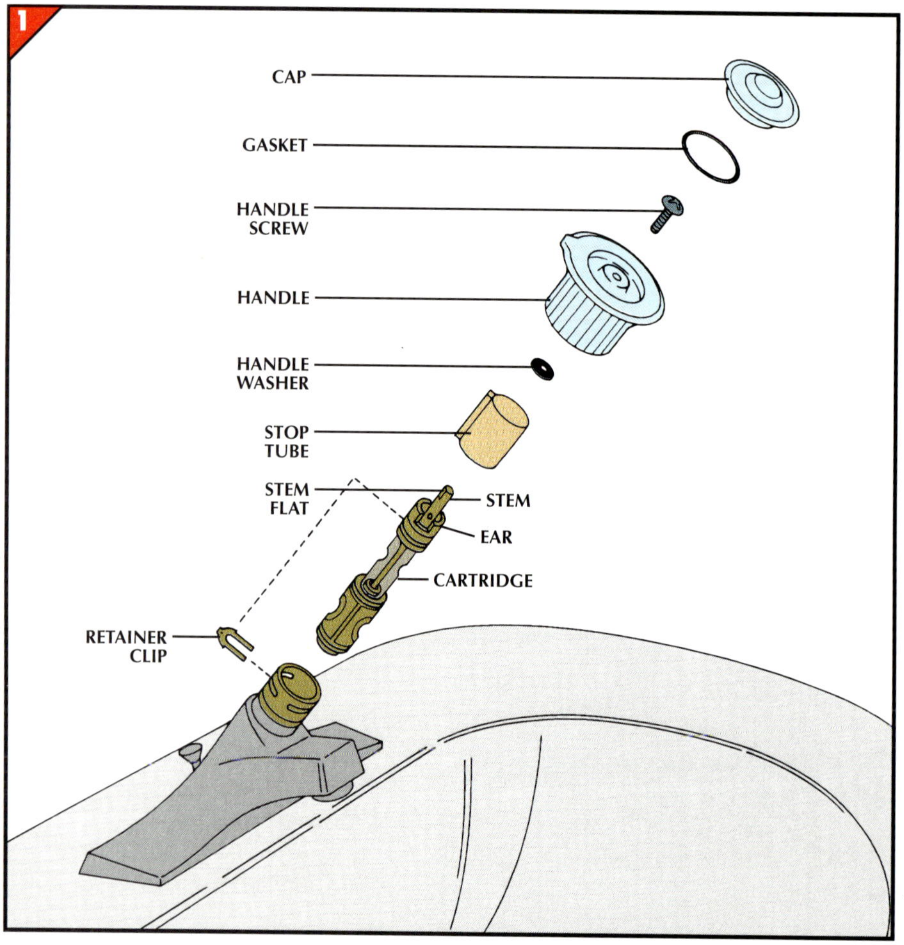

1. Repairing a single-lever cartridge faucet.

Fixing a cartridge faucet usually requires replacing the cartridge. When taking the faucet apart, carefully note the orientation of the cartridge ears and the stem flats, flat areas at the top of the stem *(diagram, left)*; position the replacement the same way.

◆ Remove the cap with a utility knife or a very small screwdriver.

◆ Unscrew the handle and remove it.

◆ Remove the stop tube, if there is one present.

◆ Complete the disassembly by removing the retainer clip and cartridge, as shown below.

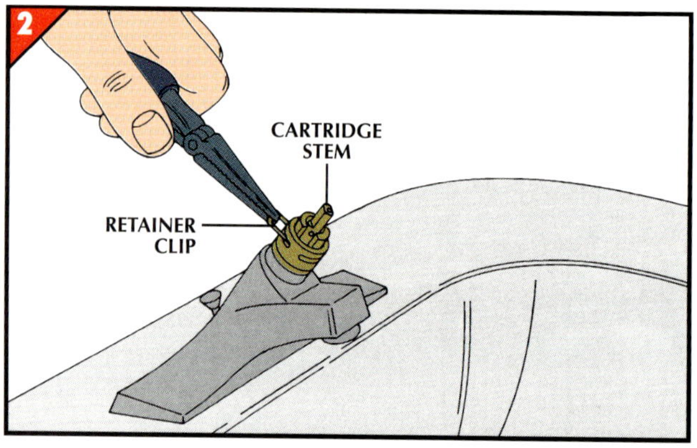

2. Removing the retainer clip.

◆ With long-nose pliers, pull out the retainer clip that holds the cartridge in the faucet body *(left)*.

◆ Lift out the cartridge, using pliers to grip the top of the stem if necessary.

3. Replacing the cartridge.

◆ Position the new cartridge to match the orientation of the old one. With the stem at its highest position, push the cartridge by its ears down into the faucet body.

◆ Align the cartridge ears with the faucet body slots; slide the retainer clip through the slots.

◆ Turn the stem to place the stem flats in the same position as in the old cartridge, then reassemble the faucet and turn on the water. If hot water comes out when you try to turn on the cold, and vice versa, remove the handle and stop tube and rotate the stem 180 degrees.

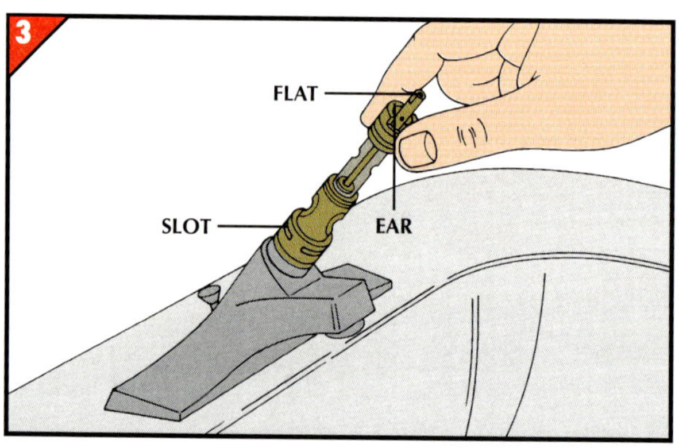

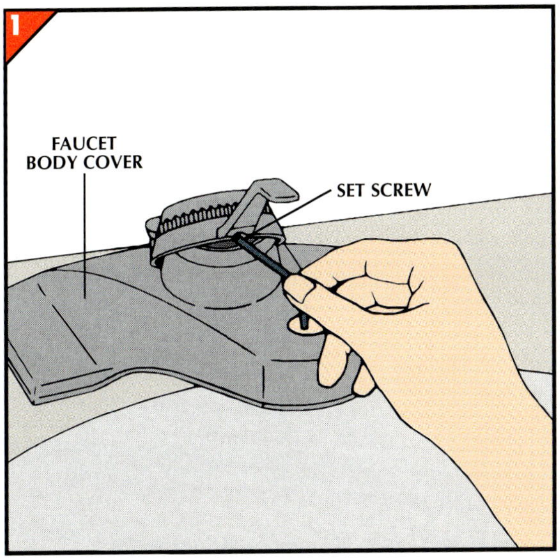

1. Getting access to a disk cartridge.
In ceramic disk faucets, leaks show up around the body of the faucet or as a puddle under the basin.
◆ Turn the faucet on full and move the handle side to side to dislodge dirt that may be lodged between the disks. If the leak persists, replace the disk cartridge.
◆ After turning off the water and draining the faucet, raise the lever as high as it can go. Unscrew the setscrew under the lever *(left)* and remove the handle.
◆ With older models, remove the pop-up lift rod *(page 18)*, remove the screws on the underside of the faucet, and take off the body cover. Newer ceramic disk faucets have a screw in the handle and a metal ring that twists off.

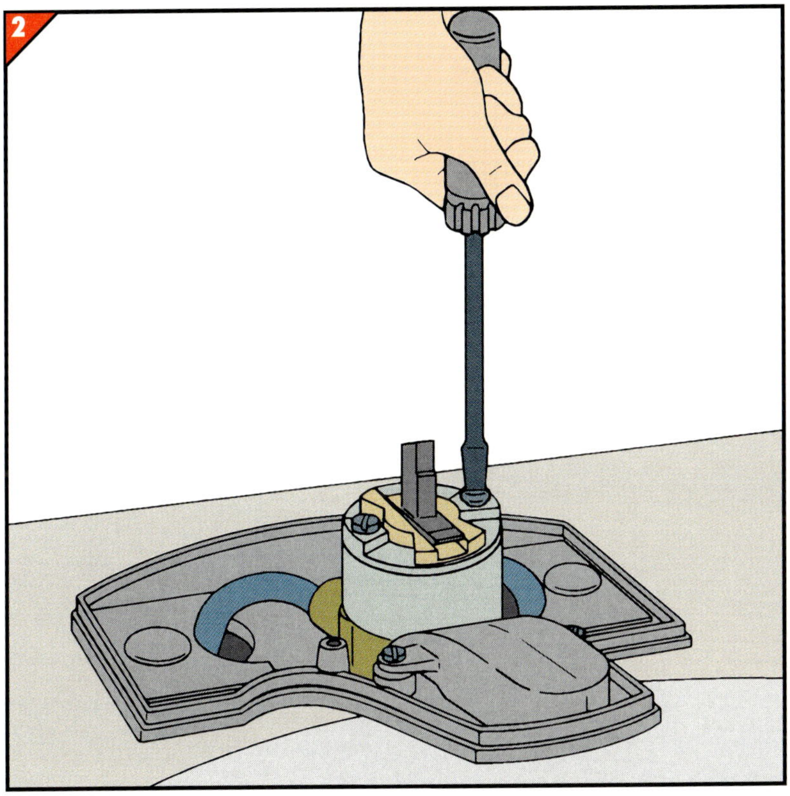

2. Removing the disk cartridge.
◆ Unscrew the bolts that hold the disk cartridge in place.
◆ Remove the cartridge and purchase an identical replacement.

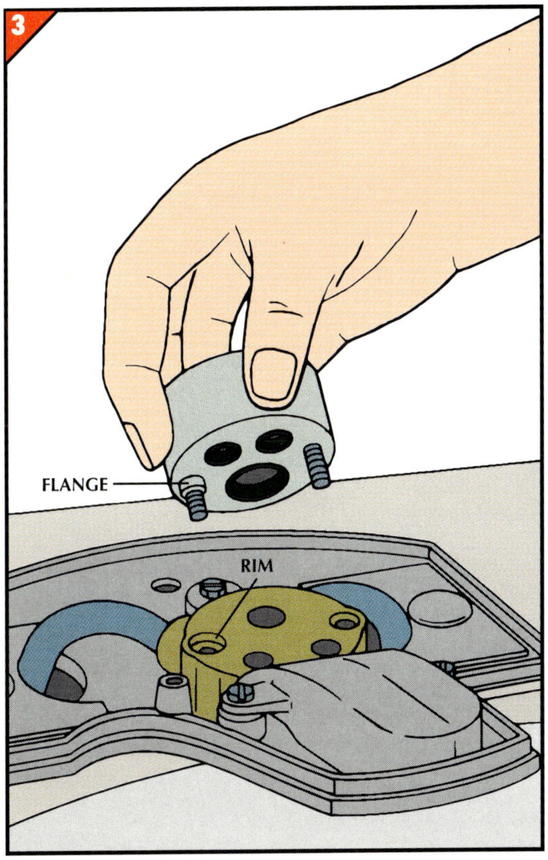

3. Installing a new cartridge.
◆ Align the three ports on the bottom of the disk cartridge with the three holes in the base of the faucet body. One of the bolt holes on the cartridge will have a flange; make sure it fits into the rim around the corresponding bolt hole in the faucet body.
◆ Replace the disk cartridge bolts, the body cover, and the handle.

SINGLE-LEVER BALL FAUCETS

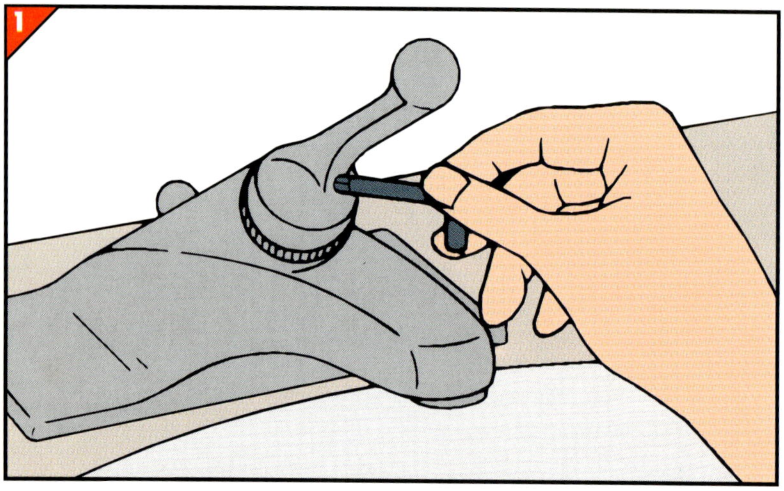

1. Loosening the setscrew.
If the spout of a ball faucet drips when the water is off, replace the two rubber valve seats and metal springs in the bottom of the faucet body.

◆ With a hex wrench, loosen the setscrew under the shank of the handle *(left)*. Do not take the screw all the way out; it is easily lost.

◆ Remove the handle.

2. Removing the cap and ball.
◆ Unscrew the cap assembly and lift out the ball by its stem; the plastic-and-rubber cam assembly will come with it.

◆ Inspect the ball; if it is rough or corroded, replace it.

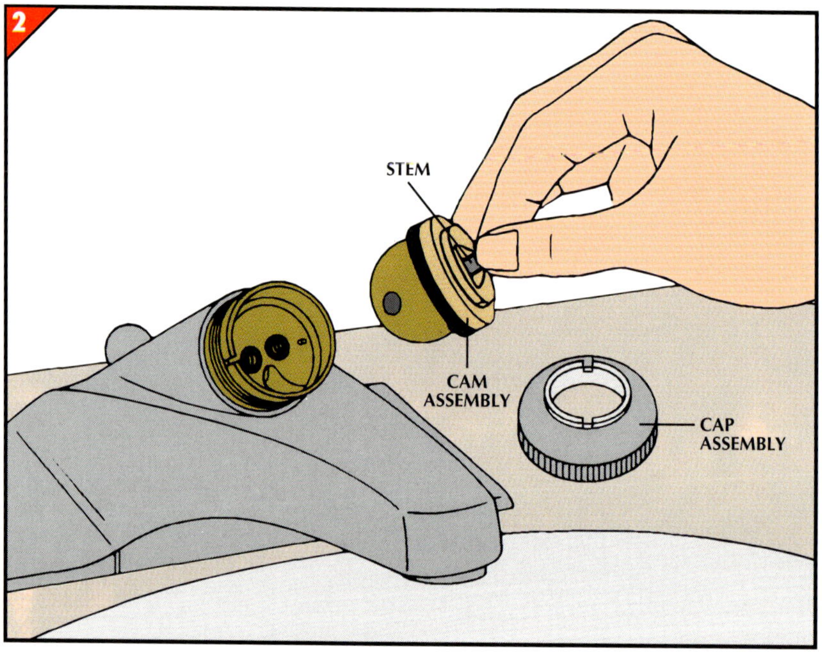

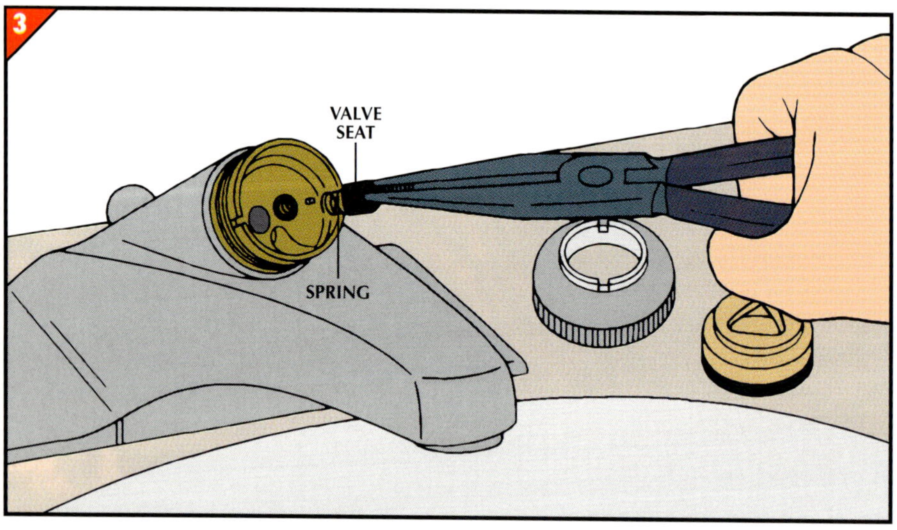

3. Installing new valve seats and springs.
With long-nose pliers, remove the valve seats and springs. Use a fingertip to push replacements firmly into place.

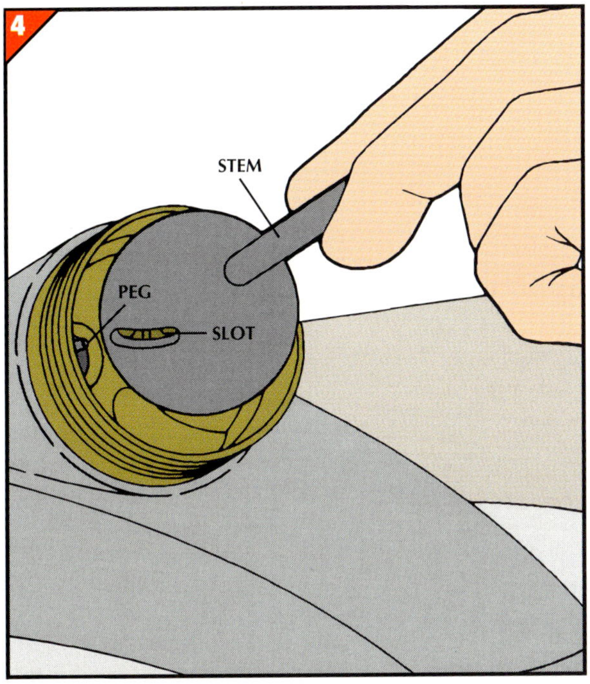

4. Replacing the ball.
A tiny metal peg projects from one side of the cavity into which the ball fits. As you replace the ball, make sure that the peg fits into an oblong slot on it.

5. Replacing the cam assembly.
◆ Replace the cam assembly so that its tab fits into the slot on the faucet body.
◆ Screw on the cap assembly.

6. Setting the adjusting ring.
◆ Turn on the water to the faucet.
◆ Move the ball's stem to the on position. If water leaks out around the stem, tighten the adjusting ring with a tool provided by the manufacturer or with the tip of a small screwdriver *(right)*.
◆ If you must tighten the ring so much that the handle is difficult to work, turn off the water, drain the faucet, and replace the entire cam assembly, including the rubber ring.
◆ Now put the cap assembly back in place. Position the handle so that the setscrew is over the flat on the stem and tighten the setscrew.

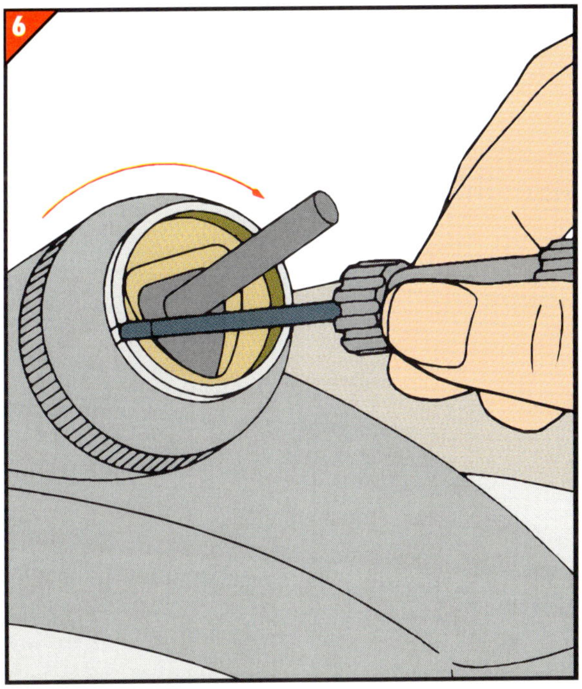

New Fittings for Basins and Tubs

Sometimes the best and easiest repair for a worn-out bathroom faucet is to throw it out and install a new one. Replacing the washbasin faucet—or any tub and shower fittings—also helps give an old bathroom a new look with relatively little effort.

Buying the Right Fitting: If you plan to keep your washbasin, you must buy a faucet that fits the spacing of the sink's side holes. Determine the spacing by measuring between the centers of the faucet handles, or remove a faucet with a single handle to check the holes directly. Most center-set faucets *(opposite, bottom)* are designed for a washbasin in which the side holes are 4 inches apart. You can replace a center-set faucet with a single-hole faucet *(page 21)* if its base plate covers the side holes. A wide-spread faucet *(page 22)* can accommodate side holes that are situated from 6 to 20 inches apart and must be replaced by a wide-spread set.

If your washbasin has a pop-up drain plug, you may want to replace the plug and the drain body to match the new faucet, as shown on pages 26-27. You can also follow the steps on the same pages to add a pop-up plug to a basin that does not have one; you will need to install a new drain body, T connector, and pop-up plug mechanism and purchase a faucet with a lift rod.

Tub and shower fittings are not as standardized as a sink's. Depending on the part, it is always best and sometimes essential to use replacements from the same manufacturer.

Preparation Steps: Several hours before disconnecting an old faucet or other fittings, spray all the threaded connections with penetrating lubricant. Cover the drain so that screws and small parts will not be lost. For work in a tub or shower, lay down padding or towels to avoid scarring the finish. After removing the old fittings, clean the surface beneath, removing crusty mineral deposits with a solution of equal parts of white vinegar and water.

TOOLS

- Pliers
- Basin wrench
- Adjustable wrench
- Pipe wrench
- Tubing bender
- Faucet-handle puller
- Small screwdriver
- Drill with a $\frac{1}{4}$-inch carbide bit
- Hacksaw

MATERIALS

- Penetrating lubricant
- Plumber's putty
- Plumbing-sealant tape
- Washers, lock nuts, and other hardware
- Braided flexible supply tubes

REMOVING AN OLD WASHBASIN FAUCET

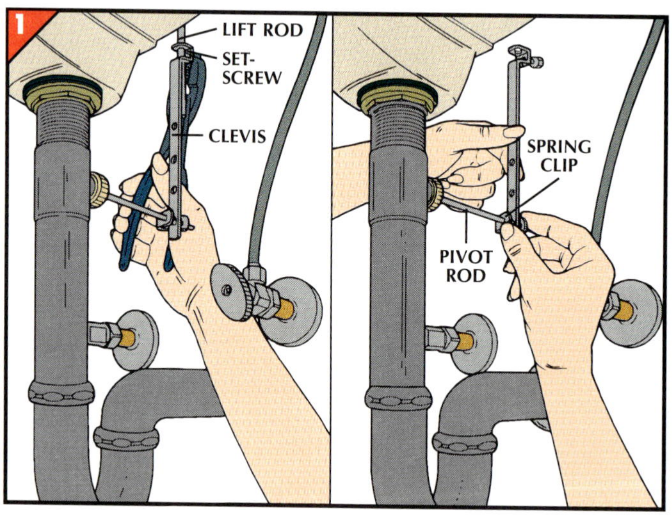

1. Freeing the pop-up plug mechanism.

Detach the pop-up plug mechanism, if any, before removing the faucet; leave the plug and pivot rod in place.

◆ With pliers, loosen the setscrew securing the pop-up lift rod to the clevis, or adapter bar, underneath the basin *(above, left)*.

◆ Above the basin, pull the lift rod up and out of the clevis.

◆ Pinch the spring clip holding the pivot rod in place *(above, right)*, and pull the clevis and spring clip free; set aside for reuse with the new faucet.

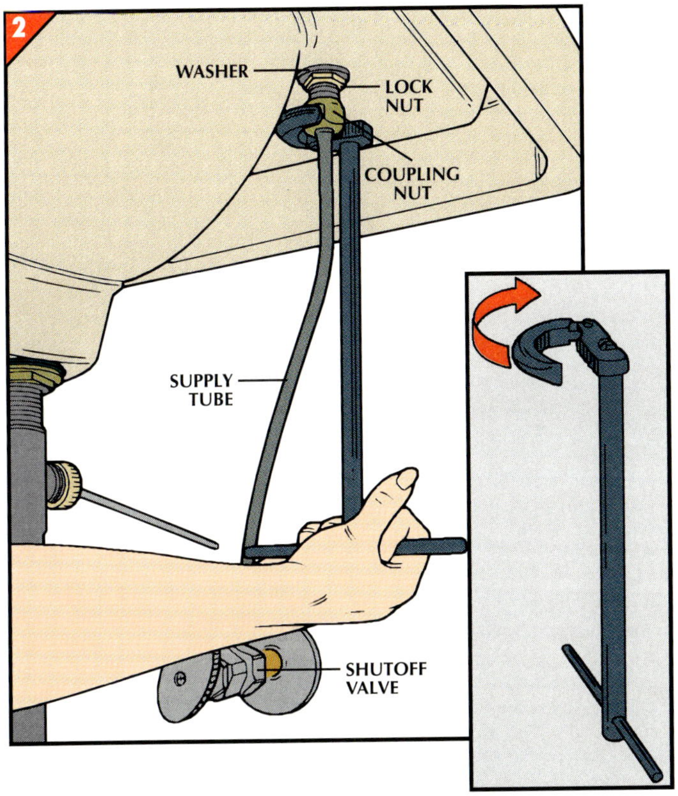

2. Disconnecting the supply tubes.

◆ Turn off the shutoff valves and drain the faucet; if you find that the valves will not turn, drain the house system as described on page 10.
◆ With a basin wrench *(inset)*, unscrew the coupling nut at the top of one of the supply tubes *(left)* and disconnect the tube.
◆ At the bottom of the supply tube, unscrew the nut attaching it to the shutoff valve.
◆ Disconnect the second supply tube in the same way.
◆ With the basin wrench, unscrew the lock nuts under the basin that secure the faucet; remove each nut and washer.
◆ Lift out the faucet, and clean the sink surface.

HOOKING UP A CENTER-SET FAUCET

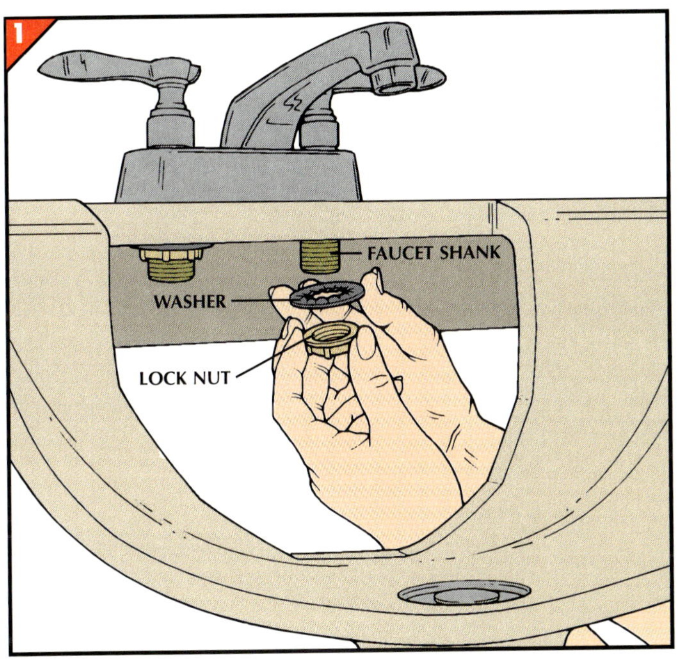

1. Attaching the faucet.

◆ Before positioning the faucet, slip a gasket and bottom plate over the faucet shanks; if these were not supplied, apply a bead of plumber's putty under the assembly.
◆ Insert the shanks into the side holes of the basin.
◆ Working underneath the washbasin, slip a washer onto one of the faucet shanks. Then thread on a lock nut and tighten by hand. Do the same with the other faucet shank.
◆ Tighten both lock nuts with a basin wrench. If you used plumber's putty, wipe off any excess with a finger.

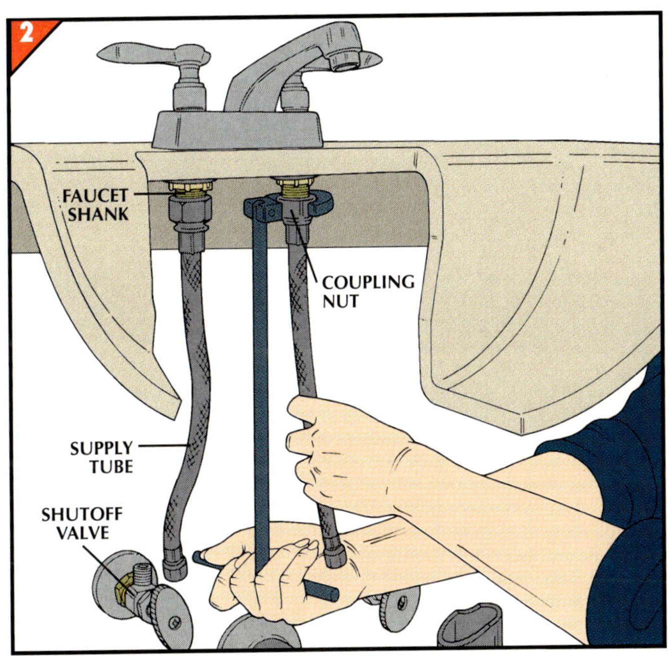

2. Attaching flexible supply tubes.

◆ Wrap plumbing-sealant tape around the threads of the faucet shanks and shutoff valves.
◆ Insert a washer into the large coupling nut at one end of a braided flexible supply tube and hand tighten the nut to a faucet shank; attach the second supply tube the same way *(above)*.
◆ Connect each tube to its corresponding shutoff valve with the smaller coupling nut at the other end of the tube.
◆ Make a final half-turn on each nut with a wrench.

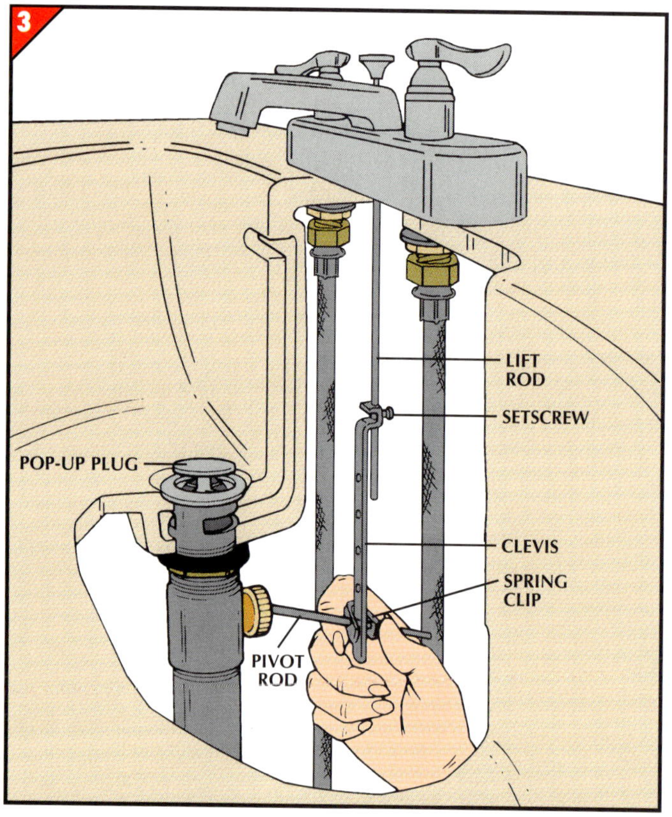

3. Installing the lift rod.

Attach the faucet's lift rod to the pop-up plug mechanism.

◆ Drop the lift rod through the hole at the back of the spout. From underneath the sink, slip the lift rod through holes in the top of the clevis.

◆ With a spring clip, secure the pivot rod to the clevis, passing the rod through one of the clevis holes. Holding the pivot rod and clevis at this connection *(left),* pull downward to raise the pop-up plug in the drain. Adjust if necessary by moving the pivot rod to a different hole.

◆ Lock the lift rod in place by tightening the setscrew at the top of the clevis.

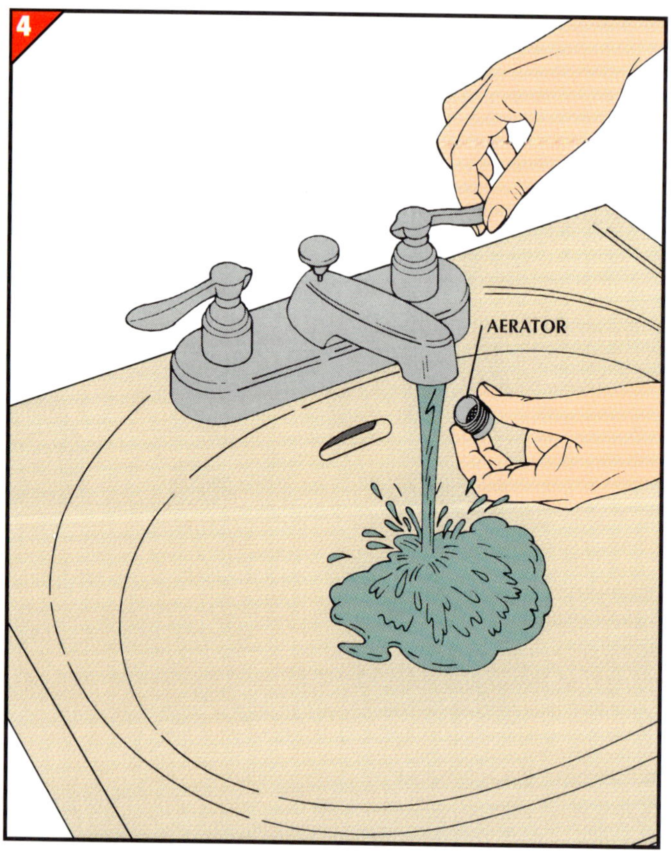

4. Flushing out the faucet.

◆ Turn on the water supply.

◆ Unscrew the aerator, an attachment in the underside of the spout that ensures an even flow of water and prevents splashing.

◆ Turn on the faucet slowly *(left)* and check under the sink for leaks. Fix leaking connections by tightening slightly with a wrench. Then turn the water on full force to flush out sediment.

◆ Turn off the faucet and replace the aerator.

MOUNTING A SINGLE-LEVER FAUCET

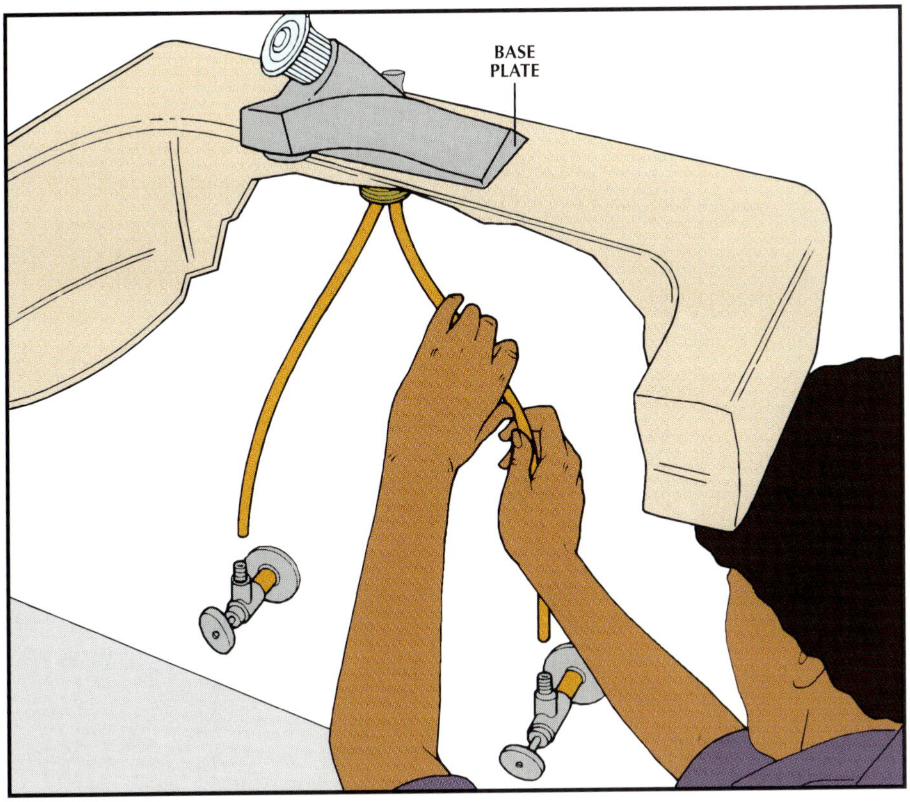

Setting the faucet in place.

◆ Place the gasket supplied with the faucet on the base plate; if there is no gasket, substitute a bead of plumber's putty.

◆ Insert the faucet's preattached supply tubes—usually flexible copper tubing—through the center hole. Position the faucet on the sink.

◆ Under the basin, push a washer up over the tubing, followed by a lock nut. Thread the nut onto the faucet shank and tighten.

◆ With your hands, gently separate the supply tubes. Do not bend them sharply, or the faucet assembly will be useless. Put your thumbs together *(left)* and shape each piece of tubing to line up with its corresponding shutoff valve. Or use a tubing bender *(box)*.

◆ If the tubing is too short, extend it with braided tubes *(below, left)*.

◆ Complete the installation as with a center-set faucet *(opposite)*.

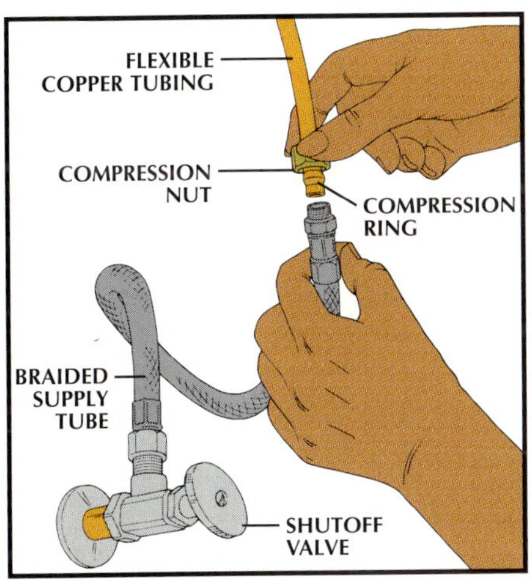

Extending the supply lines.

If the flexible copper tubing does not reach to the shutoff valves, extend each piece with a braided supply tube equipped with compression fittings.

◆ Find the end of the braided tube that has a compression nut that turns in place but stays on the tube; attach that end to the shutoff valve.

◆ At the other end of the tube, detach the compression nut and compression ring and slip them onto the corresponding piece of faucet tubing. Connect the faucet tubing and the supply tube with the compression nut *(above, left)*.

◆ Repeat the process for the second supply line.

TRICKS OF THE TRADE

To Gently Shape Tubing

A tubing bender makes it easier to shape flexible copper tubing without crimping. Slip the coiled metal over the tubing and bend to the desired shape.

INSTALLING A WIDE-SPREAD FAUCET

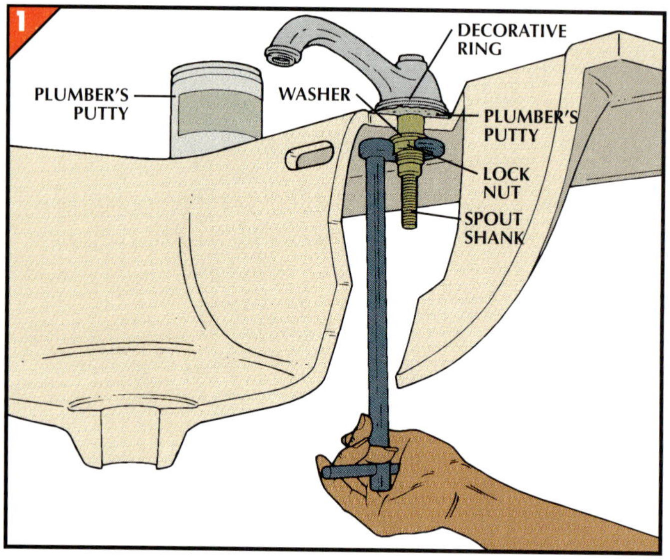

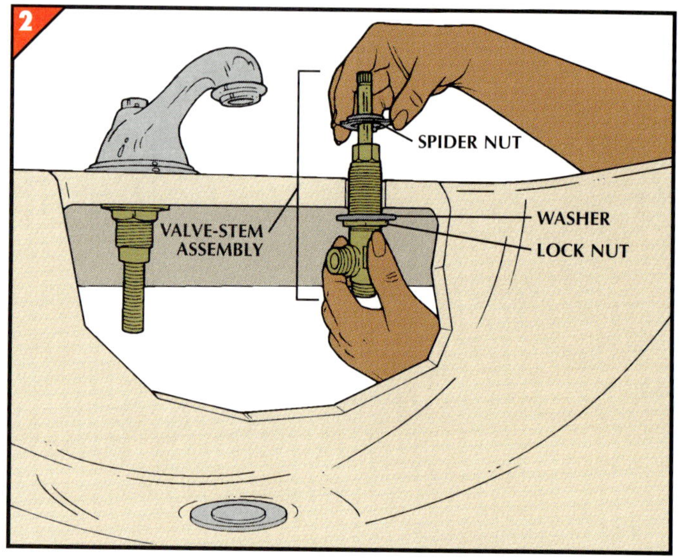

1. Mounting the faucet spout.

◆ Press a pencil-thick bead of plumber's putty around the edge of the underside of the spout.

◆ Insert the shank through the decorative ring and into the center hole of the sink. Be sure to position the spout at right angles to the back of the washbasin.

◆ Under the basin, secure the spout with a washer and lock nut; use a basin wrench to tighten the nut *(above)*.

◆ With a finger, wipe away excess plumber's putty from around the spout.

2. Installing the valve-stem assemblies.

◆ Place a washer and lock nut on one of the faucet's valve-stem assemblies. From underneath the washbasin, push the upper part of the assembly through a side hole.

◆ By hand, screw a spider nut onto the top of the assembly *(above)*.

◆ Adjust the upper and lower nuts until the stem portion of the assembly protrudes above the sink by the distance recommended by the manufacturer.

◆ Install the second valve-stem assembly in the same way.

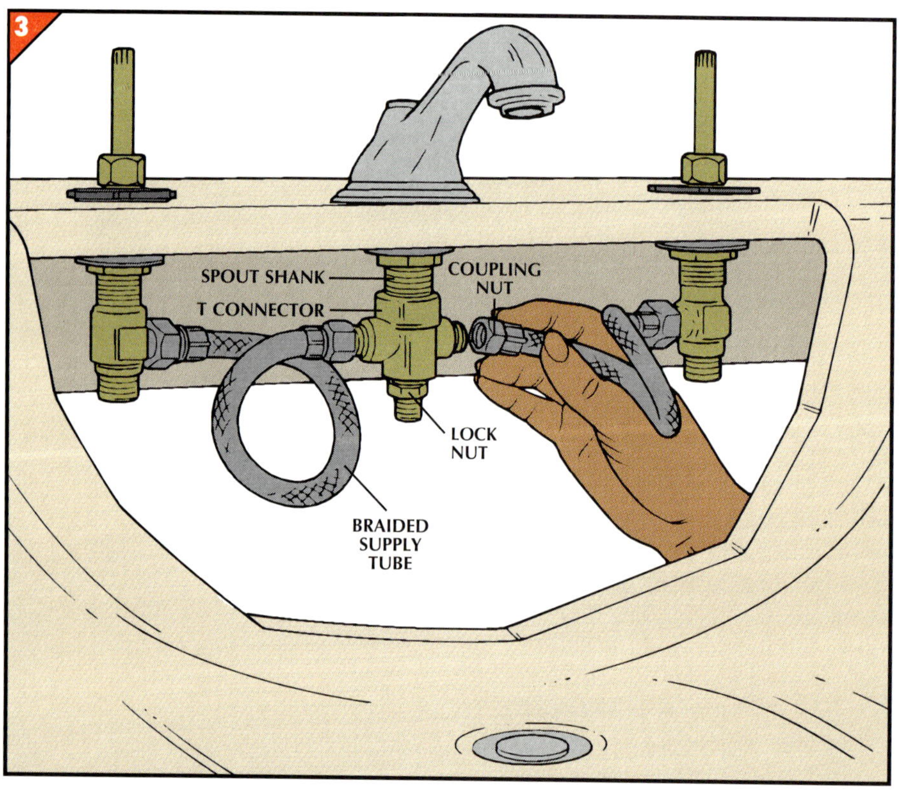

3. Connecting the spout.

◆ Place an O-ring and washer on the upper side of the faucet's T connector and slip the connector onto the spout shank; secure the connector from below with a packing nut and a lock nut.

◆ Wrap plumbing-sealant tape on the threads at each side of the T connector and around the supply connectors on each valve-stem assembly.

◆ Connect each valve-stem assembly to the T connector with a braided supply tube *(left)*. Hand tighten the larger coupling nut on the tube to the valve-stem assembly and the smaller one to the T connector. Make a final turn on each nut with an adjustable wrench.

◆ Follow the same procedures as for a center-set faucet *(page 20)* to connect the pop-up plug mechanism, attach supply tubes from the faucet shanks to the shutoff valves, check for leaks, and flush out the faucet.

A NEW LOOK FOR A THREE-HANDLE TUB FAUCET

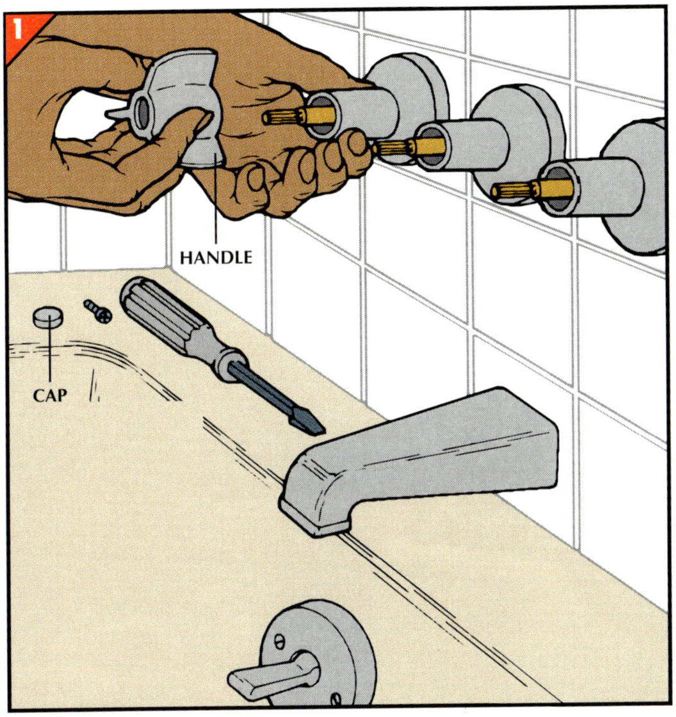

1. Removing the handles.

◆ Before starting, obtain replacement handles from the same manufacturer for best results; others can be adapted to fit *(Step 5)* but will not last as long.
◆ Turn off the water supply to the tub.
◆ Pry off the cap in the center of each faucet handle, or unscrew the cap with pliers if it has raised edges.
◆ Remove the screw holding the handle on the faucet stem, and pull off the handle *(above)*. If necessary, use a faucet-handle puller *(page 11)*.

2. Removing escutcheons and sleeves.

◆ Take off the faucet's escutcheons, or cover plates; they may be held in place by face screws or by a setscrew at the base of each escutcheon, or they may have been secured by the handles.
◆ If the sleeves are separate pieces, as here, remove them next; they may lift off, or you may need to unscrew each with a tape-wrapped pipe wrench *(above)*.

3. Installing new escutcheons.

◆ Slide each new escutcheon over a faucet stem. If the escutcheons have holes for setscrews, position the holes at the bottom.
◆ For escutcheons that are secured with face screws, center each escutcheon over a stem and line up the face-screw holes to either side of it. Mark the location of the screw holes on the wall *(left)* and make 1-inch-deep holes at the marks using a drill with a $\frac{1}{4}$-inch carbide bit. Insert the plastic screw anchors supplied with the handles into the holes, then attach the escutcheon with the face screws.

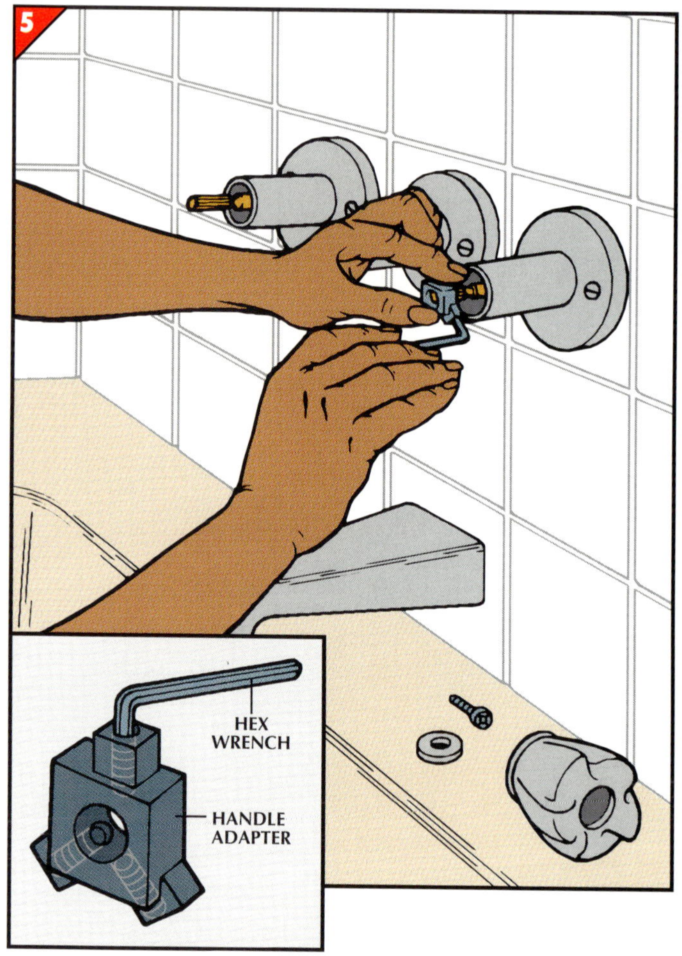

4. Inserting the sleeves.

◆ Attach separate sleeves by placing each one over a faucet stem and inserting it into the center of that escutcheon.

◆ Measure how much of the stem protrudes beyond the sleeve *(above)*; if less than $\frac{3}{4}$ inch of the stem is exposed, remove the sleeve and shorten it with a hacksaw.

◆ Attach the sleeve, usually by tightening a setscrew at the bottom edge of the escutcheon.

5. Attaching the handles.

◆ If the new handles are from the same manufacturer as the original handles, set them in place, attach with screws, and cover the screws with caps.

◆ For replacements from a different company, use handle adapters. Fit an adapter onto the ridged end of each faucet stem, then tighten the three setscrews with the hex wrench supplied with the adapter *(inset)*. Put on each handle and secure it with a screw. Snap the handle caps in place.

REPLACING OTHER BATH AND SHOWER FITTINGS

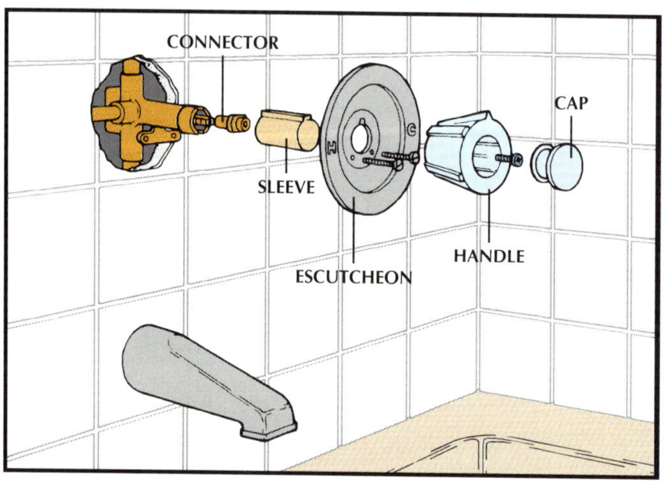

Revamping a single-handle faucet.

Always replace a single-handle tub or shower faucet with one from the same manufacturer.

◆ Pry off the faucet cap, which conceals a screw attached to the connector. Loosen the screw and pull off the handle.

◆ Unfasten the escutcheon. Remove it, the sleeve, and the connector.

◆ Install new trim by reversing the disassembly process, substituting a new sleeve, escutcheon, and handle.

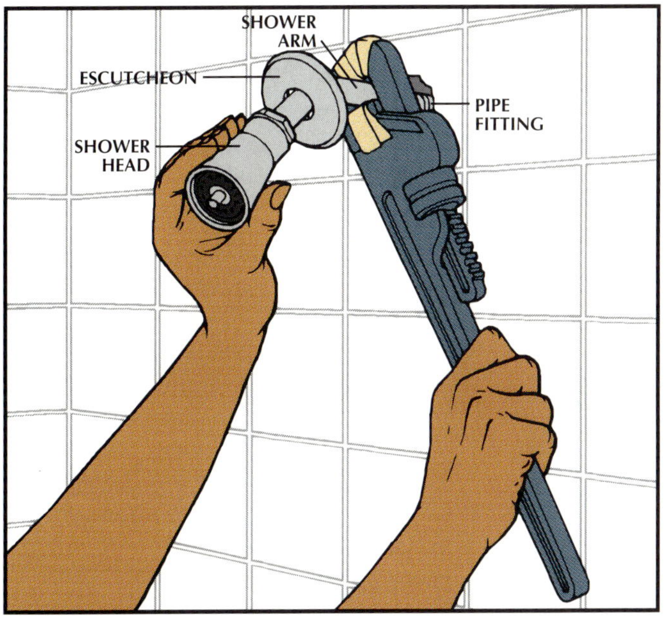

Changing a showerhead and shower arm.

◆ Pull the shower-arm escutcheon away from the wall.
◆ With a pipe wrench, carefully unscrew the shower arm from the pipe fitting inside the wall. Discard the old showerhead and shower arm.
◆ Wrap the threads on both ends of the new shower arm with plumbing-sealant tape. Screw the new head onto the arm and slide the escutcheon over the other end.
◆ Hand screw the free end of the arm into the pipe fitting. Steadying the assembly with one hand *(left),* tighten the arm with a tape-wrapped wrench until the shower head points down.
◆ Press the escutcheon against the wall.

CAUTION *Never allow the pipe fitting to turn or move inside the wall. This could break it and require extensive repairs.*

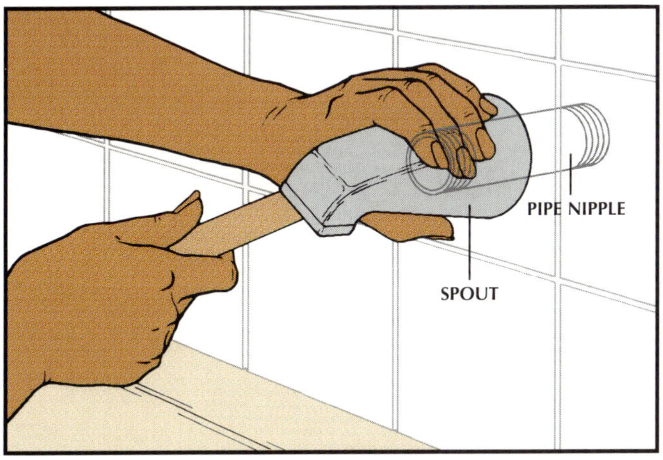

Changing a tub spout.

◆ If your spout has a setscrew at the base, loosen it and slide the spout off; replace it with any other spout using the same system.
◆ If your spout does not have a setscrew, turn the spout with a pipe wrench to remove it from the pipe nipple underneath. Take the spout to a plumbing-supply store to find a replacement with the same threading.
◆ Wrap the threads on the nipple with plumbing-sealant tape and tighten the new spout onto the nipple by hand. To finish tightening, trim a piece of wood to fit in the spout opening *(left);* use it to position the spout with its opening straight down.

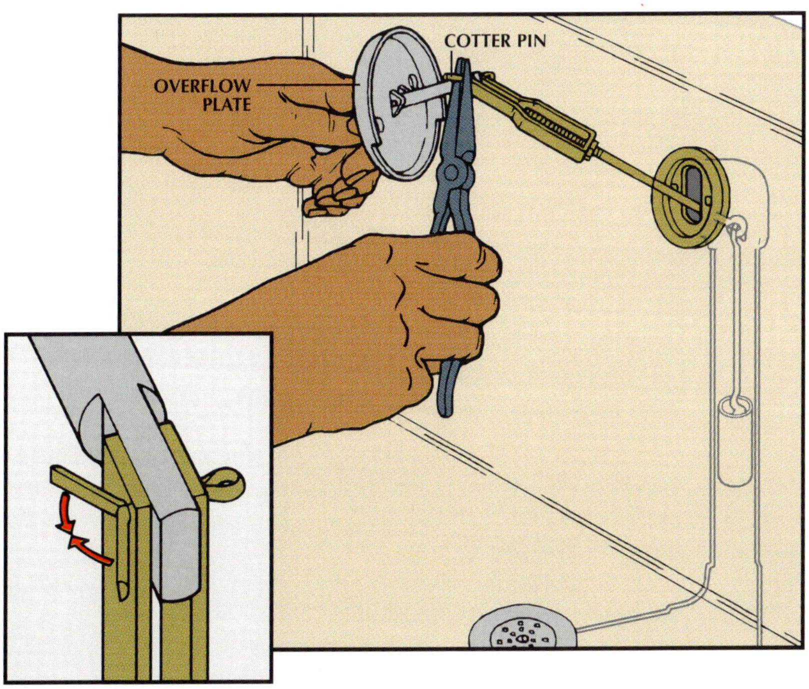

Changing an overflow plate.

◆ Remove the two screws holding the overflow plate to the tub.
◆ Pull the plate and attached mechanism out of the overflow hole far enough to reach the cotter pin *(inset)* that secures the mechanism to the back of the plate.
◆ With pliers, squeeze the ends of the cotter pin together and pull the pin out to free the plate *(left).*
◆ Attach the new plate to the old mechanism with a new cotter pin.
◆ Ease the mechanism back into the overflow hole and secure the plate with the two screws provided.

Updating Drains and Traps

Over time, corrosion in the trap and drain under your bathroom washbasin can cause leaks, which are best remedied by the replacement of all or part of the drain assembly. You may also want to replace a worn pop-up plug and drain body when installing a new faucet.

For best results, spray the threaded connections in the drain assembly with a penetrating lubricant several hours before disconnecting the old fittings. Drain configurations vary, but most include slip-nut connections that can easily be dismantled with a wrench. If you intend to reuse a trap, be sure to put new washers under the slip nuts before putting the trap back in.

Selecting the Right Parts: If the sink is mounted in a vanity top or on a pedestal, and you are replacing all of the drain assembly, use polyvinyl chloride (PVC) fittings like those depicted here. Such pipes are durable, rustproof, and easy to work with. To replace the entire drain assembly under a wall-hung basin, chrome-plated parts are an elegant alternative. If you are replacing only some of the drain fittings, match the material of those that remain.

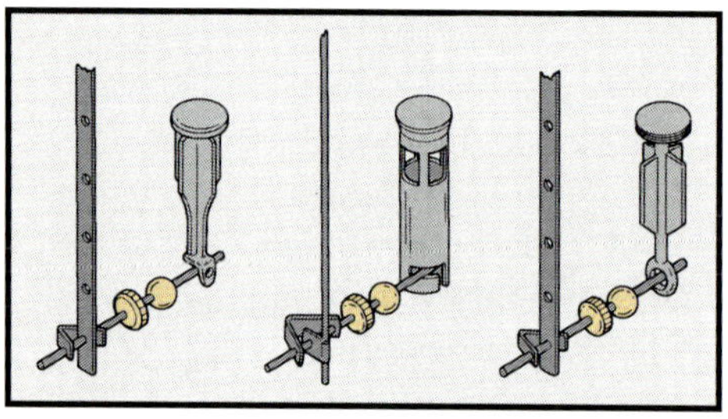

Pop-up drain plugs.

The method for removing a pop-up drain plug depends on its type. Some plugs sit atop the pivot rod and just lift out *(far left)*. Others require a quarter-turn to free them from the rod *(left, center)*. To remove the type of plug at near left, you must disengage the pivot rod from the T connector under the basin and then lift out the plug.

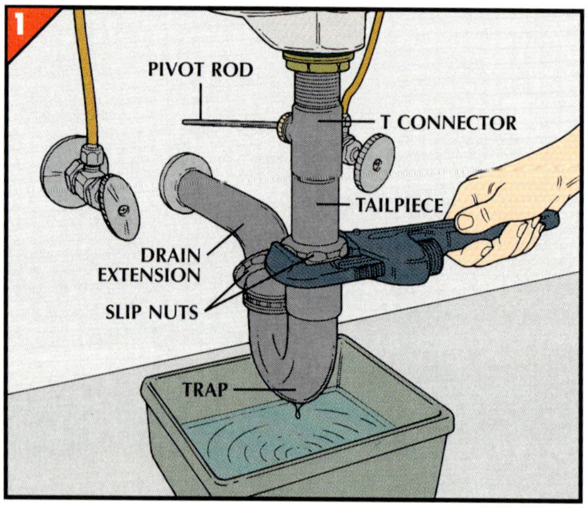

1. Removing the trap.

◆ Place a shallow container underneath the trap to catch any water remaining inside.

◆ With a pipe wrench or a monkey wrench, unscrew the slip nuts on either end of the trap, disconnecting it from the tailpiece and the drain extension *(above)*.

◆ Remove the pop-up plug as outlined above, as well as the lift rod and clevis *(page 19)*. With pliers, unscrew the retaining nut at the back of the T connector and remove the pivot rod.

2. Removing the fittings.

◆ With a pipe wrench, unscrew the T connector from the drain body, remove the lock nut and washer holding the drain body to the basin *(above)*, and push the drain body up and out through the hole in the basin.

◆ If replacing all of the drain assembly, pry the escutcheon from the wall. Unscrew the slip nut behind it, then gently remove the drain extension, being careful not to move or break pipes inside the wall. Clean the threads of the drain outlet pipe.

3. Sealing the new drain flange.

◆ Inside the washbasin, scrape off any old putty from around the drain opening and clean and dry the surface.

◆ Roll a short rope of plumber's putty and press it under the edge of the flange at the top of the drain body. Lower the drain body through the opening in the sink *(left)* and press down on the flange.

◆ Underneath the basin, push the gasket, washer, and lock nut onto the drain body. Hand tighten the lock nut against the bottom of the basin, then tighten one more turn with a pipe wrench. Wipe away any excess putty with a finger.

◆ If you are replacing the faucet, install the new one now, as well as the new lift rod and clevis.

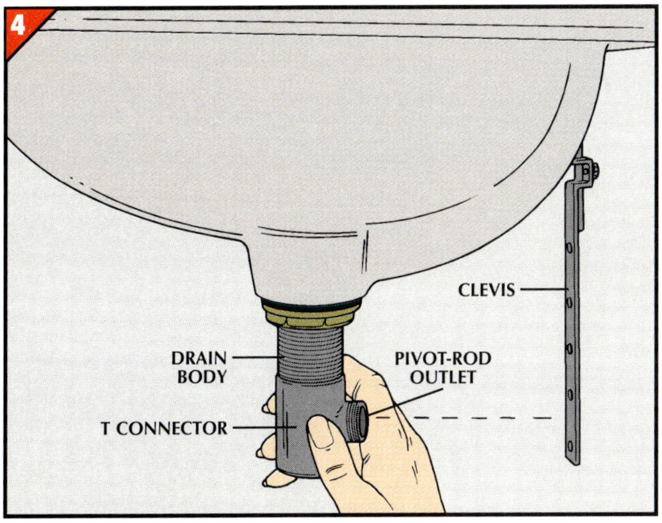

4. Aligning the T connector.

◆ Wrap plumbing-sealant tape around the threads on the lower part of the drain body.

◆ Screw the new T connector onto the drain body so that the pivot-rod outlet faces toward the clevis *(dotted line, left).*

◆ Insert one end of the pivot rod into the T connector and attach the other end to the clevis with a spring clip, following the procedure shown on page 20.

◆ Tighten the pivot rod's retaining nut on the T connector and adjust the position of the pivot rod on the clevis as necessary.

5. Installing a new plastic trap.

◆ Wrap plumbing-sealant tape around the threads of the tailpiece and hand tighten it into the T connector. Slide a plastic slip nut and washer *(not visible)* onto the tailpiece.

◆ If replacing the entire drain assembly, loosely connect the replacement trap and the new drain extension with a plastic slip nut. Slide the escutcheon, a nut, and a washer onto the extension and insert it into the drain outlet pipe. The washer fits between the extension and the outlet pipe, but the nut slips over the pipe's outside.

◆ Align the top of the trap with the tailpiece *(right).* Loosely connect the pipes with the nut.

◆ When the drain assembly is properly aligned, hand tighten the nuts at each connection. Turn each nut once more with a wrench. Push the escutcheon against the wall.

◆ Close the pop-up plug, fill the sink with water, then open the drain and check for leaks. Tighten any leaking joints slightly.

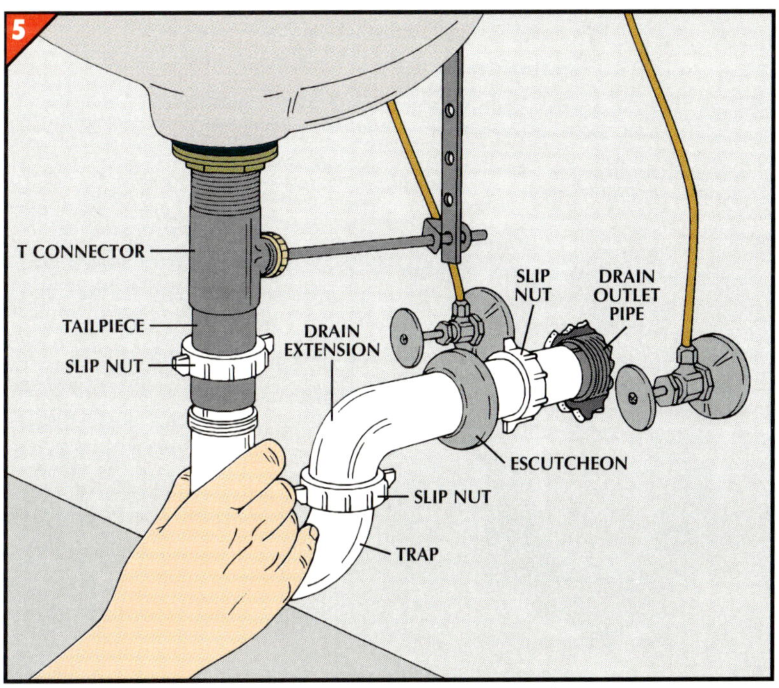

Time-Tested Methods for Unclogging Drains

When a bathroom drain stops or slows, see if other drains are affected. If so, the problem may lie elsewhere in the house's plumbing.

A Hierarchy of Solutions: If only one drain is blocked, try a plunger *(right)*. Prepare the drain by removing the strainer, pop-up plug, and overflow plate, if present; take apart a tub's drain hardware as shown in Step 1 on page 29. Stuff any overflow opening with rags.

If the plunger fails, you can sometimes clear a tub or shower drain with water *(below)*. A third method is to use an auger—a trap-and-drain auger for a tub, sink, or shower, and a closet auger for a toilet. Avoid compressed-air devices, which often compact the blockage and may cause old pipe joints to break apart.

Chemical Drain Cleaners: Do not pour chemical cleaning agents into a blocked drain. Many contain lye, and you could be exposed to the caustic as you continue work on the stoppage. Cleaners can be helpful once a tub, sink, or shower drain is open; applied regularly, they prevent buildup of debris. Never put such cleaners in a toilet, however. They do no good and can stain the porcelain.

TOOLS

- Foldout plunger
- Garden hose
- Drain flusher
- Trap-and-drain auger
- Closet auger

SAFETY TIPS

If human waste is present when you are unclogging a toilet, wear goggles and rubber gloves.

CLEARING A STOPPAGE WITH WATER

Flushing a drain with a hose.

A hose-mounted drain flusher, available at most hardware stores, will work in a shower or tub drain.

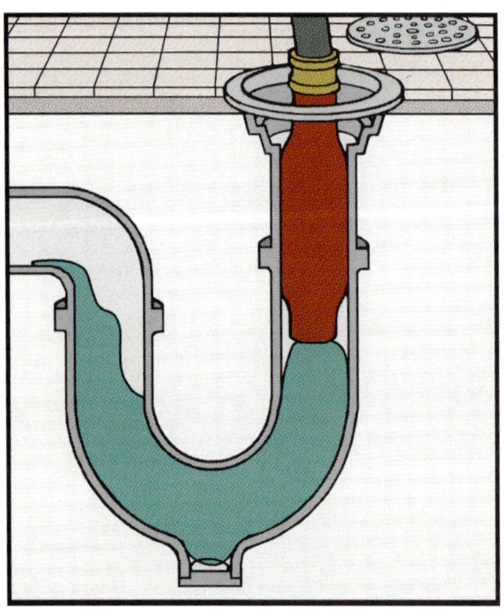

◆ Attach the drain flusher to a garden hose and push it into a shower drain; in a tub, insert it through the overflow opening past the level of the drain. Connect the other end of the hose to a faucet; for an indoor faucet, you will need a threaded adapter.

◆ Have a helper slowly turn on the hose water. The flusher will expand to fill the pipe so that the full force of water is directed at the clog.

CAUTION *Do not flush a clogged drain that contains caustic cleaners, and never leave a hose in any drain. The cleaner could splash into your face, and the hose could draw wastewater into the supply system if the pressure should drop.*

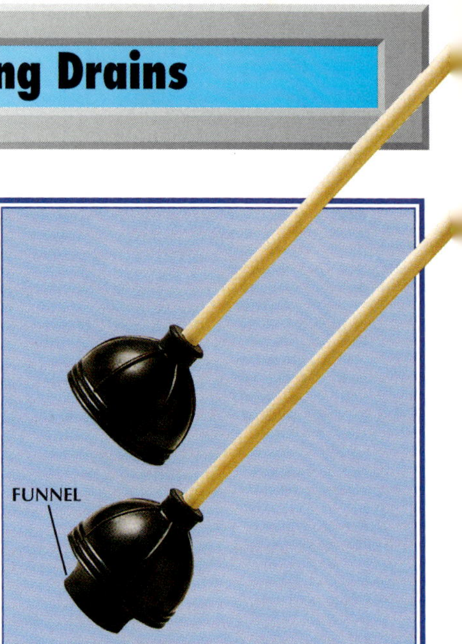

A Multi-Role Plunger

An ordinary force-cup plunger is suited to many drains, but it will not fit a toilet. For the bathroom, purchase a foldout plunger instead. As shown above, its cup can take on two different shapes.

With a tub, sink, or shower drain, keep the funnel portion tucked inside *(upper photo)*. Coat the rim of the cup with petroleum jelly and center it over the drain. Make sure that standing water covers the cup completely; if it does not, add more water. Without breaking the seal between drain and cup, pump the plunger down and up several times, then jerk it away. When the drain opens, run hot water through it to flush it clean.

For a toilet, extend the plunger's funnel lip *(lower photo)*. If a clogged toilet is too full, bail out some of the contents. If the bowl is empty, add water by hand, not by flushing. Fit the plunger over the opening near the bottom of the bowl and pump vigorously, then jerk it away. If the bowl empties, pour in water to confirm that the drain is fully opened.

BREAKING UP A CLOG WITH A TRAP-AND-DRAIN AUGER

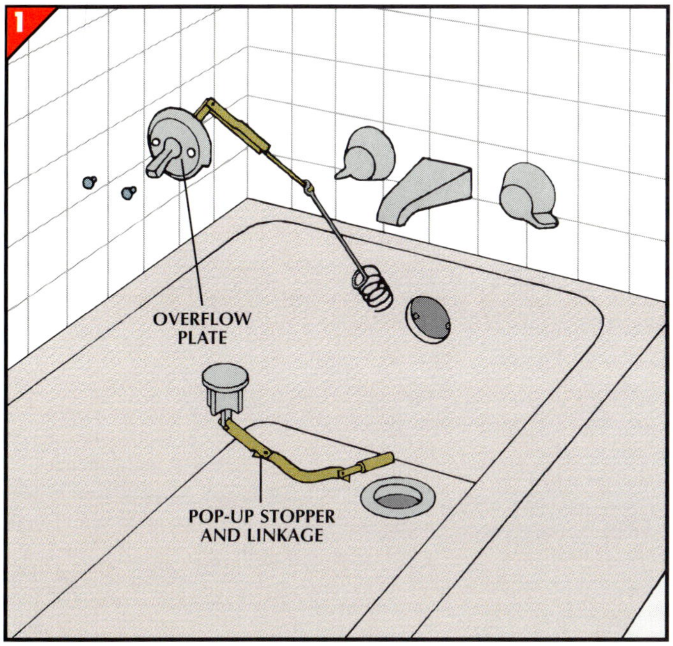

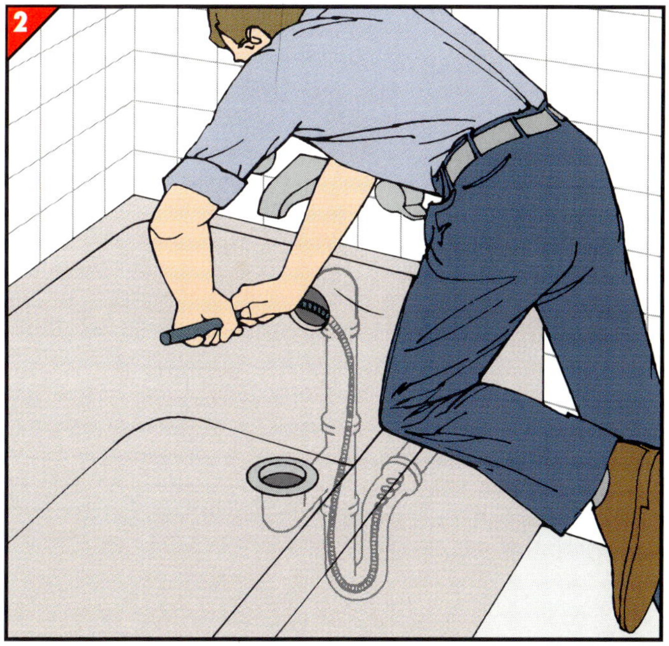

1. Gaining access to the drain.
To unclog a bathtub, unscrew the overflow plate and lift it up and out. Draw out the pop-up stopper and its linkage. Note how the parts line up so that you can put them back in the same way.

2. Inserting the auger.
◆ Cranking the auger handle clockwise, feed the auger tip through the tub overflow opening.
◆ When the auger wire reaches the blockage, move the auger slowly backward and forward while cranking. Continue to crank clockwise as you withdraw the auger wire; doing so helps to prevent you from dropping the material that caused the blockage.
◆ After clearing the drain, run hot water through it for 2 to 3 minutes.

OPENING A TOILET DRAIN WITH A CLOSET AUGER

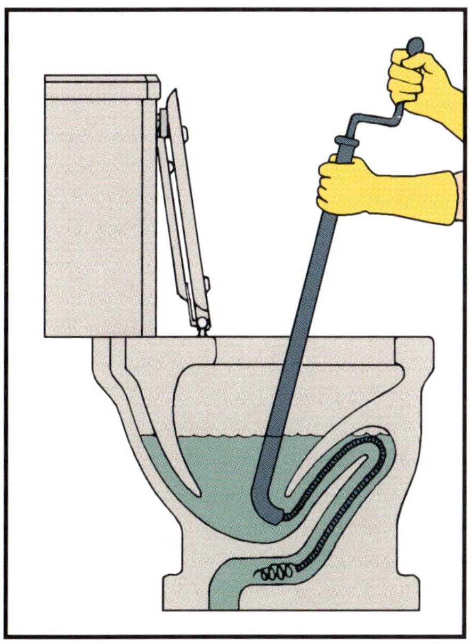

An auger meant for toilets.
The cranking handle of a closet auger attaches to a long sleeve shaped to help guide the tip of the auger into the trap. Closet augers work equally well in toilets with a front drain opening, as shown here, or with the opening at the back.
◆ Hold the sleeve near the top and position the other end against the drain opening. Crank the auger tip slowly clockwise into the trap until you hook the obstruction or break through it.
◆ Withdraw the auger while cranking the handle clockwise. If the drain remains clogged, repeat the process.
◆ When the drain seems clear, test it with a pail of water before attempting to flush the toilet.

Simple Toilet Repairs

Understanding how the mechanisms inside a toilet tank work can make their repair fairly simple. Certain parts vary, but most operate according to the same scheme. When you press the handle, a lift wire or a chain pulls a stopper off the opening to the bowl. Water rushes into the bowl. The falling water level in the tank causes a float to drop. This, in turn, opens the ball cock—the device that starts and stops the refill cycle. When the tank is nearly empty, the stopper drops into place. Rising water then lifts the float high enough to shut off the ball cock.

Diagnosing the Problem: One way to spot a mechanical breakdown is to lift the tank lid and watch a flush cycle. Also be alert to noises and leaks. The sound of water running constantly may indicate that the tank ball is not properly seated *(opposite)*. A high whine or whistle during flushing means that the ball cock needs attention *(pages 32-33)*. Visible leaks near the tank may be caused by loose bolts, worn washers, or condensation *(page 34)*.

Working Near Porcelain: Most toilets are made of vitreous china, which is easily cracked or broken. Set the lid on padding in an out-of-the-way place while working in the tank, and use gentle pressure when removing or tightening bolts. As shown on page 35, it may be safer to cut corroded seat-cover bolts than to strain to remove them with a wrench near fragile porcelain.

TOOLS

- Adjustable wrench
- Plastic cleansing pad or steel wool
- Locking-grip pliers
- Long-nose pliers
- Socket wrench with deep sockets
- Screwdriver
- Hacksaw

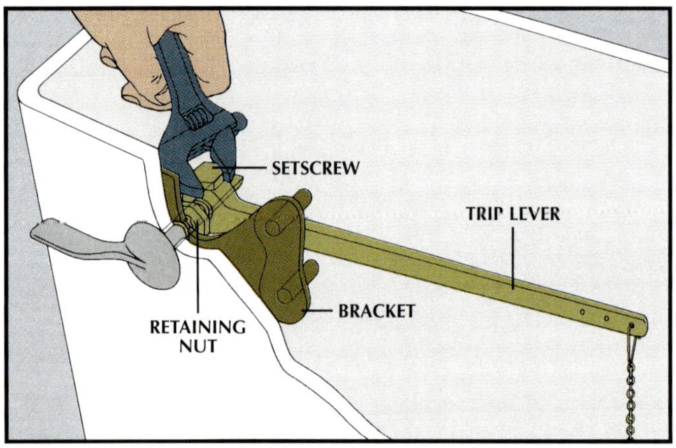

Tightening the handle.

If a toilet handle must be held down until the flush cycle is complete, the linkage between the handle and the trip lever needs to be secured.

◆ For a toilet with a bracket arrangement like the one above, tighten the retaining nut with an adjustable wrench so the bracket does not wobble but still moves freely when the handle is turned. Turn the nut counterclockwise—the opposite direction from that used to tighten most nuts. With a wrench or pliers, turn the trip-lever setscrew against the handle shaft.

◆ In models that have a one-piece handle and trip lever, tighten the nut that holds the handle on its shaft. This nut also must be tightened counterclockwise.

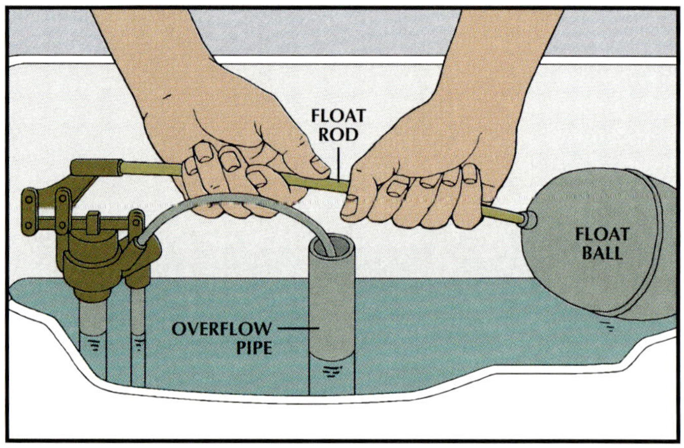

Adjusting the water level.

If water is cascading through the overflow pipe into the bowl, lower the water level by replacing the float ball or adjusting the float rod.

◆ Unscrew the float ball and examine it; if it is worn or there is water in it, replace it.

◆ If the ball is sound, bend the float rod $\frac{1}{2}$ inch downward with both hands *(above)*. Alternatively, unscrew the rod with pliers and bend it over a rounded surface, then put it back. The rod may break when bent; if that happens, replace it with a new one. Reattach the ball.

◆ Flush the toilet. The water should stop rising about $\frac{1}{2}$ inch below the top of the overflow pipe. If it does not, the rod must be readjusted.

REMEDIES FOR A LEAKING FLUSH ASSEMBLY

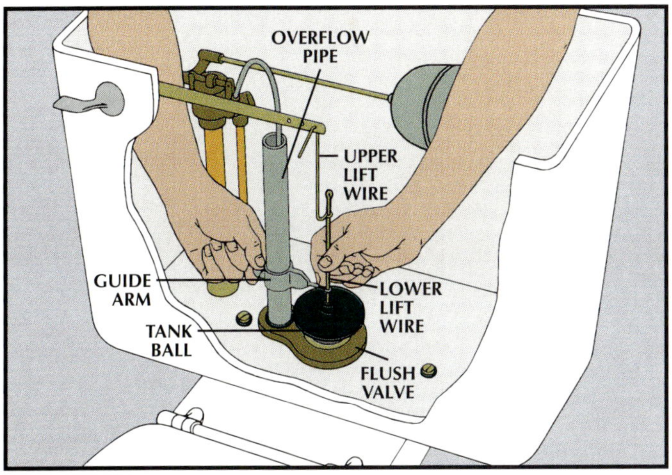

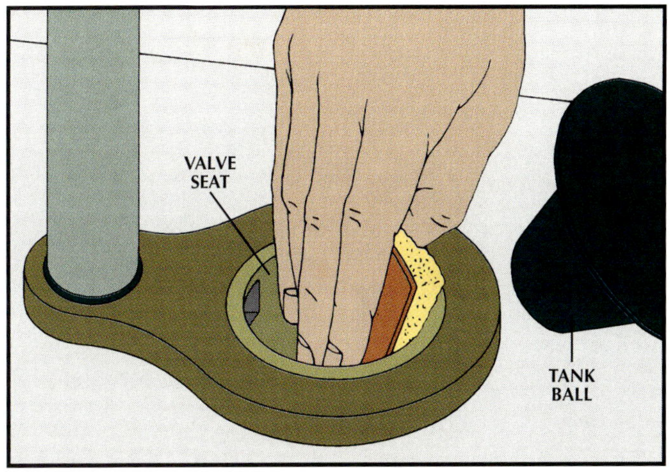

Adjusting the tank ball.

If water runs constantly into the bowl from the tank, sometimes making the toilet flush, first try reseating the tank ball.

◆ Turn off the water at the shutoff valve and remove the lid.

◆ Flush the toilet. If the tank ball does not fall straight into the flush valve opening, loosen the thumbscrew fastening the guide arm to the overflow pipe *(above)*.

◆ Reposition the arm and the lower lift wire so the tank ball is centered over the flush valve. If necessary, straighten the lift wires.

◆ Turn the water on. If the leak persists, clean mineral deposits off the ball and valve seat *(right)*.

Cleaning the tank ball and valve seat.

◆ Turn off the water and empty the tank.

◆ Unscrew the tank ball and wash it with warm water and detergent. If the ball is worn, replace it with a modern flapper ball hinged to prevent misalignment *(below)*.

◆ Gently scour the seat of the flush valve with fine steel wool or a plastic cleansing pad *(above)*.

◆ Replace the ball and turn on the water. If the valve still leaks, a special replacement flush valve seat can be placed over the old one. To replace the old valve seat completely, remove the tank as shown on page 34.

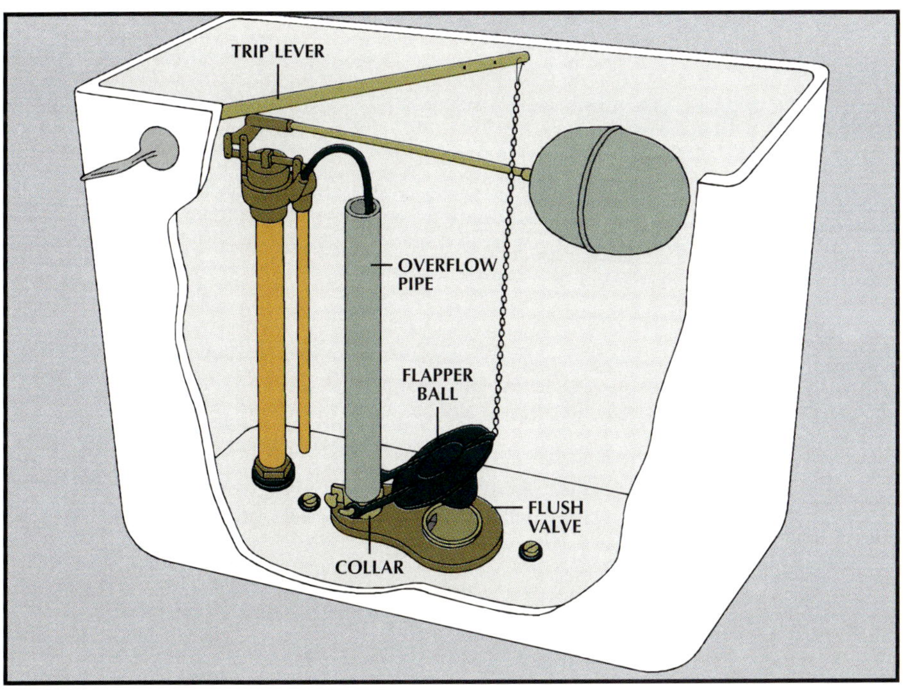

Installing a hinged flapper ball.

◆ Turn off the water, drain the tank, and remove the old guide arm, lift wires, and tank ball.

◆ Slide the collar of the flapper ball to the bottom of the overflow pipe and align the ball over the flush valve. If there is a thumbscrew on the collar, tighten it.

◆ Hook the chain from the ball through a hole in the trip lever directly above, leaving about $\frac{1}{2}$ inch of slack.

◆ Turn the water on, flush the toilet, and check whether the tank drains completely. If it does not, lessen the slack or move the chain one or two holes toward the rear of the lift arm.

REPAIRS FOR THE TANK'S FILL MECHANISM

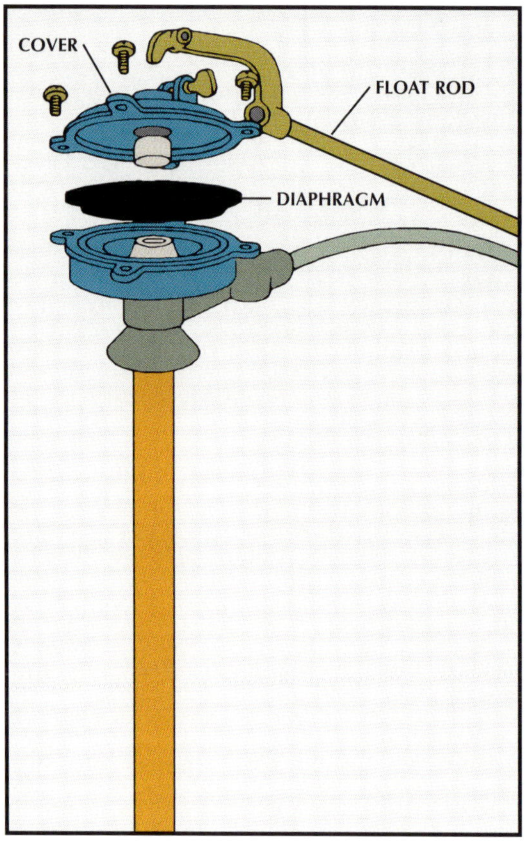

Servicing a ball cock.
When a diaphragm ball cock or a float-cup ball cock develops a minor leak, repair it with parts available at plumbing-supply stores. Replace other, older types of ball cocks *(below)* rather than attempting repairs.

◆ Shut off the water and flush the toilet.

◆ Remove the top screws and lift off the cover and float rod assembly.

◆ In a diaphragm ball cock *(left),* take out and replace the diaphragm, rubber gaskets, and washers. For a float-cup ball cock like the one shown at far right, replace the rubber valve seal and washers.

◆ Attach the ball cock cover and turn the water on. If the ball cock still leaks, or appears worn-out, replace it.

A DEVICE FOR REPLENISHING THE TANK

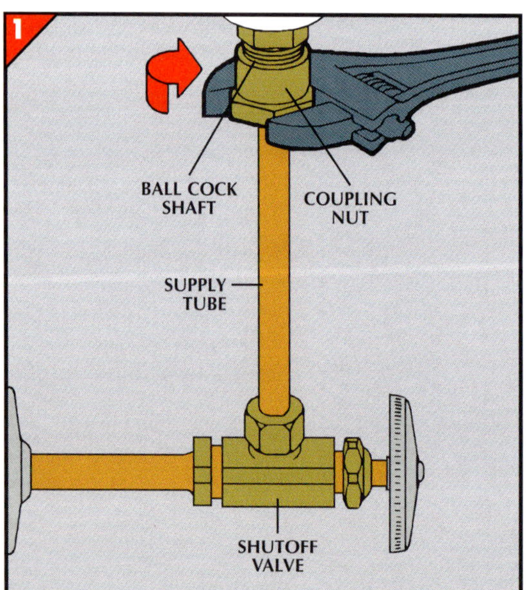

1. Disconnecting the supply tube.

◆ Turn off the water at the shutoff valve, flush the toilet, and sponge out the remaining water from the tank.

◆ With an adjustable wrench, unscrew the coupling nut on the underside of the tank that attaches the supply tube to the ball cock shaft.

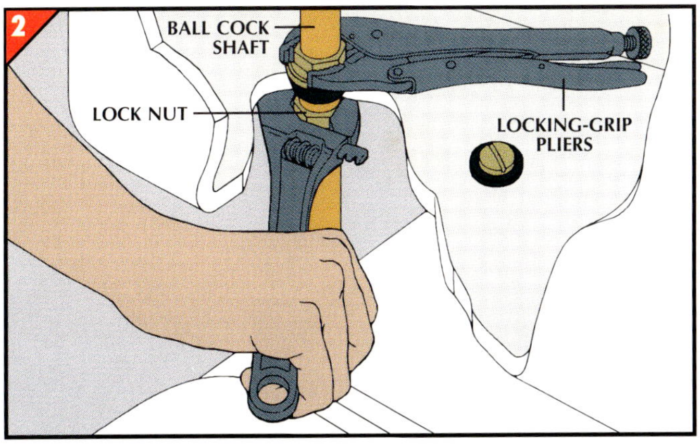

2. Removing the ball cock.

◆ Inside the tank, attach locking-grip pliers to the base of the ball cock shaft. The pliers will wedge against the side of the tank and free your hands.

◆ With an adjustable wrench, unscrew the lock nut that secures the ball cock shaft on the underside of the tank *(left)*. Use firm but gentle pressure to avoid cracking the tank.

◆ If the nut resists, soak it with penetrating oil for 10 or 15 minutes and try again. Once the nut is removed, lift the ball cock out of the tank.

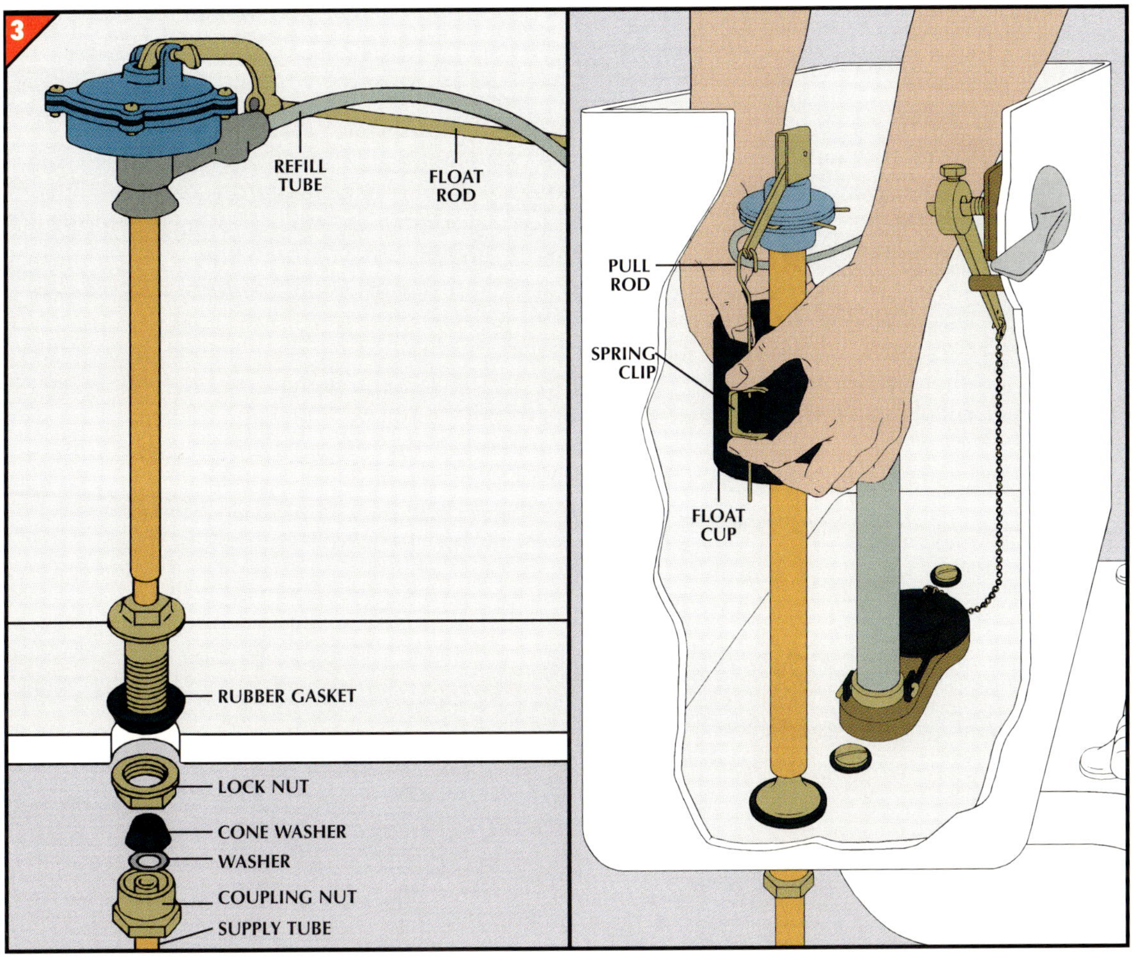

3. Installing a modern ball cock.

Diaphragm ball cocks and float-cup ball cocks are secured in place in the same way. Float-cup ball cocks require a simple adjustment as well. Float-cup ball cocks come in several heights; measure your tank depth before buying one.

◆ Put the new ball cock shank through the rubber gasket supplied with it and through the hole in the tank. Then screw a lock nut onto the ball cock shaft underneath the tank.

◆ Inside the tank, hold the base of the ball cock with locking-grip pliers. Tighten the lock nut.

◆ Insert a new washer in the coupling nut on the supply tube; some supply tubes come with built-in washers. If the tube extends through the nut and washer, place a cone washer over the tube *(above, left)*. Screw the coupling nut to the bottom of the ball cock shaft.

◆ Attach the float rod assembly and refill tube, and turn the water back on at the shutoff valve.

For a float-cup ball cock, adjust the ball cock to change the water level in the tank. To raise the level, pinch the spring clip on the ball cock's pull rod and slide the float cup higher *(above, right)*. To lower the water, move the cup down.

SEALING LEAKS AT BOLTS AND GASKETS

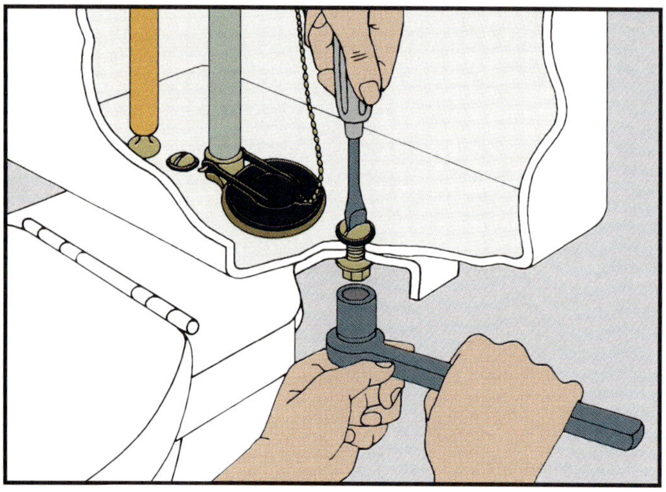

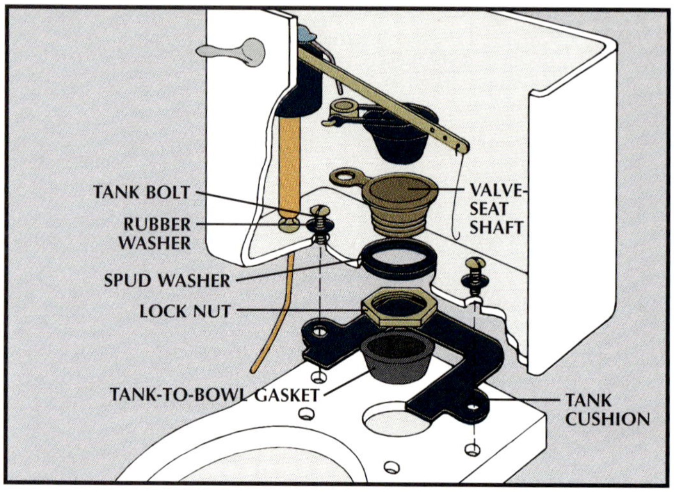

Tightening the tank bolts.
Drips at the tank bolts may be caused by condensation on the tank's exterior, or by seepage from the inside. To check, pour a few drops of food coloring into the tank and hold white tissue over the bolts. If the tissue turns that color, tighten the bolts to stop the leaks.

◆ Turn off the water and drain the tank. Hold the slotted head of the bolt with a screwdriver or have a helper do it.
◆ Tighten the nut below the tank with a socket wrench and a deep socket *(above)*, or use an adjustable wrench.
◆ Turn the water back on.
◆ If the leak persists, drain the tank, remove the bolts, and replace their washers.

Replacing flush-valve washers.
If water leaks outside the toilet at the connection between tank and bowl, you must remove the tank.

◆ Turn off the water, drain the tank, disconnect the supply tube *(page 32)*, and unscrew the tank bolts.
◆ Lift the tank off the bowl and set it on its back on a padded work surface.
◆ The components that connect the tank and bowl appear above in diagrammatic form. Remove the lock nut on the valve-seat shaft protruding from the tank bottom, then pull the shaft into the tank and replace the spud washer and tank-to-bowl gasket. Reattach the lock nut.
◆ Place the tank on the tank cushion, reconnect the tank bolts, and attach the supply tube. Turn on the water.

DETERRING TOILET TANK CONDENSATION

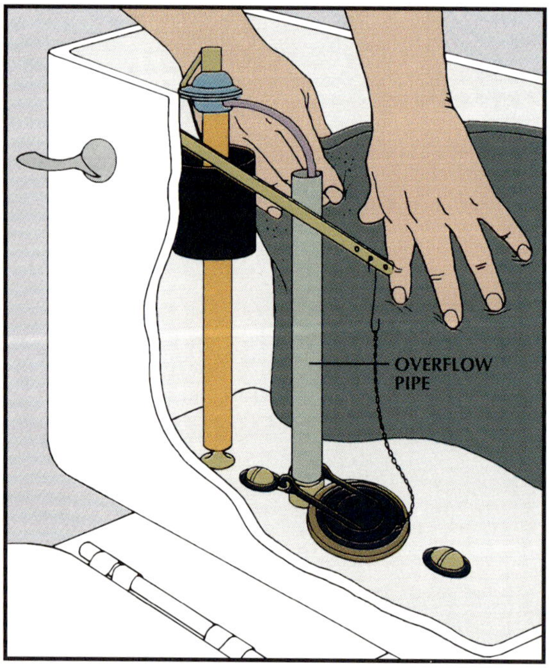

Installing insulation pads.
Condensation on the outside of a toilet tank may signal other problems, such as a constant leak from tank to bowl. If temperature or humidity is the cause, line the tank with a waterproof insulating material such as foam rubber.

◆ Turn off the water, drain the tank, and sponge it dry.
◆ Measure the inside width and depth of the tank and the height from the bottom of the tank to a point 1 inch above the overflow pipe.
◆ Cut four pieces of $\frac{1}{2}$-inch-thick foam rubber to fit the front, the back, and each side.
◆ Trim 1 inch from the width of the front and back pieces so they will abut the side pieces.
◆ Make a cutout for the toilet handle, and be sure the pads do not interfere with other moving parts.
◆ Apply a liberal coating of silicone glue or rubber cement to the inside tank surfaces; press the pads in place.
◆ Let the glue dry 24 hours before refilling the tank.

REPLACING A TOILET SEAT

Removing the seat bolts.
To take off an old toilet seat, unscrew the nuts underneath the bowl. First try to turn the nuts with long-nose pliers. Should that fail, twist gently using a socket wrench with a deep socket. If the seat bolts are too corroded to loosen, apply the methods below.

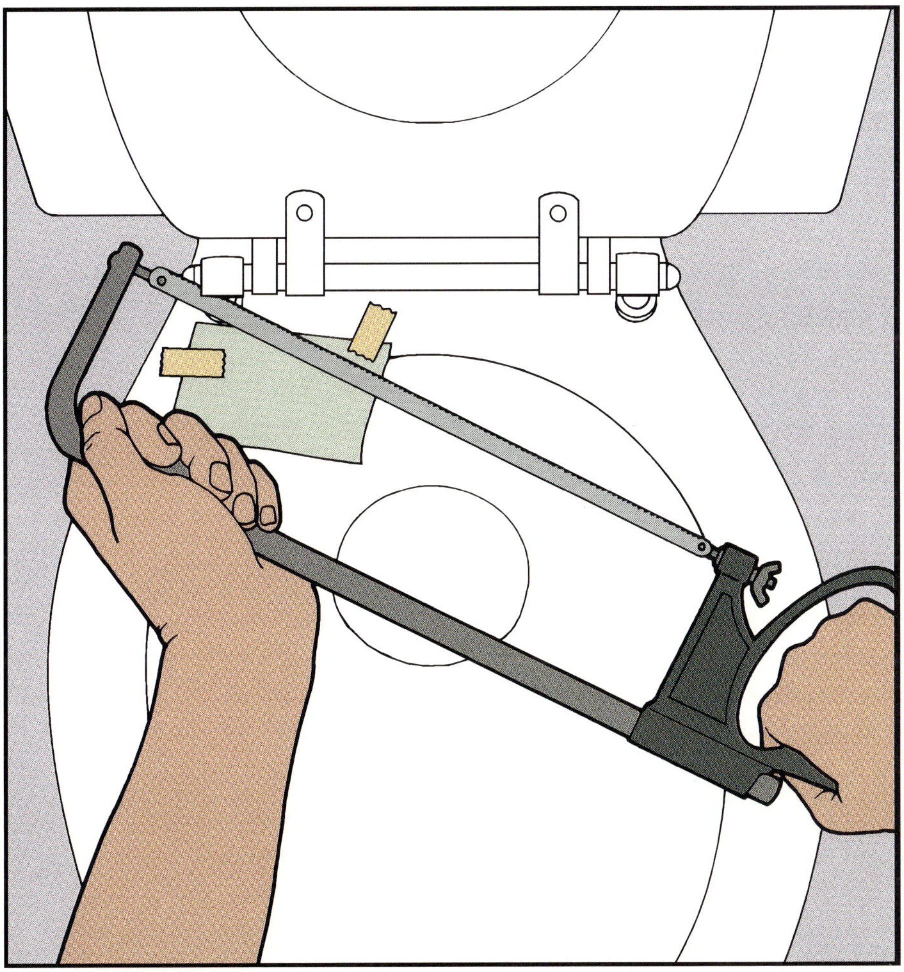

Freeing corroded bolts.
◆ Soak the bolts with penetrating oil for at least 30 minutes—overnight is better still. Then try loosening the nuts once more.
◆ If penetrating oil does not free the nuts, tape thin cardboard on top of the bowl next to the heads of the bolts to protect the china. Then, with a hacksaw, cut off the boltheads, sawing through the attached washers *(left).*

2 Updating Your Bathroom

You can noticeably improve almost any bathroom with a variety of basic amenities. From hanging a mirror to adding an exhaust fan, the installations and modifications explained in the pages that follow not only modernize a bathroom but also make it safer, more accessible, and generally more agreeable to family members and guests alike.

Framing for a recessed medicine cabinet →

Hanging a Mirror

Placing a large mirror above the bathroom washbasin not only aids grooming, it seems to enlarge the room. Buy $\frac{1}{4}$-inch glass mirror and have the dealer cut it. Ask to have the edges seamed, which removes the sharp side of each edge. In determining the dimensions, plan for at least $\frac{1}{8}$ inch of clear space around the mirror to ease installation and to allow for settling of the house.

Methods for Mounting: Hanging a mirror on the wall requires special hardware, which comes in several varieties. In the system illustrated here, J clips and L clips anchor the mirror. Made of metal, J clips support the weight of the glass and provide a $\frac{1}{8}$-inch ventilation space behind the mirror to prevent corrosion. Plastic L clips keep the top of the mirror in place.

Self-adhesive felt pads stuck to the back of the mirror help to maintain the ventilation space and prevent the mirror from flexing. In areas subject to earthquakes, a bulky adhesive called mirror mastic *(box, opposite)* not only sticks the mirror to the wall but also serves instead of felt pads as a spacer.

Avoiding Corrosion: A mirror's reflective coating is easily damaged by moisture and harsh chemicals. Never mount a mirror so that it touches a backsplash; water creeping onto the backing could ruin it. Let a freshly plastered or painted wall dry for a week before installing a mirror. When cleaning the glass, avoid preparations with ammonia.

CAUTION *If you are carrying a mirror and it starts to fall, do what the professionals do—get out of the way. Never try to catch it.*

Mirror-Handling Checklist

✔ Each square foot of $\frac{1}{4}$-inch mirror weighs more than 3 pounds. Work with a helper if your mirror is larger than 12 square feet—for example, if it is larger than 3 feet by 4 feet or 6 by 2.

✔ When you bring a mirror home, store it on edge.

✔ Salts and oils from human skin can damage mirror backing; always wear work gloves when handling the mirror.

✔ Carry the mirror on edge so it will not sag and break of its own weight. When working with a helper and navigating stairs, post the stronger person at the lower end.

TOOLS

- Electronic stud finder
- Drill
- Level

MATERIALS

- $\frac{1}{4}$-inch glass mirror, cut to size
- Self-adhesive felt pads
- J clips
- L clips
- $1\frac{1}{2}$-inch flat-head screws
- $1\frac{1}{2}$-inch round-head screws
- Mirror mastic

1. Preparing the wall.

◆ Mark the locations of the mirror's bottom corners on the wall—at least $\frac{1}{8}$ inch away from the backsplash and adjacent walls. Use a straightedge to join the marks to make a baseline for the mirror.

◆ To check for bulges in the wall, run a straight board over the area the mirror will occupy *(above)*.

◆ To determine the height of any bulge, center the board on it and, using the bulge as a pivot, push one end of the board against the wall. Have your helper measure the gap between the wall and the board at the other end and halve this distance.

◆ Flatten bulges higher than $\frac{1}{8}$ inch with a hammer.

2. Mounting the J clips.

◆ Using an electronic stud finder, locate the studs inside the mirror area nearest the ends of the baseline.

◆ Place the bottom corner of a J clip on the baseline at a stud near one end of the line. Mark the location of the clip's screw holes and drill a pilot hole $1\frac{1}{2}$ inches deep at each mark.

◆ Secure the clip with flathead screws *(above),* then cover the heads with a felt pad *(inset).*

◆ Attach a J clip to a stud at the line's other end.

◆ For a mirror wider than 5 feet, mount a J clip on every second stud.

3. Placing the mirror in the J clips.

◆ Using a level, measure up from each J clip a distance equal to the height of the mirror plus $\frac{1}{4}$ inch.

◆ Mark and drill a pilot hole into the stud at that height.

◆ Stick two or more rows of felt pads on the back of the mirror, keeping the pads several inches in from each side.

◆ With a helper, lift the mirror. Tilt the top edge forward and lower the bottom edge into the J clips. If necessary, slide the mirror sideways into its intended position.

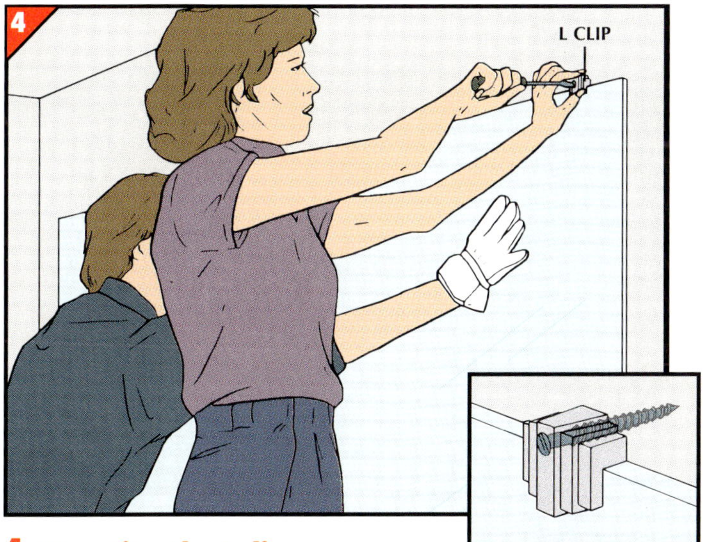

4. Mounting the L clips.

◆ Push the mirror toward the wall, listening carefully for the muted sound of felt pads making contact. A sharp sound indicates the mirror is hitting the wall; add pads on top of the first ones. Test again and add a third layer of pads if necessary.

◆ While a helper steadies the mirror, drive a round-head screw through the hole in an L clip and into each pilot hole *(inset).* Tighten each fastener no more than needed to prevent movement of the mirror when you push on it.

Mirror Mastic for a Permanent Bond

Mirror mastic helps secure a mirror to the wall without damage to the backing. Although particularly suited to earthquake zones because it remains resilient and will flex with tremors, mastic is messy to use and permanent. Attempting to remove a mirror glued with this adhesive usually damages both mirror and wall.

Mastic, which takes the place of felt pads on the back of the mirror, is applied after Step 2 of mirror installation. Lay the mirror facedown on a clean blanket. Using a wood scrap to avoid scratching the backing, scoop mastic onto the mirror in separate pats—each about $1\frac{1}{2}$ inches across and $\frac{3}{4}$ inch thick. Apply four pats for every square foot of mirror, keeping the adhesive at least $2\frac{1}{2}$ inches from the edges. Then mount the mirror as shown in Steps 3 and 4.

Installing a Glass Tub Enclosure

Replacing an old-fashioned shower-curtain rod with a glass tub enclosure not only helps to keep shower spray where it belongs but also adds an elegant touch to the bathroom. Most tub enclosures are designed to fit a standard 5-foot tub between two side walls and are made of glass and extruded aluminum. They come in many styles: Panels may be clear, frosted, or mirrored, and frames may be polished bright or anodized in gold or other colors.

Preparing the Tub Area: Before buying an enclosure kit, check your tub rim and side walls with a level and a framing square. If the tub is as much as $\frac{1}{4}$ inch off level, or if the walls are out of plumb by that amount, you can compensate by adjusting the enclosure's panel rollers; if the variance is much greater, an enclosure may be impractical.

For a tub with tiled walls that do not extend as high as the top of the enclosure frame, add filler tiles as needed, securing them with a waterproof bathroom adhesive.

A Sturdy Installation: Methods for securing the enclosure frame in place vary depending on whether there are studs located where the frame is to be attached. When studs are present, drill through the finished wall and attach the frame to the stud with $1\frac{1}{2}$-inch No. 8 wood screws. When studs are not present, the frame should be secured with hollow-wall anchors.

Care and Maintenance: To keep water from spraying between the panels into the bathroom when showering, keep the inner panel toward the shower head. The only upkeep required is periodic cleaning with a nonabrasive window cleaner and, when necessary, adjusting the panel rollers in their slots.

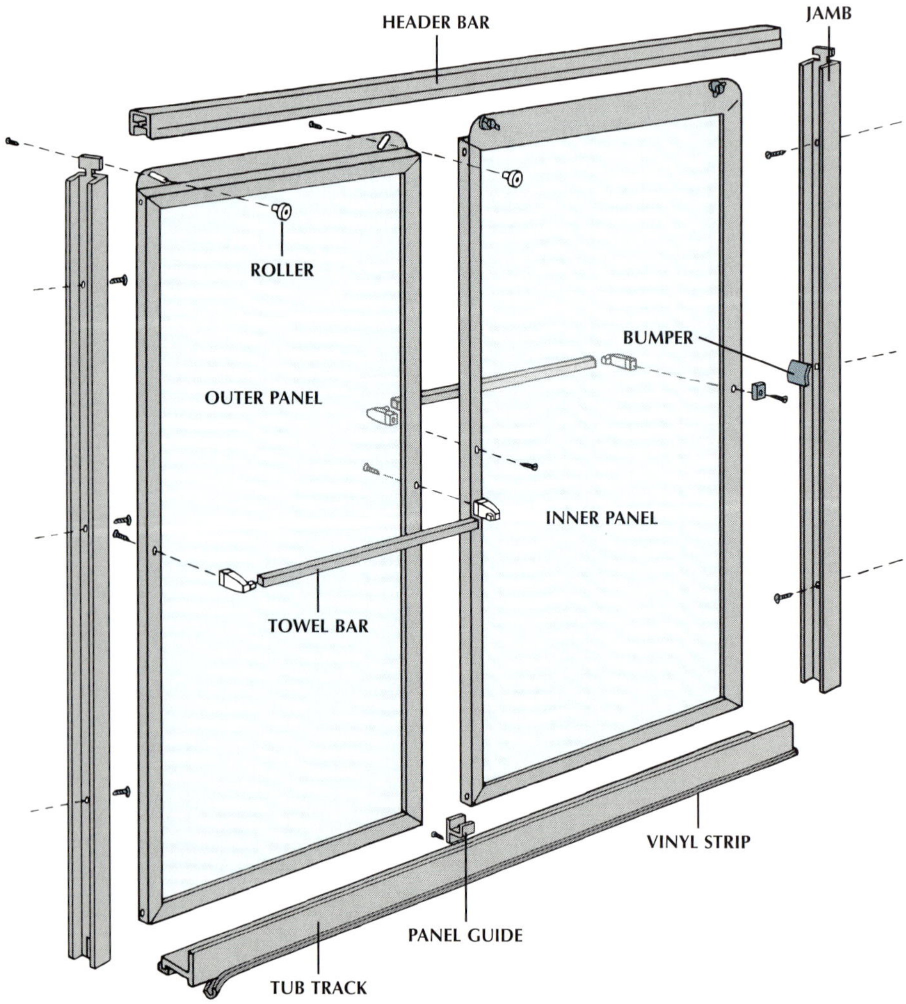

TOOLS

- Tape measure
- Hacksaw with metal-cutting blade
- Miter box
- Metal file
- Grease pencil
- Utility knife
- Level
- Electric drill

SAFETY TIPS

If you must drill into ceramic tile with a carbide bit, wear safety goggles and use a dust mask.

Anatomy of an enclosure. The typical glass tub enclosure at left consists of a frame and sliding panels. The frame includes side jambs, a header bar, and a tub track, which is sealed against the tub rim with a flexible vinyl strip. The tempered glass panels, each with a towel bar in this example, ride inside the header bar on adjustable rollers and are held in the tub track by a panel guide. Bumpers keep the panels from hitting the jambs too hard.

1. Cutting the pieces.

◆ Measure the tub rim between the two side walls, then subtract $\frac{1}{16}$ inch to avoid too tight a fit. Mark the tub track to this length and cut it with a hacksaw, using a miter box to ensure a square cut *(left)*.

◆ To measure for the header bar, set one of the jambs on the tub rim against a side wall and mark the wall at the top of the jamb. Mark the second wall the same way, then determine the distance between the two marks. Subtract $\frac{1}{16}$ inch and cut the header bar to that length.

◆ Smooth the cut edges of both pieces with a metal file.

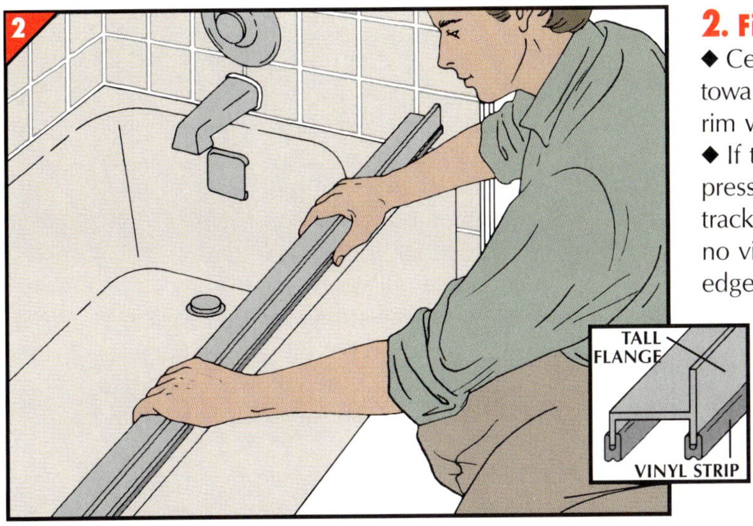

2. Fitting the tub track.

◆ Center the tub track on the tub rim, with the tall flange toward the room. Mark the position of the track on the tub rim with a grease pencil.

◆ If the enclosure kit includes vinyl sealing strips *(inset)*, press them onto the flanges on the underside of the tub track; trim off any excess with a utility knife. For kits with no vinyl strips, apply a bead of silicone caulk along the edges at the bottom of the track.

◆ Set the track on the tub rim between the marked lines. Secure it in place with masking tape until both of the jambs are installed.

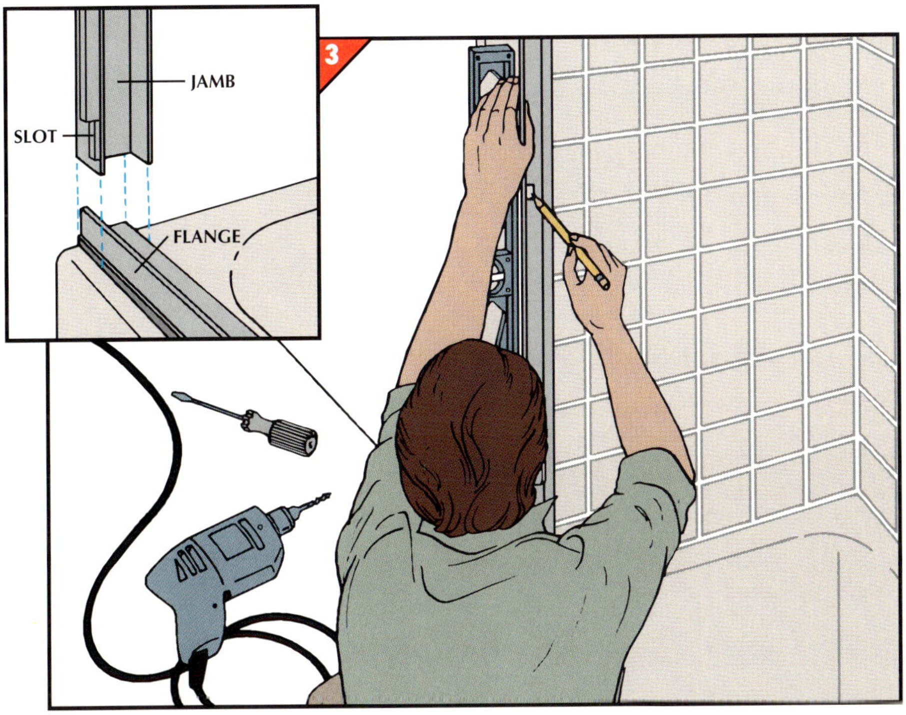

3. Marking the walls.

◆ Place a jamb at one end of the tub track so that the slot in the jamb goes over the track flange *(inset)*. Adjust the jamb against the wall with a level to get it upright, then mark the wall through each screw hole. Set the jamb aside. Repeat the process for the facing wall with the other jamb.

◆ Drill holes at each mark for the fasteners: $\frac{3}{32}$-inch pilot holes for wood screws if a stud is present behind the wall, or larger holes for hollow-wall anchors. Use a carbide-tipped bit for ceramic tile.

◆ Put the bumper in place on one of the jambs, place the jamb on the track as before, and fasten the jamb to the wall. Do not install the other jamb yet.

4. Completing the frame.

◆ Place the bumper on the unattached jamb and set the jamb aside.
◆ Slide one end of the header bar into the top of the installed jamb, inserting the bar into the jamb's T-shaped fitting.
◆ Angle the free end of the bar slightly outward and connect it to the T fitting on the unattached jamb *(inset).*
◆ Gently lift the bottom of the jamb into place on the tub track and fasten the jamb to the wall.
◆ Remove the masking tape from the tub track now that the track is held in place by the jambs.

5. Hanging the panels.

With the frame installation complete, put the door panels in place.
◆ Place a roller in each of the diagonal slots at the tops of the door panels; do not tighten the roller screws yet.
◆ Hold the inner panel with its rollers facing the tub. Lift the panel to set the rollers over the lip of the header bar's inside flange. Install the outer panel so that its rollers rest on the outside flange of the bar *(inset).*
◆ Slide the panels against the jambs. If a panel does not slide freely or does not hang straight, adjust it by removing the panel from the frame and shifting the position of one or both of the rollers within the diagonal slots. Tighten each roller screw and rehang the panel.

6. Attaching the hardware.

◆ Secure the panel guide *(inset)* to the tub track so that it will retain the bottom edges of both panels.
◆ Attach any accessories supplied with the kit—in this case, two towel bars.
◆ Apply a thin bead of silicone caulk where the frame meets the tub and walls. Smooth the caulk if necessary with a finger dipped in liquid detergent. Let the caulk cure overnight before using the tub.

Making the Bathroom Safe and Accessible

Most bathrooms combine at least three potentially dangerous elements: electricity, water, and slick surfaces. You can improve the safety of your bathroom and the ease with which you can use it by undertaking some or all of the modest projects described here and on pages 44-47.

Measures against Falls: A water-slicked shower floor or tub can be dangerous. To reduce the likelihood of accident, add texture to either surface with grip strips *(below)*.

Also consider installing grab bars *(page 44)* as handholds on walls surrounding the bathing area. Towel bars are too weak to rely on. Choose grab bars made from metal tubing without sharp corners. And avoid hanging towels on them; someone could accidentally grasp the towel instead and fall.

Preventing Electric Shock: To minimize the hazards of operating electrical appliances near water, the National Electrical Code requires that new bathroom electrical circuits be equipped with a device that is called a ground-fault circuit interrupter, or GFCI. If your bathroom does not have this protection, you can add it by installing a GFCI outlet in place of the receptacle that already exists *(page 45)*.

Adaptations for Disabilities: For someone with a disability, the typical bathroom can be difficult, or even impossible, to use. Ideally, a bathroom for a family member who needs a wheelchair, a walker, or simply some assistance with standing up or sitting down is designed from the outset for their comfort and capabilities. As described on pages 46 and 47, you can also make an old bathroom somewhat more accessible with a variety of products and modifications.

APPLYING GRIP STRIPS

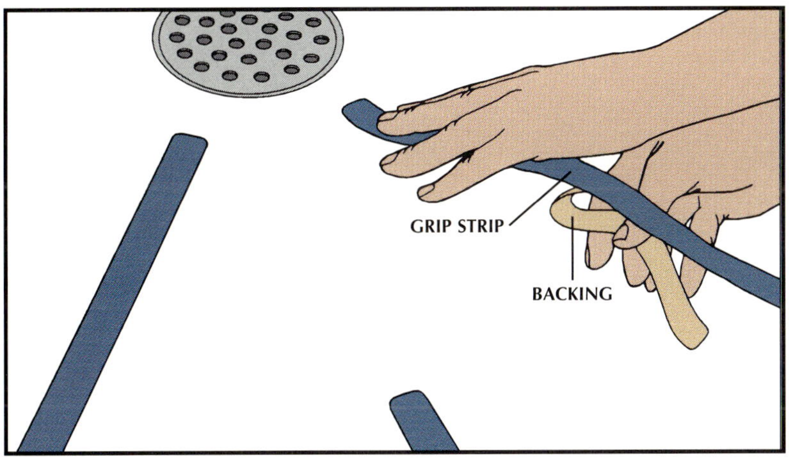

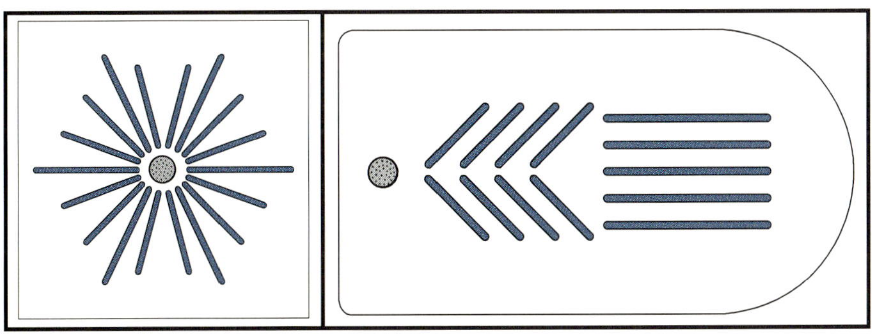

Laying a safe pattern of strips.

◆ Wash the shower or tub floor, clean it with rubbing alcohol, and let it dry.

◆ For a shower, plan a star pattern of strips *(below, far left)*; for a tub, arrange strips both in a chevron pointed at the drain and in parallel lines *(below, left)*.

◆ To apply each strip, peel the backing from one end and press it firmly in place, then continue peeling as you work *(left)*. If you must cut a strip, round the corners so they will not curl later.

GRAB BARS FOR SHOWER AND TUB

1. Positioning the bar.
The grab bar shown here is de signed so each flange is anchored by two screws in a stud and a toggle bolt through the wall. (To support someone weighing more than about 250 pounds, double the studs from the other side of the wall and use three screws.)
◆ Locate studs above the tile with an electronic stud finder.
◆ Drop a plumb line at the center of each stud and mark the width of the stud with masking tape at the height you intend to anchor the flanges.
◆ Place the grab bar so that two mounting holes in each flange lie on the tape. Mark all six hole locations with a pencil *(above).*

2. Drilling holes.
◆ At each hole location, tap a punch with a hammer to break through the slick tile glaze.
◆ Wearing safety goggles, use carbide-tipped bits to drill a $\frac{1}{2}$-inch hole through the wall for each toggle bolt. For the screws, drill a hole through the tile slightly larger than the screw diameter, then use an ordinary bit to drill a smaller hole into the wooden stud.
◆ Remove the tape from the wall.

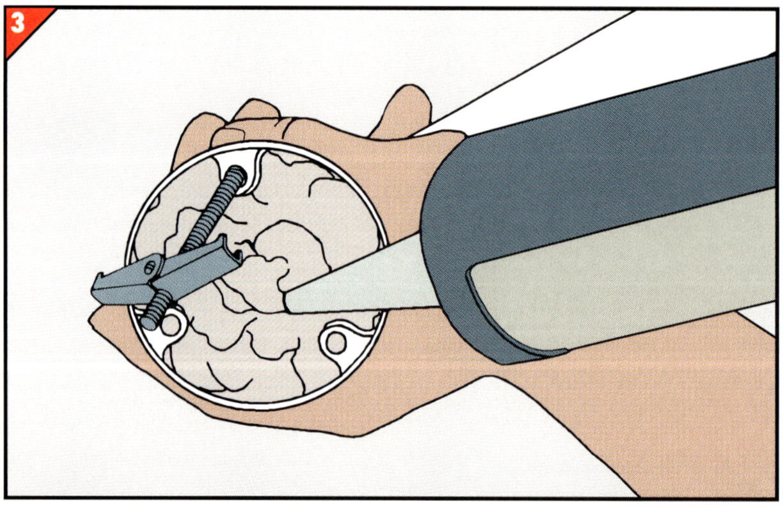

3. Mounting the bar.
◆ Insert a $\frac{3}{16}$-inch toggle bolt into its hole on a flange and fill the inside of the flange with silicone caulk *(above).* Prepare the other flange the same way.
◆ Position the bar on the wall, pushing the toggle bolts into place. Insert 3-inch-long screws into the remaining holes and tighten screws and toggle bolts with a screwdriver.
◆ Caulk around each flange and let dry for 24 hours.

SHOCKPROOFING AN ELECTRICAL OUTLET

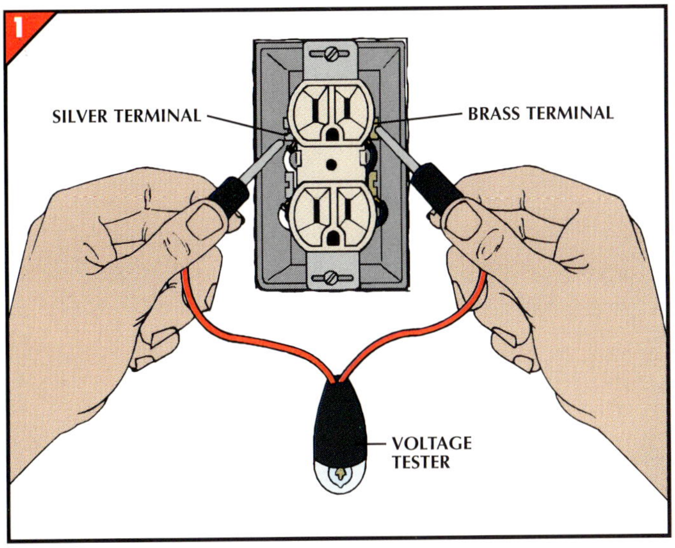

1. Checking for power.

◆ Turn off the electricity to the bathroom receptacle at the service panel. Then unscrew and remove the cover plate.

◆ Test for power at the receptacle with a voltage tester *(left)*. Holding the tester by its insulated wires, touch the probes to each pair of brass and silver terminals; the tester will not light if the power is off.

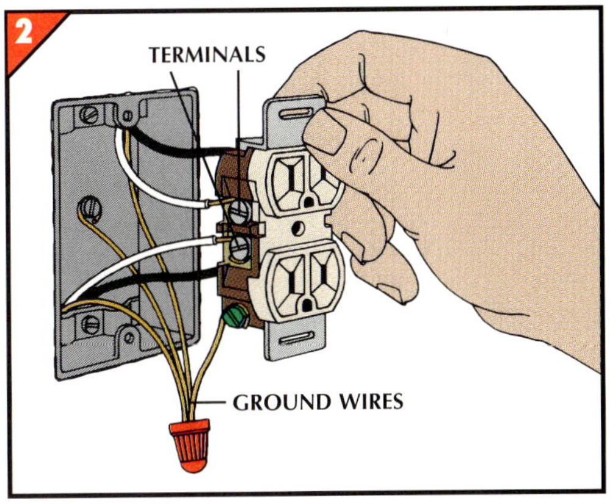

2. Removing the receptacle.

Unscrew the receptacle and pull it from the box. Look inside; consult an electrician if the wiring is aluminum, if there are no ground wires, or if the box is less than $2\frac{3}{4}$ inches deep. Otherwise, detach all wires from the receptacle terminals.

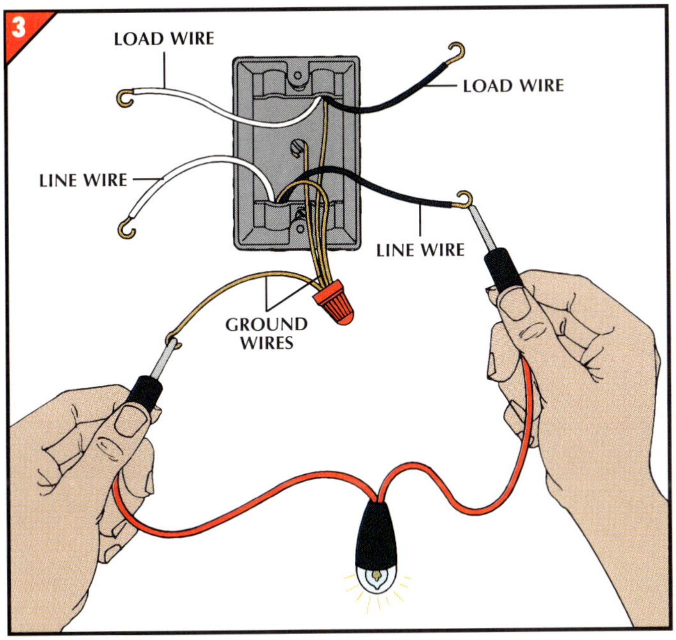

3. Identifying line and load wires.

To install a GFCI receptacle, you need to know which black wire in the box brings power from the service panel.

◆ To identify this so-called line wire, stretch out all the wires so they touch neither each other nor the box. Then turn the power on.

◆ Keeping your hands away from any bare wires, touch one probe of the voltage tester to a ground wire and the other to each black wire. The one that causes the tester to glow is the line wire *(above)*; the other is called the load wire.

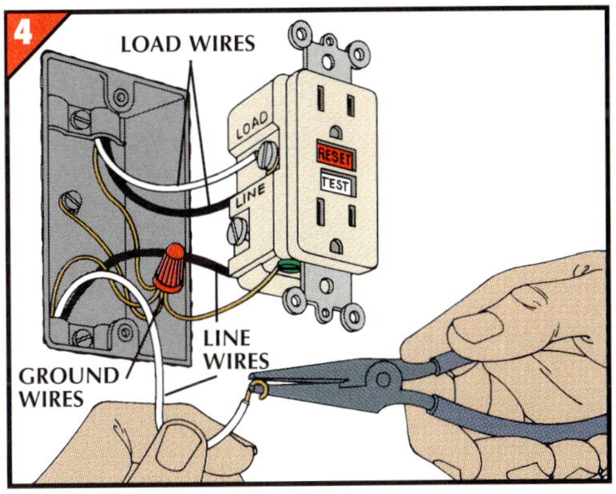

4. Installing the GFCI.

◆ Turn the power off. Attach the wires of the line and load cables to the corresponding terminals on the GFCI, connecting the black wires to the brass terminals. Attach the ground wire to the green terminal.

◆ Screw the GFCI into place and replace the cover plate. Turn on the power, then press the test button. If the wiring is correct, the reset button will pop out, interrupting the power going to the receptacle. Depress the button to reset the GFCI.

ADAPTING A BATHROOM FOR SPECIAL NEEDS

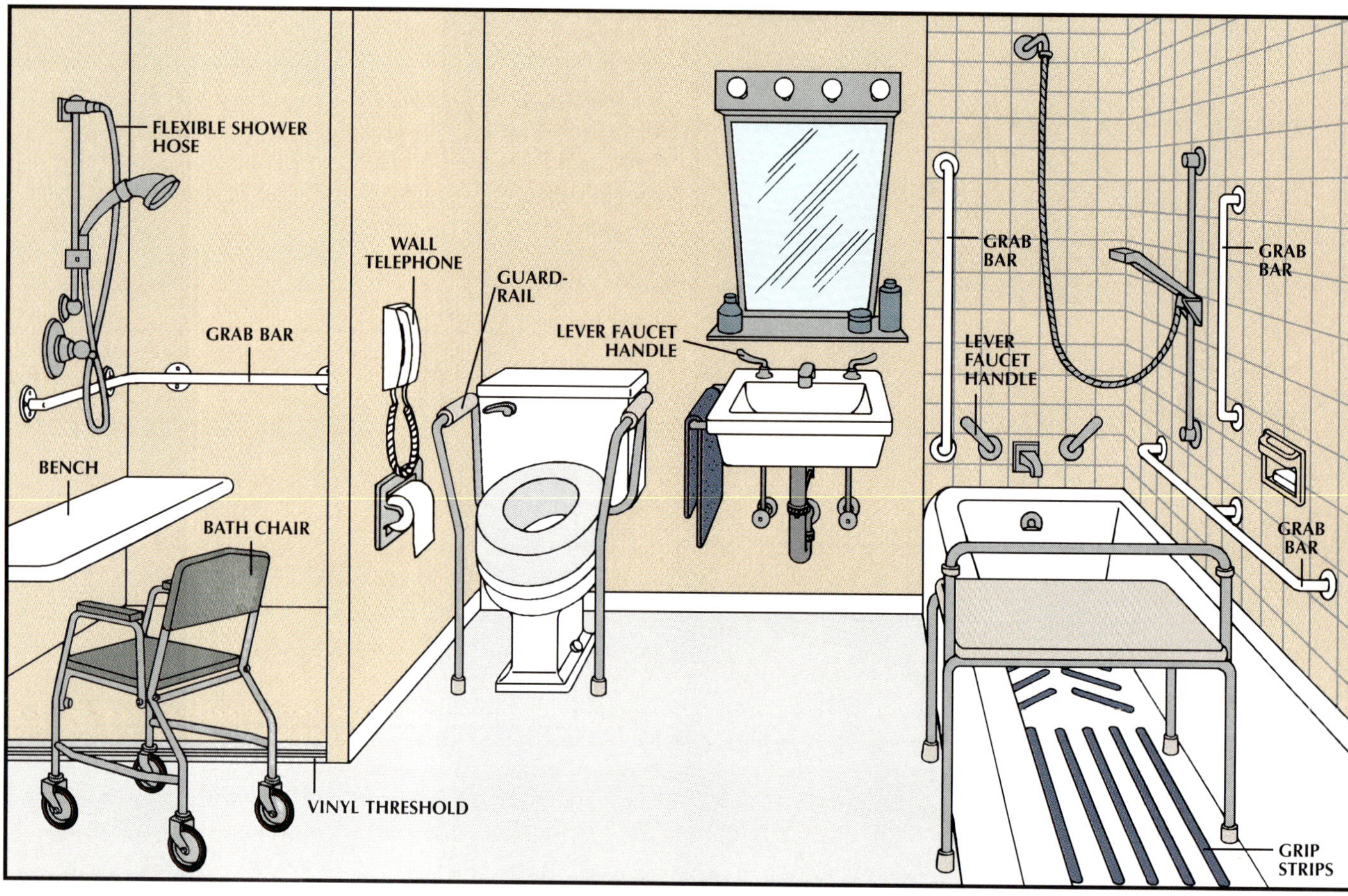

Helpful modifications.
Few bathrooms offer all the features in the composite illustration above, but a person with a disability may find several of them beneficial.

A roll-in shower. For a family member who uses a wheelchair or bath chair, consider a shower with a low flexible-vinyl threshold; either vehicle can easily roll across, and the vinyl keeps water from flowing out. Once inside, a bather may transfer to a bench seat.

An accessible telephone. A wall phone with the dial or keypad in the handset provides a link to help.

An easier-to-use toilet. A thicker-than-usual toilet seat and adjustable guardrails may help someone who has difficulty sitting down or standing up. Alternatively, install a grab bar beside the toilet.

A nonslip floor. Floor tiles in a bathroom are a poor choice for someone who may slip and fall. Carpet or vinyl sheet flooring are among the alternatives.

A convenient mirror. Tilt mirrors downward a bit to make them useful for a person in a wheelchair.

Lever handles. Equip faucets with long handles, rather than knobs that must be grasped.

Washbasin access. A wall-hung basin lets someone in a wheelchair roll up to the sink; insulate the hot-water pipe to prevent burns.

Grab bars and grip strips. As in any bathroom, grab bars and grip strips in tubs and showers help to prevent falls while bathing.

Seating in the bath. Place a bench or bath chair in a tub or shower; install a showerhead with a flexible hose, and mount it on a sliding bar or within easy reach.

Easing the Way for a Wheelchair

- A door opening 32 inches wide is usable if the bathroom opens onto a wide hallway, but an opening of 36 inches is better.
- Inside the bathroom, the clear floor space should be at least 60 inches square to allow a wheelchair to turn around completely.
- Sinks must be no more than 34 inches high, and they must not rest on a vanity.
- Buy an add-on toilet seat from a medical-supply store to raise the seat 4 inches—the same height as most wheelchair seats.
- Mount such items as the telephone at 33 to 36 inches.

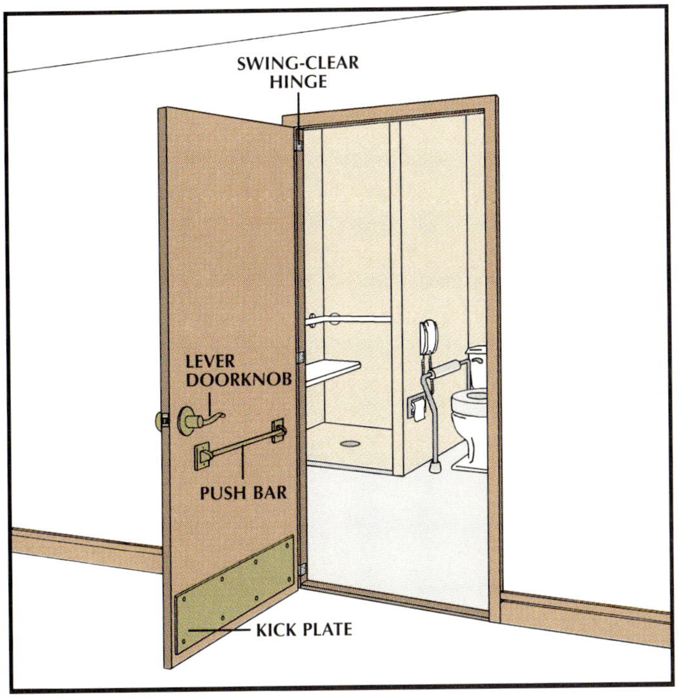

A doorway that provides easier access.

To maximize the width of a door opening, install a pocket door or a sliding door. Rehang a hinged door to open outward *(above)*; you can increase its effective width with swing-clear hinges *(right)*, which add $1\frac{1}{2}$ to 2 inches to the opening. Other useful door hardware includes a kick plate, a lever doorknob *(below)*, and a push bar to help open and close the door.

Installing a swing-clear hinge.

◆ Buy swing-clear hinges that fit the cavities that were cut into the door edge and jamb for the old hinges.

◆ Unscrew the old hinges from the door and the jamb; set the door aside.

◆ If new screw holes are required, pack lengths of dowel, coated with glue, into the existing holes. Let the glue dry overnight, then drill pilot holes for the new screws.

◆ Attach the swing-clear hinges and rehang the door.

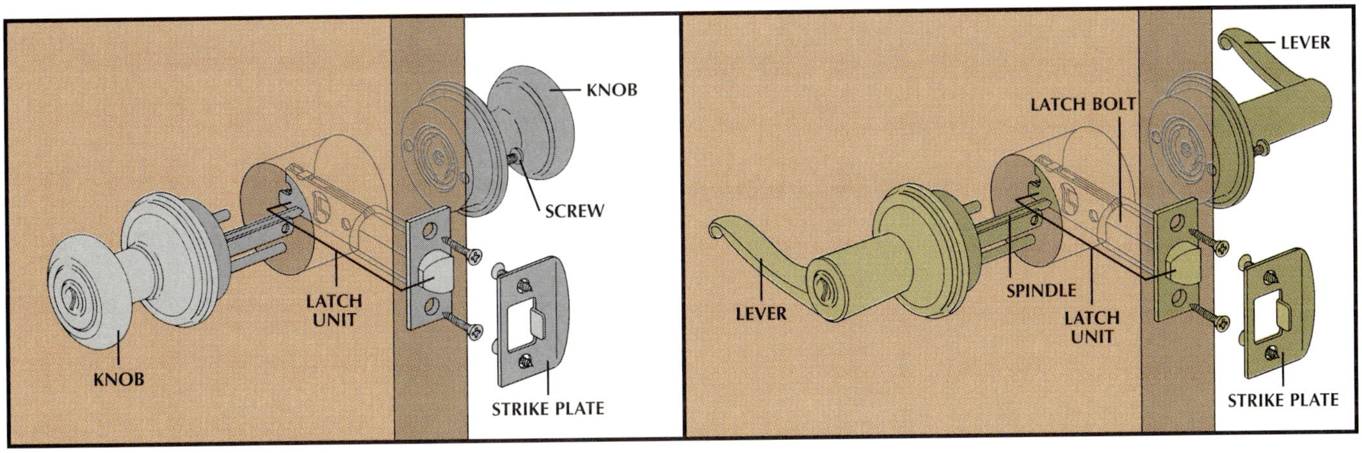

Putting in place a lever-knob assembly.

◆ Unfasten the two screws that secure the knob plate and pull it off with the knob *(above, left)*. If no screws are visible, depress the metal tab that holds one knob on its shaft. Then remove the knob and the underlying cover plate to reveal the screws.

◆ Pull off the other knob.

◆ Remove the two screws holding the latch unit in place and slide it out of the door.

◆ With a half-round rasp, enlarge the lock and latch holes as needed to accommodate the new mechanism.

◆ Set the latch unit of the lever knob in the door. Screw it to the door edge.

◆ Insert the spindle attached to one of the two lever handles so that it engages the latch unit; then install the other lever. Secure the assembly with screws *(above, right)*.

◆ Check to make sure the strike plate aligns with the latch bolt.

How to Increase Storage Space

Storage space is often at a premium in a bathroom. A simple way to make more room is to install a larger medicine cabinet or a supplementary one, mounted on the wall or recessed into it. For even more space, you can discard a stand-alone washbasin and instead install a vanity with a sink in the countertop.

Considerations for a Vanity: Ready-made cabinets are available in many widths. Choose a vanity that is at least wide enough to cover the holes left in the wall by the bracket for the old washbasin but not so large that the bathroom becomes cramped *(page 88)*. For ease of installation and maintenance, choose a one-piece countertop like the one shown on page 51.

If you plan to tile, wallpaper, or paint the bathroom walls, do so before installing the vanity. This way the new cabinet will cover the edges of the finish.

Installing a Medicine Cabinet: A surface-mounted cabinet can be hung virtually anywhere *(page 52)*, but recessed cabinets require more consideration. Most are designed to fit in the space between existing studs, commonly $14\frac{1}{2}$ inches but sometimes $22\frac{1}{2}$ inches. If the cabinet location is not critical, simply fit it between the studs *(page 52)*.

A unit wider than a single stud space—or one that must be centered on a wall or above the washbasin—requires cutting out sections of one or more studs.

A Suitable Wall: The technique for cutting away studs shown on these pages applies only to nonbearing walls, which carry no weight from the structure above. Usually such walls run parallel to joists. A basement ceiling or attic floor is the best place to find exposed joists, which usually have the same orientation from floor to floor. Treat all exterior walls, and any walls about which you are uncertain, as load-bearing walls. Avoid them.

Making Holes in Walls: Whenever possible, avoid cutting into a part of a wall that might conceal pipes or wires. To check for wires, note the locations of switches, outlets, and lights on both sides of the wall and in the rooms above and below. Also observe where pipes and drains enter and leave walls and floors.

Before you cut or drill, turn off electricity to any circuit that might run through the wall. Drill only enough to penetrate the wallboard or plaster and lath, usually less than 1 inch; plan to cut studs, if necessary, as a second step. Stop at once if the drill bit hits a hard surface; it might be a pipe or electrical junction box. If you puncture a pipe, turn off the main water supply and call a plumber. Severed cables usually require an electrician's help.

TOOLS

- Wrenches
- Screwdriver
- Cold chisel
- Saber saw
- Electronic stud finder
- Utility knife
- Pry bar
- Level
- Electric drill with screwdriver bit
- Backsaw
- Dry-wall saw

MATERIALS

- Wood shims
- $2\frac{1}{4}$-inch No. 6 dry-wall screws
- Adhesive caulk
- $1\frac{1}{2}$- and $2\frac{1}{2}$-inch finishing nails
- $\frac{3}{4}$-inch brads
- Scribe molding
- Shoe molding
- Hollow-wall anchors
- 2-by-4s
- Wallboard

SAFETY TIPS

To protect your eyes, wear safety goggles when drilling or sawing at or above the level of your waist.

CLEARING THE WAY FOR A VANITY

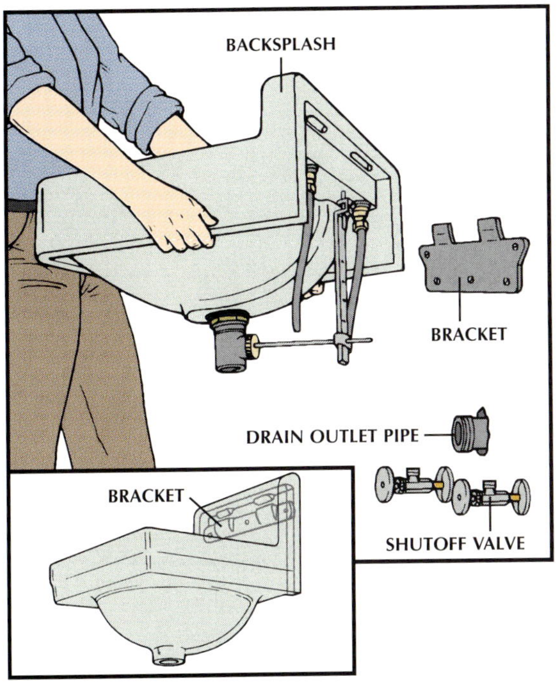

Dismounting wall-hung basins.

◆ Turn off the water at the basin shutoff valves or at the house's main valve. Disconnect the supply lines and the drainpipe assembly *(pages 19 and 26)*.

◆ To remove a basin hung on a bracket behind the backsplash as shown in the drawings at left, simply lift the basin straight up.

◆ Unscrew the bracket from the wall.

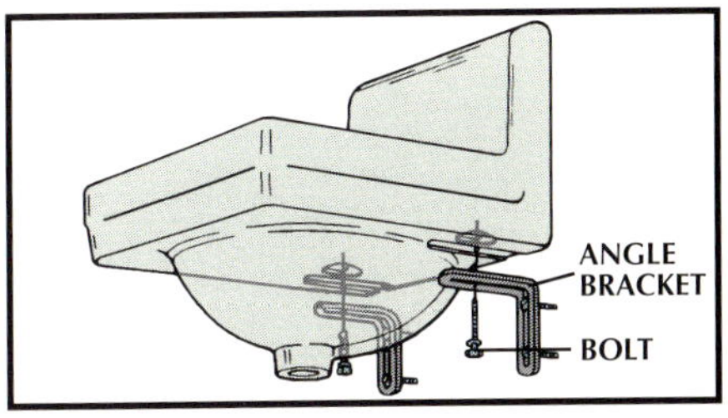

An angle bracket mounting.

To detach a basin supported from below by angle brackets, have a helper hold the basin while you loosen the mounting bolts with a wrench and remove them. Set the basin aside and unscrew the brackets from the wall.

DISASSEMBLING PEDESTAL BASINS

1. Removing a two-piece pedestal basin.

◆ Shut off the water and disconnect the water-supply lines and drainpipe assembly *(pages 19 and 26)*.

◆ Look inside the pedestal for a long threaded rod connecting the basin to its base. In the absence of such a rod, simply lift the basin from its wall bracket and set it aside. Otherwise, reach inside the pedestal with a wrench and remove the nut at the lower end of the rod *(above)*. Lift the basin off its pedestal and wall bracket, then remove the rod from the basin.

2. Removing the pedestal.

◆ Unscrew any fasteners you find holding the pedestal base to the floor *(above)*, then lift the pedestal away.

◆ If the pedestal is secured to the floor with grout, gently rock it back and forth to break the seal. Loosen old grout from the floor with a cold chisel.

◆ For a pedestal and basin molded as a single unit, unscrew the pedestal from the floor. Then lift the entire fixture free of the basin wall bracket.

◆ Detach the basin bracket from the wall.

ANCHORING A VANITY BASE AND COUNTERTOP

1. Aligning the cabinet.

◆ Position the vanity so that shutoff valves and drainpipe are roughly centered within the frame. If the vanity has a back, mark openings for the pipes, then cut the holes with a saber saw.

◆ Push the vanity against the wall. Mark the outline of the cabinet on the wall with light pencil lines, then set the cabinet aside.

◆ With a stud finder, locate wall studs that fall within the cabinet outline. Mark the center of each stud above the outline as shown here.

2. Dealing with baseboard.

◆ For wooden baseboard, run a utility knife along the joint between the wall and the top of the baseboard section extending across the planned area for the vanity, breaking any paint seal.

◆ At one end of the baseboard section, tap a small pry bar into the joint. Place a shim behind the bar *(above)*, then lever the molding away from the wall. Slip a shim into the gap.

◆ Continue prying and shimming to loosen the baseboard section, then pull it free and set it aside.

To remove vinyl molding, cut it at the cabinet outline with a utility knife guided by a straightedge. Peel away the piece below the pipes.

3. Securing the vanity.

◆ Reposition the vanity against the wall and level it from side to side by inserting shims under the cabinet *(far left)*. Level the cabinet from front to back by shimming it away from the wall *(left)*.

◆ Mark each shim at cabinet edges. Remove one shim at a time, saw it to length, and slide it back into place.

◆ For wallboard or plaster walls drive $2\frac{1}{4}$-inch No. 6 dry-wall screws through the back of the cabinet about $\frac{3}{4}$ inch from the top and into the studs that were marked earlier.

4. Mounting the countertop.

◆ Attach as many of the faucet and drain fittings to the countertop as possible *(pages 19-22 and 27).*

◆ Apply a bead of adhesive caulk along the top edges of the cabinet, then press the countertop into place. Wipe off excess caulk immediately.

5. Finishing up.

◆ Connect the water-supply lines and the drain *(pages 19, 21, and 27).*

◆ If you detached a section of wooden baseboard earlier, use a backsaw to cut the baseboard at the lines marking the sides of the vanity. Discard the center section and nail the others to the wall with $2\frac{1}{2}$-inch finishing nails.

◆ Cover gaps at the sides of the vanity with scribe molding that matches the cabinet finish; attach the molding with $\frac{3}{4}$-inch brads *(above).* Cover a gap at the floor with shoe molding secured with $1\frac{1}{2}$-inch finishing nails.

SURFACE-MOUNTED MEDICINE CABINETS

1. Hanging the cabinet.

◆ Locate studs where the cabinet will go. Have a helper hold it with at least one upper mounting hole on a stud. Mark through the upper holes and lower the cabinet. With a level, align the marks.

◆ If both marks are over studs, drive screws into the studs until the heads are $\frac{1}{8}$ inch from the wall.

◆ Otherwise, mark for the lower mounting holes as well. For marks not on a stud, drill holes for hollow-wall anchors, tap the anchors into place, and tighten. Loosen both anchor screws $\frac{1}{8}$ inch from the wall.

◆ Slip the cabinet's mounting holes over the screwheads. Drive screws through the other holes and tighten them all.

2. Adding shelves and doors.

◆ Position the shelves on the interior brackets.

◆ Attach the door hinges and the doors. Mounting systems vary, but doors commonly are first attached to the upper hinge, then adjusted for fit at the bottom hinge *(above)*.

◆ Complete the installation by affixing door catches and any hardware provided by the manufacturer.

A MEDICINE CABINET BETWEEN TWO STUDS

Cutting an opening.

◆ Use a stud finder to locate the studs on each side of the cabinet location.

◆ Draw the dimensions of the desired opening on the wall between the studs. With a level, ensure that the top and bottom lines are horizontal.

◆ Cut away the outlined section, using a dry-wall saw for wallboard. A saber saw fitted with hacksaw blades works well for plaster walls; change blades as they dull.

◆ Drive a dry-wall screw partway into each stud, $1\frac{1}{2}$ inches above the top edge of the opening.

◆ Cut a 2-by-4 header to fit snugly between the studs, and push it up against the screws. To anchor the header, angle two screws through each end into the stud.

◆ In the same way, install a 2-by-4 sill at the bottom of the opening *(left)*.

◆ Set the cabinet into the recess. Through the predrilled holes on each side, drive screws partway into the studs. Level the cabinet and tighten the screws while maintaining the level.

RECESSING A WIDE MEDICINE CABINET

1. Cutting out studs.

◆ Mark the proposed opening on the wall, then with a stud finder locate a stud to the right and left of the outline.

◆ On the wall between these studs, mark horizontal lines $1\frac{1}{2}$ inches above and below the proposed opening.

◆ Cut away the rectangle of wall bounded by these lines and the studs.

◆ Use a backsaw to cut through studs in the cabinet space, flush with the edges of the opening *(above)*.

◆ Gently pry the stud segments away from the wall behind them. Nails that hold the wall surface to the studs may pull through, and you may have to repair some damage on the other side.

2. Framing the opening.

◆ From 2-by-4s, cut a header and a sill to fit snugly between the studs at the left and right of the opening. Screw the header and sill to the cut ends of the studs *(above)*. Fasten header and sill ends with screws that are angled into the studs at the sides of the opening.

◆ Screw vertical 2-by-4s to both end studs to provide a surface for patching wallboard.

3. Customizing the fit.

◆ If the cabinet does not fill the framed opening, cut two 2-by-4s to the height of the opening. At the sides of the planned recess, secure them to the sill and header with angled screws *(left)*.

◆ Cut and fit wallboard patches to cover the sides of the opening to the inner edges of the cabinet framing.

◆ Position the cabinet inside the framing, using shims at the bottom and sides to make it level and plumb. Drive at least two screws through each side of the cabinet, through the shims and into the framing.

Fresh Air for the Bathroom

Often stale and humid, the atmosphere in a bathroom fogs mirrors and promotes mold and mildew. Over time, the moisture can damage paint, wallpaper, and even walls.

An exhaust fan solves these problems by venting odors and humidity outdoors. The fan shown on these and the following pages also incorporates an infrared bulb to add a measure of heat on cold mornings.

Planning Steps: Before buying a fan, first determine how you will vent it. Through an unfloored attic to the roof is often the most direct route from a second-floor bathroom. With a finished floor overhead, you must run the ventilation duct between floor joists to an outside wall.

After estimating the length of duct required, use the estimator below to determine the air-handling capacity, in cubic feet per minute (CFM), of a fan that will renew the bathroom air every $7\frac{1}{2}$ minutes.

Ducting Choices: Flexible duct, best for runs of less than 16 feet, can be bent around corners or obstructions. It comes in sections that stretch to 8 feet and can be bought in kits that include a weatherproof wall or roof cap *(opposite)*, and the plastic bands needed to clamp the duct to the fan and to the cap.

Rigid duct is often a better choice for longer runs; its inner surface is smooth and offers less resistance to air flow. Rigid duct cannot be bent, so special elbow fittings are needed to detour around obstacles.

Wiring Considerations: Before planning any wiring, first check local building and electrical codes for possible restrictions. Because exhaust fans require little power, they can usually be added to an existing circuit. The most convenient power source is often a junction box mounted on an attic joist.

Switching: Since the fan and heat lamp are designed to run separately or together, you will need two switches. You can mount separate switches in side-by-side boxes, or you can use a dual switch that fits into a single box. In either case, you will need three-conductor cable to serve the two switches.

CAUTION *Do not open any electrical box without shutting off power to the circuit at the fuse or circuit-breaker box and double-checking with a voltage tester.*

TOOLS

- Electric drill
- Keyhole saw
- Hammer
- Carpenter's pencil
- Utility knife
- Saber saw
- Tape measure
- Putty knife
- Nail set
- Voltage tester
- Pliers
- Cable ripper
- Wire stripper
- Screwdriver
- Fish tape
- Socket wrench

MATERIALS

- Duct kit
- Dual switch
- Switch box
- Wire caps
- Electrician's tape
- Two- and three-conductor 14-gauge cable
- Cable clamps
- $\frac{1}{2}$-inch plastic staples
- $1\frac{1}{4}$-inch roofing nails
- Roofing cement

SAFETY TIPS

Wear goggles to protect your eyes from dust and flying debris while hammering or sawing. A hard hat guards against painful encounters with rafters and exposed roofing nails. Before handling insulation in an attic, put on a long-sleeved shirt, gloves, and a disposable dust mask.

Length Width Height

_____ x _____ x _____ ÷ 7.5 = _____ (CFM)

Calculating fan capacity. Use your bathroom dimensions in the estimator at left to determine the minimum air-handling capacity for an exhaust fan. If the result falls between two fan sizes, choose the larger. And for long duct runs—more than 8 feet of flexible duct or 16 feet of rigid duct—pick the next larger fan.

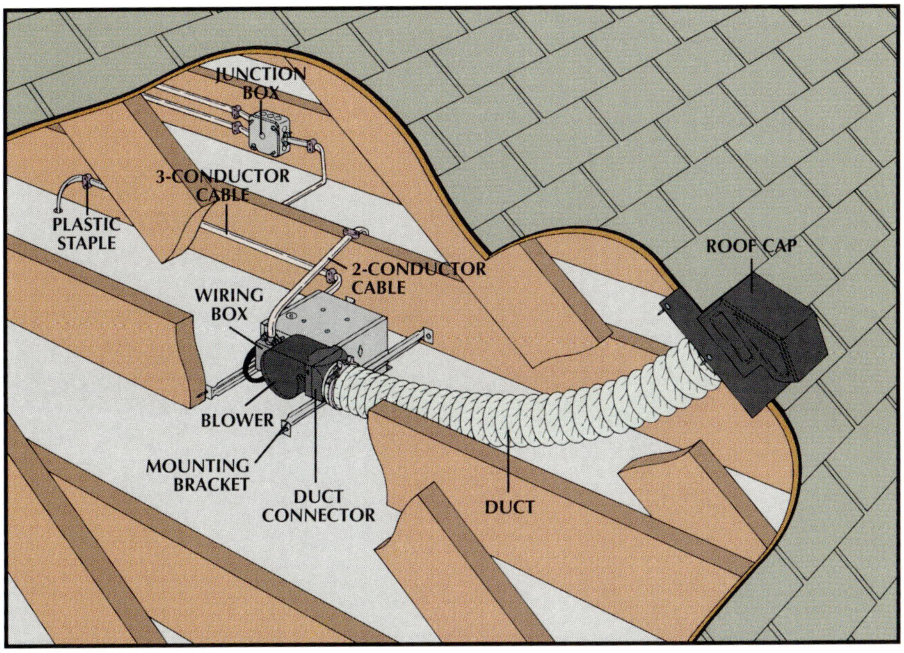

Anatomy of a fan installation. Seen at left in an attic above a bathroom ceiling, a heater fan consists of a lamp housing fitted with a blower and a wiring box. Designed for a 250-watt heat lamp, the unit is fastened to joists with adjustable mounting brackets. A length of flexible duct, extending from the blower outlet to a hole cut through the roof, carries moisture outdoors through a roof cap. Dampers at the roof cap and inside a duct connector at the blower outlet prevent backdrafts when the fan is off. Power comes to the unit from a junction box by way of a two-conductor electrical cable. A three-conductor cable leads to a pair of switches in the bathroom below; one is for the fan, and the other is for the heat lamp.

MOUNTING AN EXHAUST FAN HOUSING

1. Cutting a ceiling opening.

◆ In the bathroom, drill a $\frac{1}{8}$-inch test hole in the center of the ceiling. If the bit hits a joist, fill the hole with spackling and drill another hole several inches away. Push a length of wire up through the test hole to mark the spot.

◆ Lay plywood across attic joists to support you and your tools and the mounting brackets for the fan. Push aside any insulation you find, then remove the marker wire. Center the lamp housing between the joists on either side of the test hole and outline the housing on the ceiling *(above)*.

◆ Drill a $\frac{3}{4}$-inch hole at each corner of the outline, then cut along the lines with a keyhole saw, stationing a helper in the bathroom to support and catch the cutout.

2. Fastening the mounting brackets.

◆ Slide a mounting-bracket section into each end of the channel on one side of the lamp housing, then push the pieces together until they overlap. Repeat this procedure for the channel on the opposite side of the housing.

◆ While your helper in the bathroom holds a board across the ceiling opening, orient the blower outlet toward the exit point for the duct, then lower the housing through the ceiling to rest on the board *(inset)*.

◆ Extend the mounting brackets until their nailing flanges touch the joists, and fasten both brackets with a $1\frac{1}{4}$-inch nail in each end *(above)*.

CHANNELING THE AIR FLOW OUTDOORS

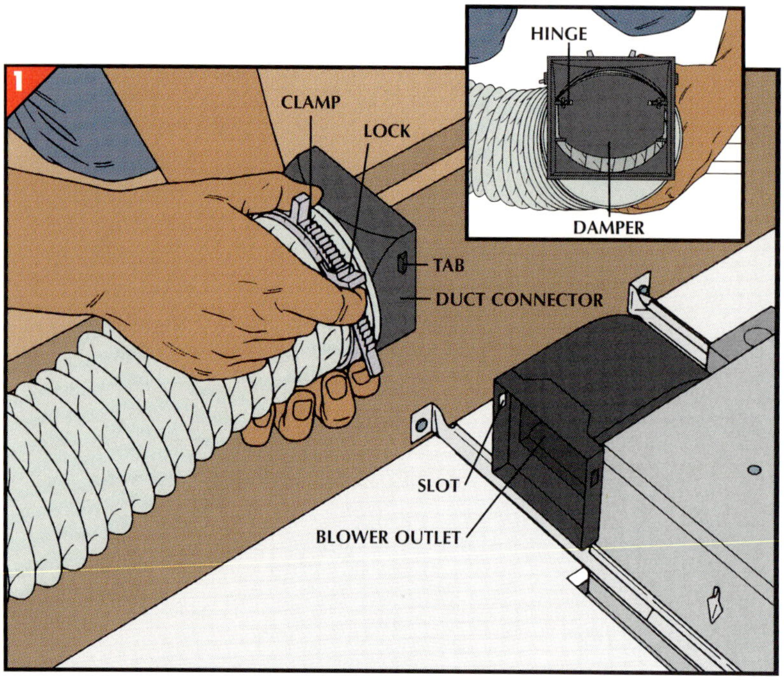

1. Attaching the flexible duct.

◆ Check that the damper inside the duct connector swings freely on its hinges, then slide a length of duct onto the circular end of the connector.

◆ Wrap a plastic clamp around the connection, then thread the clamp's serrated end through the lock. Tighten the connection by squeezing together the two projections on the clamp *(left).*

◆ Holding the connector so that the damper hinge is at the top *(inset),* attach the connector to the blower outlet. In this unit, tabs on the connector snap into matching slots in the outlet.

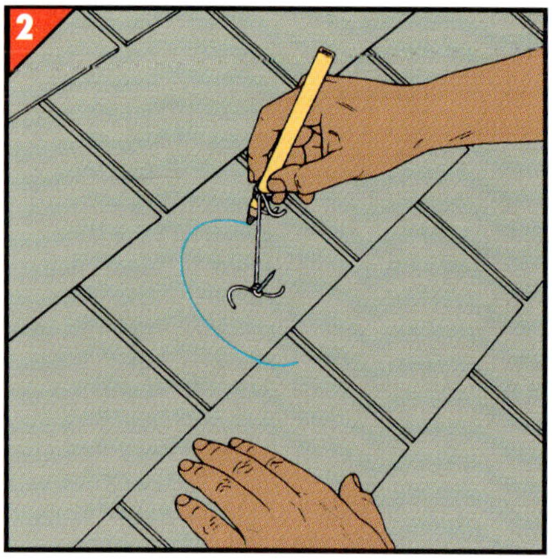

2. Making a roof opening.

◆ In the attic, hold the other duct end on the roof midway between two rafters. Mark around the duct with a carpenter's pencil, then drive a nail through the center of the circle.

◆ On the roof, find the marker nail. Draw a 5-inch-diameter circle, with it as the center *(above).*

◆ Within the circle, pull out all roofing nails. Cut away shingles and roofing paper with a utility knife. Drill a starter hole inside the circle, then saw around the circumference.

CAUTION *If the slope of your roof is greater than 15 degrees, have the roof work performed by a professional.*

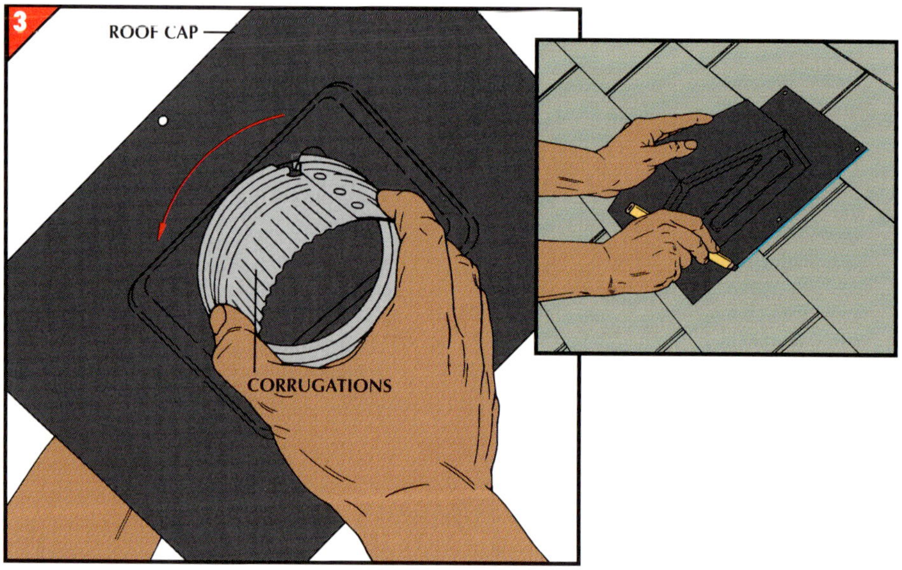

3. Assembling the roof cap.

◆ Holding the corrugated end of the duct connector *(above),* insert it into the underside of the roof cap. Lock the connector to the cap by turning it clockwise for some models, counterclockwise for others.

◆ Insert the connector into the roof opening, and mark the outline of the roof cap on the shingles *(inset).*

4. Installing the roof cap.

◆ Lift the roof cap out of the hole and set it aside.
◆ Within the outline marked in Step 3, measure 2 inches from the upper edge and draw a line. In the same manner, mark lines $1\frac{3}{4}$ inches in from the sides and bottom edge.
◆ Within this smaller area, cut away the shingles, but not the roofing paper *(left, top)*.
◆ Holding the cap at a 45-degree angle, slide the upper edge and sides of the flange under the shingles, and fit the duct connector into the 5-inch roof hole *(left, bottom)*.
◆ Nail the flange to the sheathing through the holes provided, lifting shingles as needed to do so. Apply roofing cement with a putty knife to seal the nailheads and shingle edges to the roof cap flange.
◆ In the attic, use a plastic clamp to connect the flexible duct to the roof cap's duct connector.

MAKING ELECTRICAL CONNECTIONS

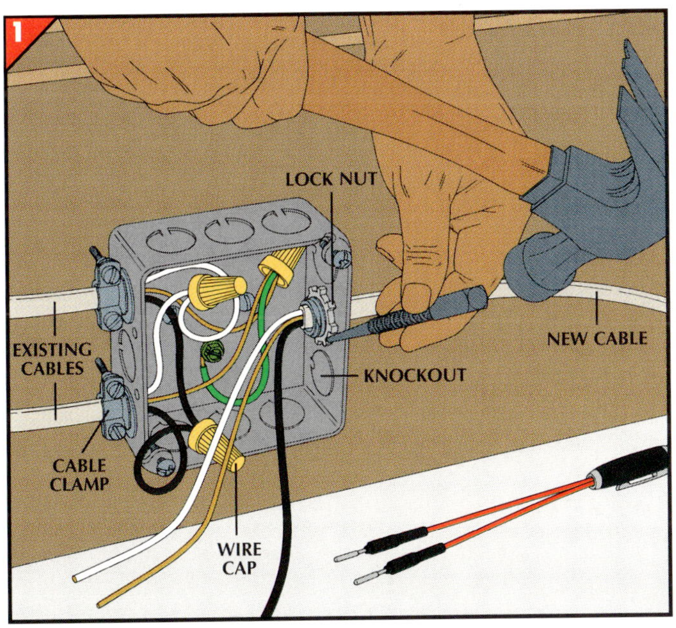

1. Tapping power.

◆ At the service panel, turn off power to the circuit you plan to extend.
◆ Remove the junction box cover, then, with a hammer and nail set, dislodge one of the removable disks called a knockout. Break it off with pliers.
◆ With a cable ripper, strip 8 inches of sheathing from a length of two-conductor cable. Use a wire stripper to remove $\frac{3}{4}$ inch of insulation from the ends of the black and white wires. Slip a cable clamp onto the cable and tighten the clamp on the cable sheathing with a screwdriver.
◆ Insert the clamp into the knockout hole and screw a lock nut onto the clamp. Tighten the nut with a hammer and nail set as shown at left.
◆ Include the new wires under the wire caps that join the old wires, connecting black to black, white to white, and bare wire to bare wire. (In some cases, larger wire caps will be needed to accommodate the added wires.)
◆ Route the cable from the junction box to the fan wiring box, securing it to joists with plastic staples *(page 55, top)*.

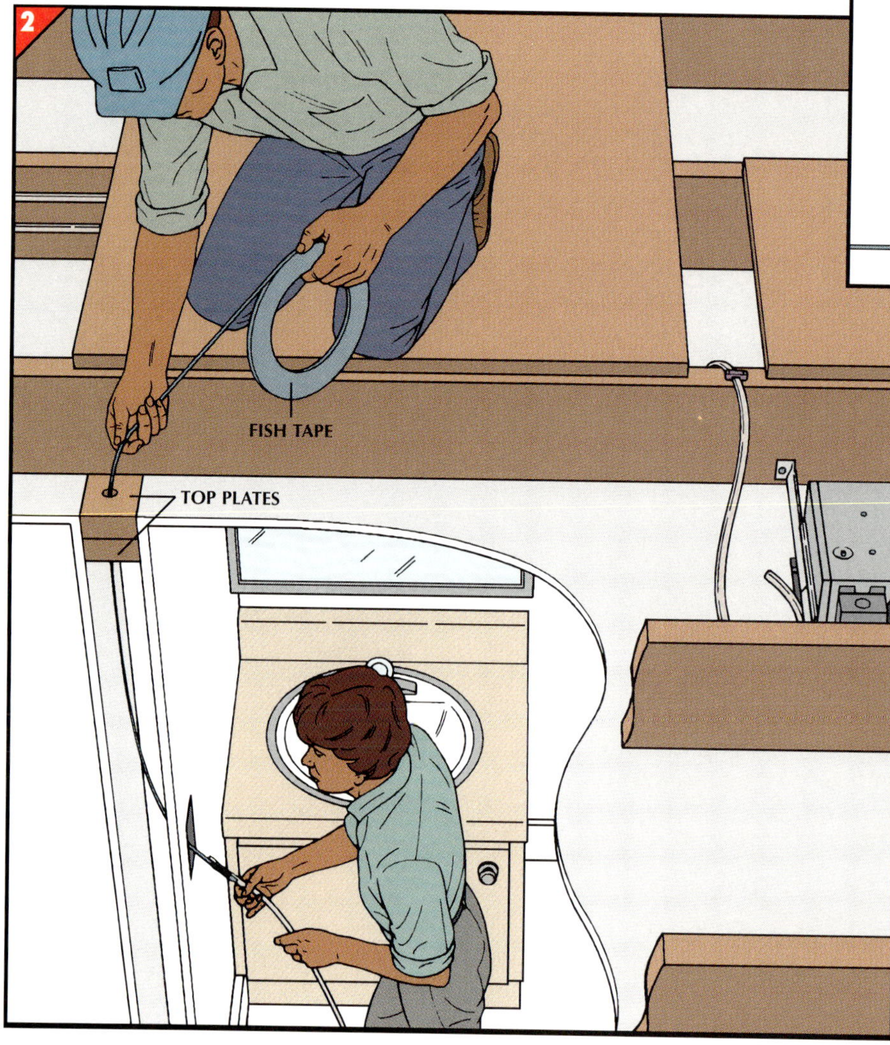

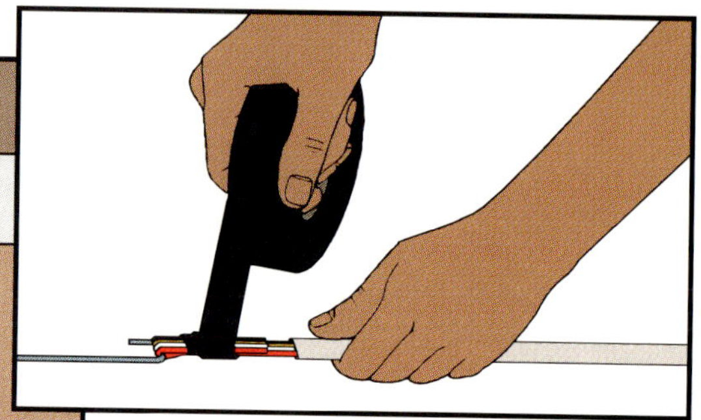

2. Fishing cable.

◆ In the bathroom, cut an opening for a new switch box in the wall near the doorway. Use the template included with the box, or the box itself, to outline the opening.

◆ In the attic, locate the top plates of the bathroom wall that has the new opening. Drill a $\frac{3}{4}$-inch hole through the plates above the opening.

◆ Push the end of a fish tape through the hole. Maneuver the tape until a helper below can pull it out through the switch opening *(left)*.

◆ Have your helper strip 8 inches of sheathing from a length of the three-conductor cable and attach the wires to the fish tape *(inset)*.

◆ With your helper feeding cable from below, pull it into the attic with the fish tape. Unhook the cable and route it to the fan wiring box.

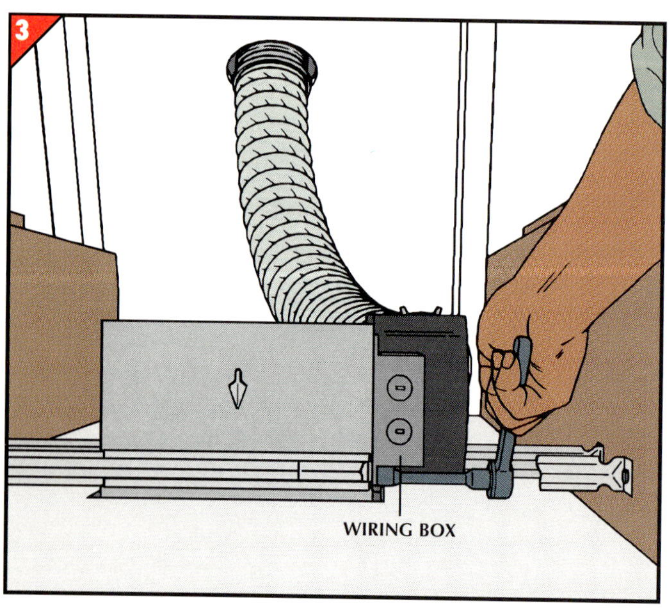

3. Preparing the wiring box.

◆ Unfasten the screw holding the wiring box to the housing. As shown at left, a socket wrench can be handy for hard-to-reach screws, most of which have hexagonal heads. Set the screw aside and remove two knockouts from the wiring box.

◆ Strip 8 inches of sheathing from the ends of both the two-conductor and three-conductor cables, then remove $\frac{3}{4}$ inch of insulation from the insulated wires in each. Attach each cable to the wiring box with a cable clamp as shown on page 57.

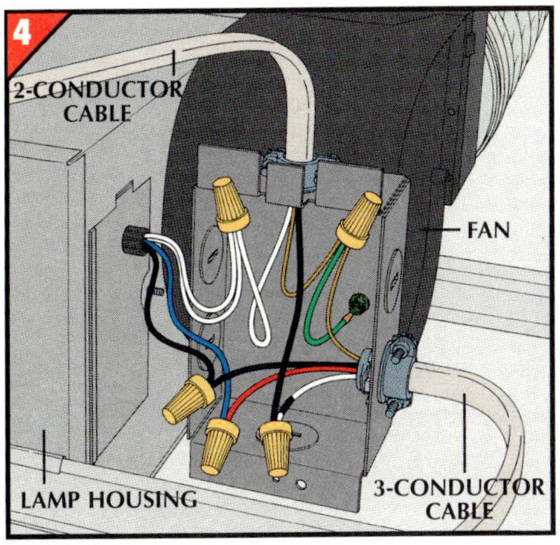

4. Wiring connections.

Using wire caps, make the following connections:

◆ Black wire of the switch cable to the black wire from the lamp housing.

◆ Red wire of the switch cable to the other colored wire from the lamp housing, blue in this case.

◆ White wire of the switch cable to the black wire of the power cable. Color the white insulation black to indicate a current-carrying wire.

◆ Bare wire of the switch cable to the bare wire of the power cable and to a jumper wire *(green)* screwed to the wiring box.

◆ White wire from the power cable to the two white wires coming from the lamp housing.

◆ Fold all connections into the box, and refasten it to the housing.

5. Adding a switch box.

◆ In the bathroom, remove a knockout from a switch box with built-in cable clamps top and bottom.

◆ With a screwdriver, loosen the clamp at the top of the box.

◆ Cut the switch cable to length, then strip off 8 inches of sheathing.

◆ Thread the cable wires into the box through the knockout, and tighten the clamp on the cable sheathing.

◆ Insert the box into the wall opening so both ears touch the wall surface.

◆ Turn the screw on each side of the box to draw the wall clamps against the inside of the dry wall *(left)*. Continue turning until the box fits tightly.

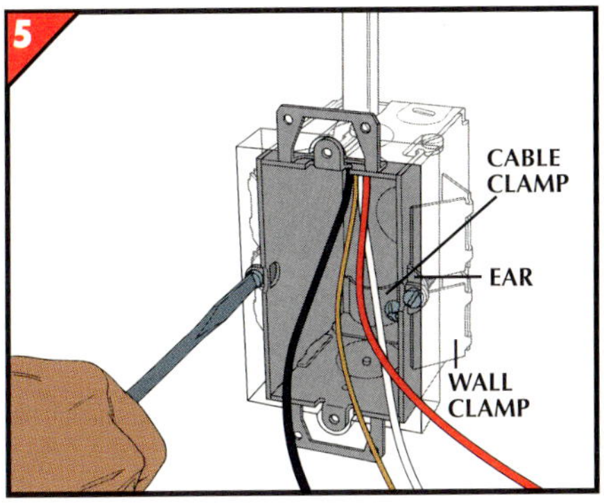

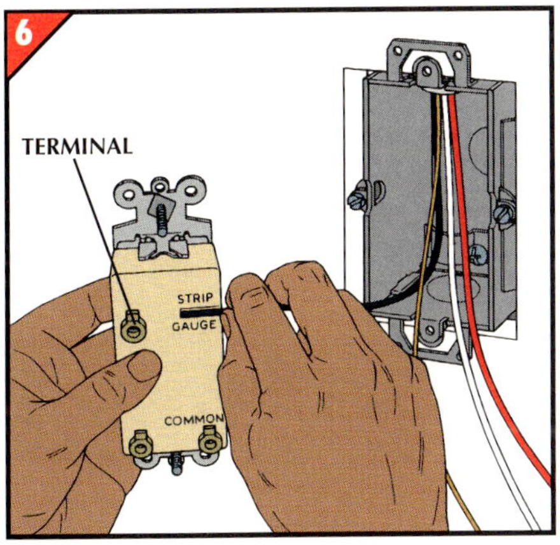

6. Wiring the switch.

◆ Using the strip gauge on the back of a two-function switch, mark the insulation of all three conductors for stripping *(left)*. The gauge shows how much insulation must be removed so that no bare wire is exposed when the conductors are inserted in the terminals.

◆ After stripping the wires, push the end of the white wire all the way into the terminal marked COMMON. Color the white insulation black.

◆ Insert the red wire into either of the two remaining terminals, and insert the black wire into the other. Screw the bare wire to the box.

◆ Fold the wires into the box and screw the switch to the box, then install the cover plate provided.

FINAL ASSEMBLY AND TESTING

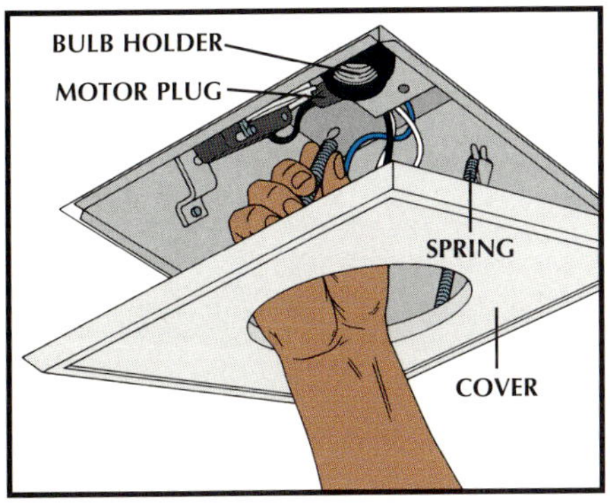

Final assembly and testing.

◆ From the bathroom, plug the fan motor into the base of the bulb holder.

◆ Hook the two cover springs to clips inside the housing.

◆ Screw an infrared heat bulb into the socket; adjust the cover to center the bulb in the opening.

◆ At the service panel, restore power to all circuits turned off for safety, then check that the switch in the bathroom operates the fan and heat lamp both separately and together.

◆ At the roof cap, confirm that the damper opens with the fan running and closes when the air flow stops.

3 Refinishing Floors and Walls

The floor and walls of a bathroom face a daily challenge from water and humidity unequaled in any other room. The following pages show how to seal the bathing area against leaks and seepage with a variety of new wall treatments—from prefabricated panels to ceramic tiles—as well as how to repair rotted areas in a bathroom floor and lay a new finish floor of tiles.

A tiled wall and floor →

Putting in a New Tub Surround

The walls surrounding a tub or shower must be durable, moisture resistant, and easy to clean. A variety of specially designed wall treatments, many in kit form, can meet these requirements handily as well as dress up an existing bathroom or complement a new one.

A Choice of Materials: Molded units of fiberglass, plastic, or acrylic are lightweight, economical, flexible, and easy to handle. Many come in three- or five-panel kits that adjust to fit standard 5-foot or smaller tubs. Extension panels sometimes are available to fit longer tubs.

The nonporous polyester and acrylic products known as solid-surface materials are heavier, more rigid, and more expensive. These walls are composed of the same material throughout, so they are very sturdy and easy to maintain.

You can install both types over nearly any clean, dry, structurally sound subsurface, including tile, plaster, wallboard, and cement.

Preparing the Area: Turn off the water supply and remove the faucet handles, tub spout, showerhead, soap dish, towel bars, and any other fittings on walls to be covered. Remove or reattach loose ceramic tiles or peeling wallpaper.

Wash the subsurface and let it dry. For wallboard, plaster, and cement walls, first seal with primer; alternatively, replace or cover these surfaces with moisture-resistant wallboard and then seal.

To avoid cracking or chipping the tub during the job, pad it with blankets or cardboard. Keep the bathroom well ventilated when working with adhesives or caulk.

TOOLS

- Level
- Circular saw
- Coarse file
- Orbital sander
- Caulking gun
- Electric drill with hole saw or spade bit
- Jigsaw
- Hot melt glue gun

MATERIALS

- Primer
- Panel adhesive
- Silicone caulk (color-matched or clear)
- Masking tape
- 120-grit sandpaper
- $\frac{1}{16}$-inch-thick laminate shims
- Denatured alcohol
- Hot melt glue sticks
- Clean white rags

SNAPPING IN PREFABRICATED PANELS

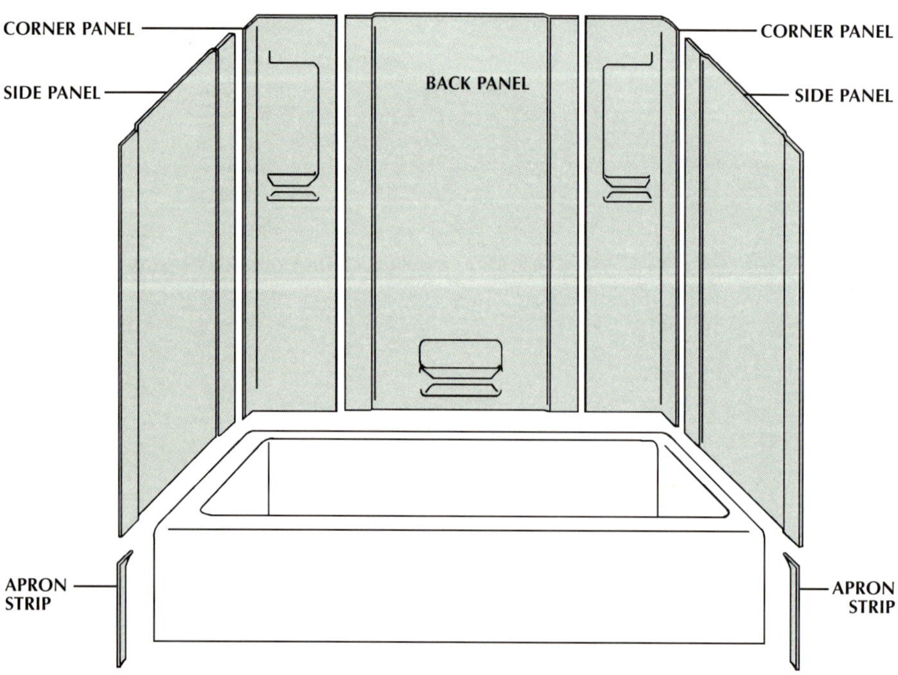

1. Preparing to install a molded tub surround.

A typical molded tub surround consists of five pieces: two corner panels, a back panel, and two side panels. Some kits, like the one at left, also include apron strips for installation on the walls in front of the tub.

◆ First, trial fit each panel. Level the top of each panel and, if the bottom edge does not meet the tub's rim evenly, draw a line across the panel marking the excess below the tub rim.

◆ With a circular saw or coarse file, trim the panel bottoms along the marked lines. Sand any rough edges.

2. Creating outlets for plumbing.

◆ If you are using apron strips, remove their backing and affix them to the wall in front of the tub.

◆ Measuring from the front edge of the tub or of the apron strip and the top of the tub *(above, left)*, make a cardboard template of the plumbing outlets. Transfer the measurements to the correct side panel.

◆ Drilling from the finished side of the panel with a hole saw or a spade bit, cut holes in the panel that are slightly larger than the pipe diameters *(above, right)*.

3. Setting corner panels.

◆ With a caulking gun, apply a $\frac{1}{4}$-inch bead of adhesive to the back of a corner panel, about 1 inch from both the panel edges and any factory-installed tape strips. Follow the pattern of straight lines around the edges and curved lines in the middle *(above)*. Put extra adhesive around shelf areas.

◆ Remove backing from the tape strips, if any, and press the corner panel into position, making sure all of it makes contact with the wall.

◆ Install the other corner panel in the same way.

4. Attaching the back and side panels.

◆ Apply adhesive to the back panel as directed in Step 3.

◆ Rest the back panel on the edge of the tub, center it between the corner panels, and press it firmly against the wall *(left)*.

◆ Apply adhesive to the side panel that attaches opposite the wall with the plumbing.

◆ Line up the panel's outside edge with the front of the tub or with the front of the apron strip, overlap the corner panel, and press it firmly onto the wall.

◆ Apply adhesive to the plumbing-wall panel and an extra ring of adhesive $\frac{1}{4}$ inch away from the edges of the cutouts. Firmly attach the panel to the wall.

◆ Caulk the top and bottom edges of the tub surround, as well as the overlapping edges of the panels.

INSTALLING SOLID-SURFACE WALLS

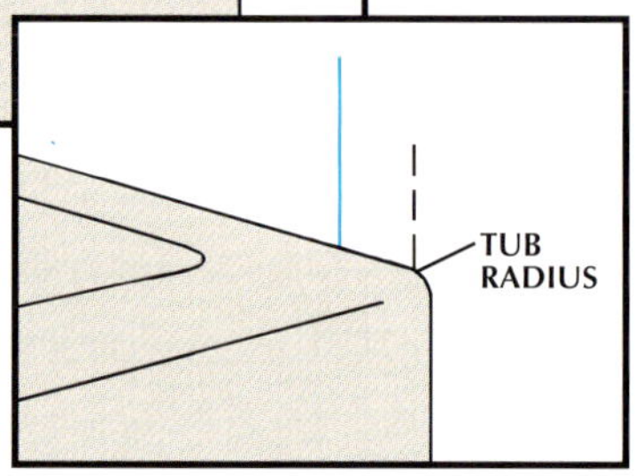

1. Preparing for installation.

A solid-surface tub wall kit usually contains two back and two side panels, corner pieces, and matching T molding and mitered trim strips.

◆ To provide a gap for caulking, tape $\frac{1}{16}$-inch-thick laminate shims around the perimeter of the tub edge *(left),* setting them where the ends of the panels, corners, and trim pieces will rest. Place the shims for the outside edges of the side panels $2\frac{1}{2}$ inches in from the point known as the radius, where the edge of the tub begins to curve down *(inset).*

◆ Trial fit all panels and trim the bottom edges, if necessary, with a circular saw or jigsaw. Smooth rough edges, using an orbital sander or sandpaper.

◆ Clean the walls and the backs of the panels, corners, and trim pieces with denatured alcohol and clean white rags.

◆ Mark the center of the back wall.

2. Attaching the panels.

◆ Apply a $\frac{1}{4}$-inch bead of silicone caulk $\frac{1}{2}$ inch from the bottom edge of a back panel and a bead of adhesive 1 inch above the caulk. Apply additional adhesive as in Step 3, page 63.

◆ Resting the bottom edge on the shims, position the back panel about $\frac{3}{8}$ inch to one side of the marked centerline, and press it onto the wall.

◆ Pull the top of the panel out slightly, apply a dab of hot melt glue to the wall at each corner, then press the panel back into position and hold it in place for 10 to 15 seconds.

◆ Attach the second back panel in the same way, thus leaving a gap of about $\frac{3}{4}$ inch between the two panels.

◆ Attach the side panel opposite the plumbing wall, its outside edge $2\frac{1}{2}$ inches from the tub radius.

◆ Starting from a line drawn $2\frac{1}{2}$ inches from the tub radius on the plumbing wall, measure and cut outlet holes in the remaining side panel as in Step 2 on page 63. Apply extra adhesive $\frac{1}{4}$ inch from the edges of the cutouts and attach the panel to the wall *(left).*

3. Fitting corners and trim strips.

◆ On the back of a corner piece, apply silicone caulk $\frac{1}{2}$ inch from the bottom and side edges and hot melt glue at the top edge; press the corner piece into place.

◆ Install the other corner panel.

◆ Measure and cut the back wall top trim to fit between the corner pieces. Attach it with a bead of caulk applied $\frac{1}{4}$ inch from each edge. Align the top edge of the trim with the top edge of the corner pieces, press the trim into position, and secure it with masking tape.

◆ To position the side trim, mark a level, horizontal line from the top of one corner piece to about 4 inches beyond the side panel edge. Place the trim piece next to the side panel, check it for plumb, and draw a vertical line along its outside edge to about 4 inches above the horizontal line.

◆ Rest the mitered end of the trim piece on the shim located between the side panel and the tub radius. Mark, then squarely cut off, the portion of the trim piece that extends above the horizontal line. Sand the cut edge.

◆ Similarly fit the side wall's top trim piece by resting its mitered end against the edge of the corner piece; mark and squarely cut off the portion extending past the plumb line.

◆ Attach the trim pieces by applying a bead of caulk $\frac{1}{4}$ inch from all edges. Secure the trim with masking tape.

◆ Repeat for the other side.

4. Finishing the job.

◆ Rest the vertical trim piece called the T molding on its shim and position it between the back panels. On the T molding, mark the length from the shim to the top trim piece and cut the molding to fit.

◆ Apply a bead of caulk about $\frac{1}{4}$ inch from the edges of the T molding, press it into place and secure it with masking tape.

◆ Mount shampoo shelves and soap dishes in the corners with caulk and small dabs of hot melt glue. Secure them with masking tape.

◆ Wait 8 to 10 hours for the adhesives to partially set. Then, remove the shims and masking tape, and caulk the gap around the tub, all of the vertical edges, and the tops of the trim and corners. Also caulk around shelves and plumbing openings.

◆ Wait 24 hours before using the tub.

Smoothing the Way for a New Floor

The first step in replacing a bathroom floor is to examine the condition of the existing one. Damage and rot are not always visible, since the floor actually consists of three layers—the surface, or finish flooring; an underlayment of particle board or plywood; and the subfloor, which is nailed or screwed directly to the joists.

Inspecting Below the Surface: Before beginning your survey, remove the toilet *(pages 91-92)*. If the floor feels suspiciously soft or yielding in places, take up a section of finish flooring and probe for rot with a screwdriver. The damage may be confined to the underlayment or it may extend through to the subfloor.

Also check for lifted seams, buckling in the finish flooring, dampness, odors, discoloration, or other signs of water seepage around sinks, tubs, and toilets. The toilet flange presents special problems in patching the underlayment and subfloor *(pages 68-69)*.

Preparing the Surface: Once the damage is repaired—or if the three existing layers are solid to begin with—the next step depends on your choice of replacement material. Resilient vinyl—either sheet or square tiles—can be laid over the old flooring. Makers of vinyl flooring sell a variety of products to level and smooth the existing surface.

Laying a ceramic tile floor over vinyl requires a new underlayment for support *(page 67)*. Exterior-grade $\frac{5}{8}$-inch plywood or particle board is preferred because of its water resistance. You may need to trim door bottoms to add this layer—plus the tile—to the floor. Do not tile over an existing ceramic tile floor unless it is structurally sound—no cracks or water damage.

CAUTION

Asbestos

If your resilient bathroom floor was installed before 1986, the flooring and the adhesive underneath may contain asbestos. When disturbed, these materials can release microscopic asbestos fibers into the air, creating severe long-term health risks. Unless you know for certain that your floor does not contain asbestos, assume that it does and follow these precautions when making any repairs:

- *Always wear a dual-cartridge respirator. Asbestos fibers will pass right through an ordinary dust mask.*
- *Never sand resilient flooring or the underlying adhesive.*
- *Try to remove the damaged flooring in one piece. If it looks likely to break or crumble, wet it before removal to reduce the chance of raising dust.*
- *When scraping off old adhesive, always use a heat gun to keep it tacky or a spray bottle to keep it wet.*
- *If vacuuming is necessary, rent or buy a wet/dry shop vac with a HEPA (High Efficiency Particulate Air) filtration system.*
- *Place the damaged flooring, adhesive, and HEPA filter in a polyethylene trash bag at least 6 mils (.006 inch) thick, and seal it immediately.*
- *Contact your local environmental protection office for guidance as to proper disposal.*

TOOLS

Electric drill with screwdriver bit
Utility or linoleum knife
Heat gun
Putty knife or stiff-bladed scraper
Chisel
Screwdriver
Circular saw
Pry bar

MATERIALS

Vinyl-tile adhesive
Latex patching compound
$\frac{5}{8}$-inch plywood or particle board
$2\frac{1}{4}$-inch dry-wall screws
Construction adhesive

PREPARING AN UNDAMAGED FLOOR FOR CERAMIC TILE

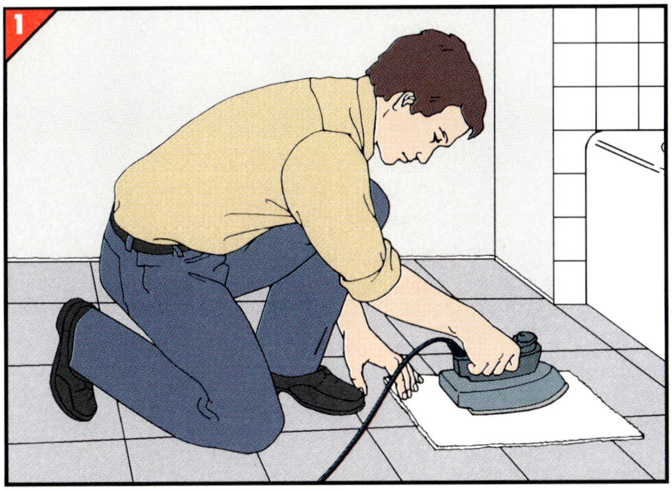

1. Leveling the finish flooring.

◆ Remove the shoe molding and baseboard as described on page 50.
◆ Clean the floor thoroughly, removing all dirt and old wax.
◆ For a vinyl tile floor, rebond any loose tiles by using a hot iron, protecting the surface with an old towel *(left)*. If heat fails to activate the adhesive, lift the tile, scrape off the old adhesive, and reset the tile with new adhesive.
◆ Fill any spaces that are left with a latex patching compound available from flooring retailers.

2. Installing new underlayment.

◆ Arrange plywood or particle board sheets in a staggered pattern. The sheets should span any joints in the existing floor. To allow for expansion, leave about $\frac{1}{32}$ inch between the sheets and about $\frac{1}{8}$ inch between the outside edges and the walls.
◆ With an electric drill and a screwdriver bit, secure each sheet with drywall screws set $\frac{3}{8}$ inch in from the edges and spaced 6 inches apart over the whole surface of the sheet *(left)*.

PATCHING OLD UNDERLAYMENT

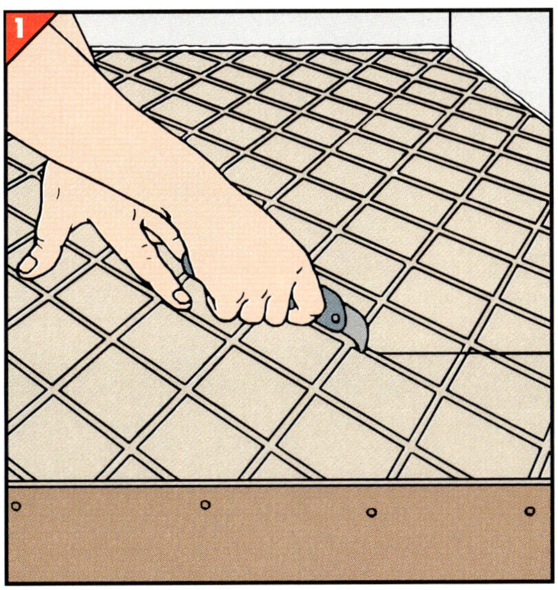

1. Removing the finish flooring.

◆ For sheet vinyl, make several parallel cuts from wall to wall with a utility or linoleum knife *(left)*.
◆ Use a heat gun to soften the adhesive along the cuts or, in the case of tiles, along the joints between them. Hold the nozzle a few inches above the floor and sweep it back and forth for about 15 seconds. Then work a putty knife blade under the flooring and gently pry it loose.
◆ Continue until the entire strip or tile comes off, then soften and scrape any remaining adhesive off the underlayment with the heat gun and putty knife.

2. Cutting out the damaged area.

◆ Poke a chisel or screwdriver through a soft spot in the underlayment to determine its thickness and set your circular saw to that depth.

◆ Cut out and remove a rectangular section of underlayment around the damaged area *(left)*.

◆ Fit an underlayment patch to the opening; make the patch the same thickness as the original. Attach the patch to the subfloor with a construction adhesive and dry-wall screws.

WORKING AROUND A TOILET FLANGE

1. Lifting out the underlayment.

◆ Stuff the toilet drain hole with rags to prevent odors and possible loss of small tools.

◆ With a circular saw, cut a rectangular section of underlayment around the damaged area *(right)*. Then cut the section in half, sawing as close as possible to the flange.

◆ Remove any screws that are attaching the toilet flange to the floor, and pull the nails out of the underlayment cutout. Ease each side of the underlayment out from under the toilet flange without putting upward pressure on the flange that would disturb the seal between the flange and the drain beneath.

2. Inserting a patch.

◆ Cut a patch of $\frac{5}{8}$-inch plywood or particle board that is the size and shape of the hole in the underlayment.

◆ Saw the patch in two so that the seam will not coincide with any subflooring joint, then notch both pieces to fit around the flange.

◆ Apply a bead of construction adhesive to the underside of both pieces of the patch, and slip them into place under the flange *(left)*. Attach them to the subfloor with dry-wall screws.

1. Cutting out the damaged area.

◆ First, increase the size of the cutout in the underlayment so it is larger than the proposed patch to the subfloor.

◆ For a plywood subfloor, cut out and remove the damaged area in the same way you removed the underlayment in Step 1 on the previous page.

◆ For a lumber subfloor *(above)*, remove the nails or screws from the joists on either side of the damaged area. Saw above the centerline of the joists through the empty nail or screw holes, then lift out the boards.

2. Patching the subfloor.

◆ Cut a plywood patch to fit the cutout in the subfloor.

◆ Mark the center of the toilet drain hole on an edge of the patch that will be parallel to the joists when installed.

◆ Saw the patch in two at that point, then cut a notch in each piece to fit the flange.

◆ Run a bead of construction adhesive along the tops of the exposed joists, then slip the two pieces under the lip of the flange *(left)* and anchor them to the joists with dry-wall screws.

Installing Ceramic Floor Tiles

The challenge of laying a floor in a bathroom depends in part on the material chosen. Laying sheet flooring, for example, is more demanding than installing tiles because of the multiple cutouts required. An error can ruin an entire sheet of material but may spoil only a single tile.

Either vinyl tile or ceramic tile—shown on these and the following pages—is suitable for a bathroom floor. Both are installed in much the same way, beginning with sound subflooring and underlayment *(pages 66-67)*.

Ceramic tile, which is the more durable of the two materials, also requires the extra step of grouting to fill the seams between the rows *(pages 74-75)*.

Both jobs begin with dividing the room into four roughly equal quadrants *(below)*. Work proceeds by quadrant, with the quadrant next to the bathroom door tiled last. Tiles may be laid in rows as shown here or diagonally in an adaptation of the method for walls on page 79. In either case, you have the option of not laying partial tiles around the perimeter of the room until you have laid all the whole tiles.

Tiles and Thresholds: Most ceramic tiles have spacer lugs on their edges that assure joints of equal width. If you use tiles without lugs, buy spacers separately. Choose tiles no thicker than will come flush with the toilet flange. Always buy a few extra tiles to allow for breakage, and save fragments to practice cutting *(pages 72-73)*.

For the threshold at the bathroom door, you can use real or synthetic marble if the tiles are flush with the floor outside the bathroom. If not, shape the underside of a wood threshold to bridge the two different levels.

Adhesive and Grout: When laying ceramic tile on any surface but particle board or concrete, the strongest bonding agent is thin-set latex adhesive, a powder that is mixed with water. Use mastic with particle board, and on concrete, lay an isolation membrane—thin fiberglass backed by rubber—to prevent small cracks in the slab from shifting the tiles. Affix the membrane with mastic, and then use thin-set latex adhesive for the tile. Grout for tile joints is available with sand or without, for a smoother look.

TOOLS

Notched trowel
Hammer
Chalk line
Tile cutter
Tile nippers
Rod saw
Grout float
Caulk gun
Small brush
Small saw

MATERIALS

Ceramic floor tiles
Tile adhesive
2-by-4
Solvent
Sandpaper, 80-grit
Grout
Denatured alcohol
Silicone caulk
Silicone grout sealant

SAFETY TIPS

When cutting tile, wear safety goggles and work gloves to protect yourself against chips and sharp edges. Put on rubber gloves to work with adhesive or grout.

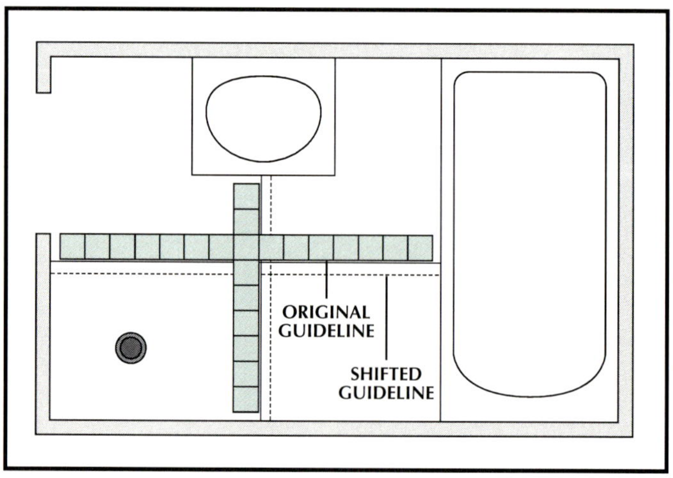

Planning a pattern.

◆ Mark the center of the rectangular area to be tiled, ignoring encroachments such as a vanity. Draw two guidelines through the center, perpendicular to each other and parallel to the walls.
◆ Position a tile with one corner at the center point, then add tiles to make a cross at the center of the area *(right)*. Use spacers between tiles without lugs.
◆ If a gap narrower than half a tile remains at the ends of either row, shift the guidelines *(right)*, widening these spaces to eliminate awkward cuts on tiny pieces of tile. Reposition the tiles on the floor to check your work.
◆ Pick up all the tiles except for the one at the center of the cross. With a chalk line, establish new guidelines along adjacent edges of the tile.

LAYING WHOLE TILES

1. Preparing the surface.

◆ Spread a thin layer of adhesive on the entire floor with the unnotched side of a trowel. Work one quadrant at a time, ending at the area by the door. Avoid obscuring the guidelines.

◆ Allow this preliminary coat to dry for about 2 hours.

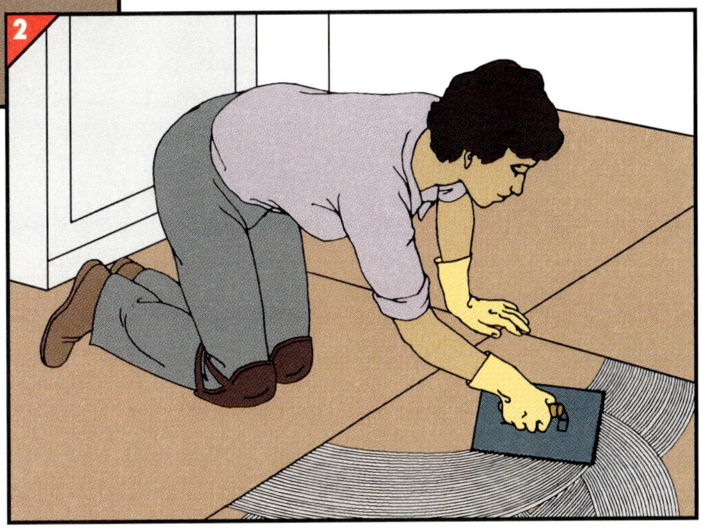

2. Applying adhesive.

◆ Pour about a cup of adhesive onto one quadrant. Pull the notched edge of the trowel through the adhesive at a 45-degree angle, assuring that the teeth penetrate to the floor.

◆ Use sweeping strokes to spread the adhesive evenly in the corner of the quadrant.

3. Setting tiles.

◆ Starting at the center of the room, set a row of tiles along the guideline, toward the wall. Work carefully; these tiles determine the alignment of all that follow. Place tiles lug to lug, pressing each into the adhesive with a slight twisting of your fingertips.

◆ Complete the quadrant in the same manner. Take care to align the first tile in each new row precisely with the tile next to it. Avoid kneeling directly on freshly laid tiles. If you can't reach across them to continue, either stop work for 24 hours while the adhesive cures or lay plywood on the tiles to protect them.

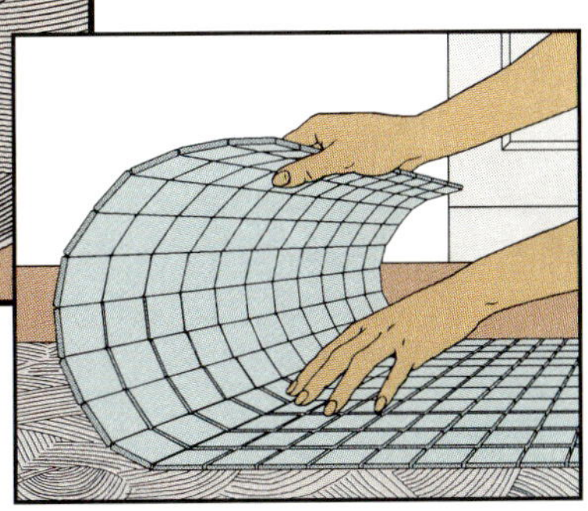

Lay mosaic tile sheets in rows, unrolling each sheet onto the surface in turn, leaving the same space between sheets as between individual tiles *(inset)*.

4. Beating in the tiles.
Cushion a straight 2-by-4 with cloth and set it on the tiles you have laid. Move the board around, gently tapping it with a hammer to force protruding tiles into the adhesive. Wipe away excess adhesive with a solvent recommended by the manufacturer.

CUTTING AND SETTING PARTIAL TILES

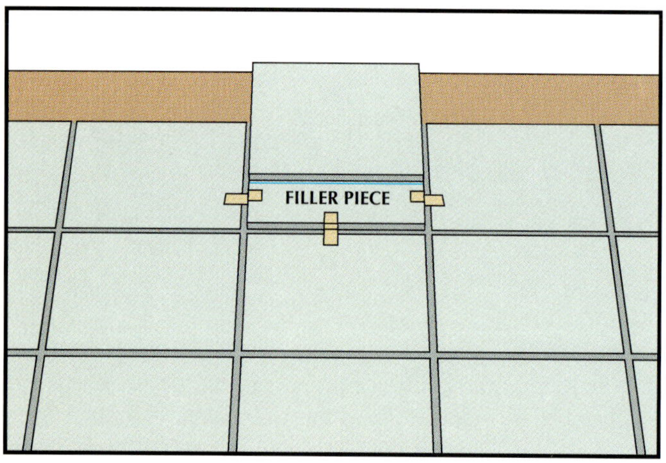

Marking edge tiles.
- To make filler pieces for gaps at walls, cabinets, and bathtubs, tape a tile on top of a tile that borders the gap. This second tile will become the filler piece.
- Set a third tile on top of the second and slide it to the wall.
- One joint width from the edge of the topmost tile, mark the filler piece for cutting as shown at left *(blue line).*

For mosaic tile, cut tiles from a sheet, trim them as needed, and set them individually.

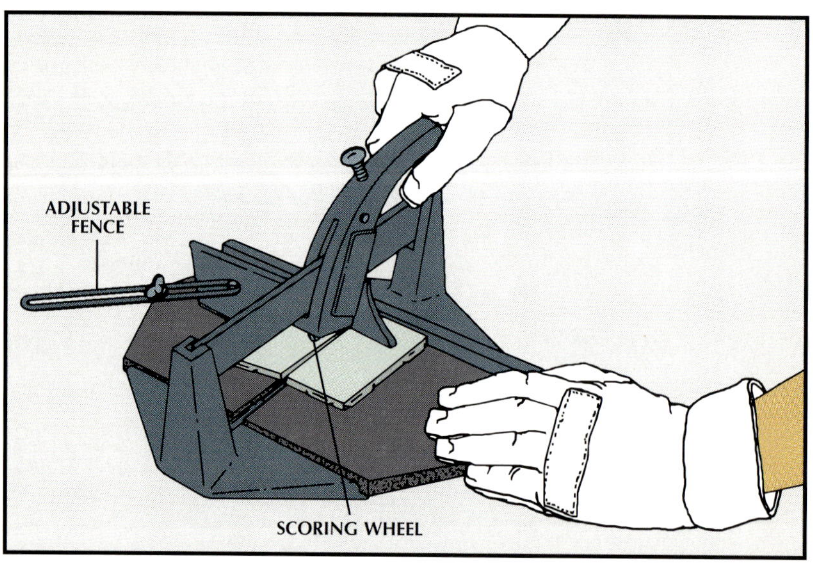

Cutting perimeter tiles.
- Position the cut line under the tile cutter's scoring wheel and set the adjustable fence to hold the tile in place.
- Score the tile with the wheel, then press down firmly with the lever to snap the tile along the line.

CAUTION: *Cut tiles are sharp. Dull the edges with 80-grit sandpaper.*

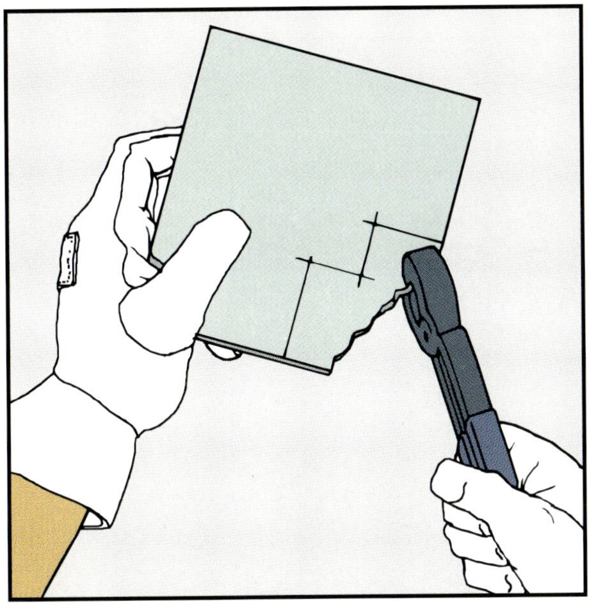

Making irregular cuts.

Use nippers to fit tiles to corners, doorjambs, or a toilet flange.

◆ First, make a paper pattern for the cut, then transfer the outline to the glazed side of the tile. Hold the glazed side up and break tiny pieces from the tile—less than $\frac{1}{8}$ inch at a time—to avoid splitting it.

◆ Smooth and dull the cut edges of the tile with 80-grit sandpaper.

TRICKS OF THE TRADE

An Alternative to Nippers

Nibbling at the edge of a tile with nippers sometimes fractures tiles and nearly always leaves a ragged edge. A rod saw solves both problems.

A variety of hacksaw blade, a rod saw is a wire coated with carbide, an abrasive that cuts quickly through ceramic. The cylindrical blade allows abrupt changes in direction to make cutting a square corner as easy as shaping a wide curve.

To cut a tile, rest it on a low work surface such as a bench or a stool with the cut line near the edge. Saw vertically, repositioning the tile as needed to keep the blade close to the supporting edge. Sandpaper the cut edge.

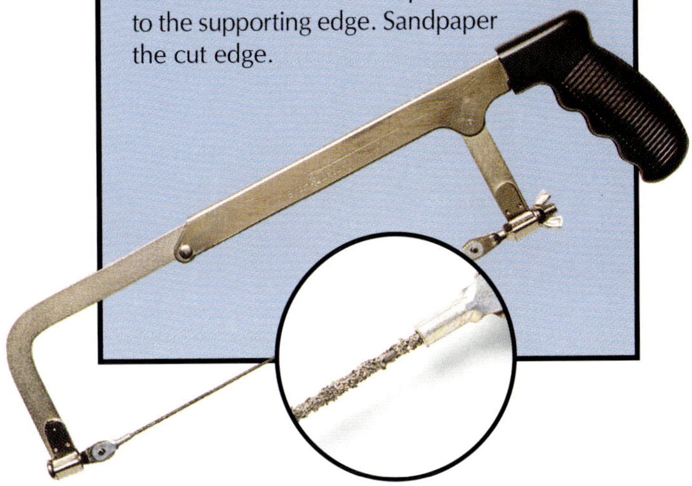

Setting partial tiles.

◆ Position each partial tile in line with its row as you did with whole tiles and press it into the adhesive.

◆ If the tile is to fit under a molding at the wall, slide the cut edge under the trim, then press the tile in place.

◆ Let tile adhesive cure for at least 24 hours before grouting the joints.

1. Grouting.
◆ Temporarily stuff perimeter joints with rolled paper towels to prevent grout from entering.
◆ Pour a cup or two of grout onto the tiles and drag it diagonally across the joints with a rubber grout float. Work in an area of 5 square feet or so, pressing grout to the bottoms of joints. Wait 15 minutes, then wipe up excess grout with a damp sponge.
◆ Grout the rest of the floor in the same manner.
◆ Keep the grout damp as it cures by mopping the floor twice daily for 3 days. Then wipe any haze of grout from the tiles with a soft cloth.

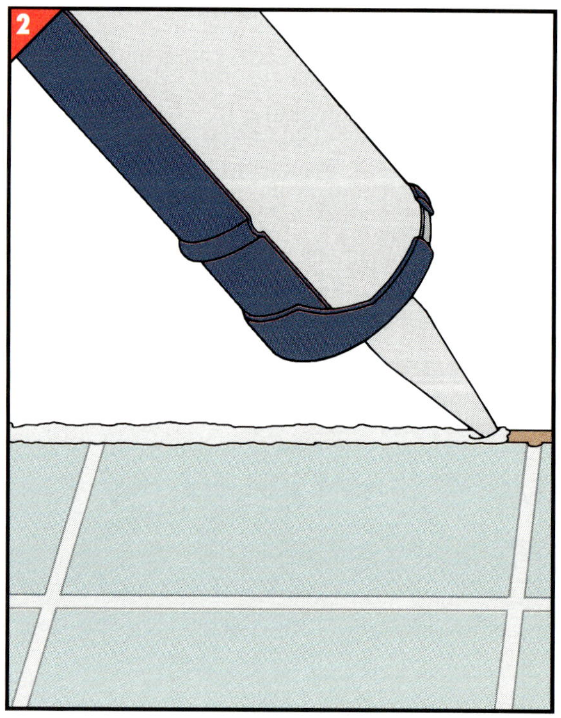

2. Caulking perimeter joints.
◆ Load a caulk gun with a tube of silicone caulk, its tip cut at a 45-degree angle, to lay a bead of caulk in each perimeter joint. Pushing the caulk ahead of the gun, as shown at right, fill the joints to the same depth as the grout between the tiles.
◆ When the silicone is tacky, dampen a rag with denatured alcohol and clean excess caulk from around the joints.

3. Sealing grout.

◆ Brush grout sealant on the joints only after the grout has fully cured. The curing period varies among sealants; check the manufacturer's instructions. Apply sealant liberally, wiping up the excess with a soft cloth.

◆ Allow the sealant to dry completely before letting the floor get wet.

ADDING A THRESHOLD

1. Cutting the doorstop.

◆ Position one end of the threshold against the doorstop to mark the doorstop for trimming.

◆ Lay a pencil flat on the threshold and drag the point across the doorstop to make a cutting line slightly higher than the threshold.

◆ Repeat this procedure for the other side of the doorway, then use a small saw to trim both doorstops *(left)*.

2. Positioning the threshold.

◆ Apply tile adhesive to the bottom of the threshold with the notched edge of a trowel.

◆ Hold the threshold as shown at right. Without allowing the adhesive to touch the floor, slide the threshold under the doorstops to the edge of the tiles and press it into place.

◆ Wipe away excess adhesive with a damp sponge.

Tiling the Walls around a Tub

Few improvements add as much life and sparkle to an older bathroom as a newly tiled tub alcove, which can also provide the classic finishing touch to a renovation or new bathroom. Tile offers the practical advantage of a waterproof, durable, and easy-to-clean surface. Moreover, by replacing old, cracked tiles you may also prevent water damage to the walls and floor.

A Solid Backing: For a tiling job that will last, cement board *(page 123)* is the best choice of backing material. In an old bathroom, strip the surrounding walls to the studs *(page 94)* and nail cement board to them. During a renovation, install cement board on any wall that is intended for tiling.

Selecting Materials: For best results with tub walls, choose full-size or field tiles that are $4\frac{1}{4}$ inches square with spacer lugs on each side. Such tiles are easier to handle than larger specimens and are less likely to shift under their own weight during installation; the lugs ensure even spacing for the grout lines between tiles.

Tub surrounds are commonly tiled to a height of 72 inches above the floor—just below the shower arm, which is normally placed between 74 and 76 inches above the floor. Estimate how many field tiles you will need to cover your surround, then add extras to allow for imperfections, breakage, and cutting mistakes. Also purchase trim tiles *(opposite, top)* as edging. Trim tiles usually lack spacer lugs; establish the correct spacing between them and the field tiles with 2-inch finishing nails *(page 80)*.

When practical, buy soap dishes and other ceramic accessories from the wall-tile manufacturer. They are often the size of one or two field tiles; leave the space open as you tile, then add the accessory as shown on page 8.

Choose a Type 1 organic or mastic tile adhesive formulated for wet areas. Follow the directions on the container to select the right trowel to properly spread the adhesive. Serrated trowels—rather than the notched trowels used for floors—are common for wall tiling. To fill spaces between tiles, look for a grout with a latex additive. It is stronger, more flexible, and more water resistant than other grouts.

Final Preparations: Before beginning any work in the bathtub, pad the bottom with cardboard and old blankets to prevent shoes, tools, or falling tiles from chipping the finish. Cover the drain and overflow openings with masking tape to keep out dust, adhesive, and other materials.

TOOLS

- Level
- Chalk line
- Hammer
- Serrated trowel
- Tile cutter
- Tile nippers
- Grout float
- Caulk gun

MATERIALS

- 1-by-2 lumber
- Dry-wall nails
- Adhesive
- $4\frac{1}{4}$-inch field tiles with spacer lugs
- Ceramic accessories
- Trim tiles
- 2-inch finishing nails
- Latex grout
- Silicone caulk
- Grout sealant

SAFETY TIPS

Protect your eyes with safety goggles and hands with work gloves while cutting or nipping tiles. Wear rubber gloves when mixing or applying tile adhesive and grout.

Trim tiles for a finished edge.
Although square field tiles cover most of the walls above a tub, two kinds of trim tiles are needed to complete the installation. The first are 2- by 6-inch bullnose tiles, which run along the top and ends of the tiled area. Where the end walls of a tub alcove meet the back wall, the bullnoses butt together as the field tiles do—the edge of one against the glossy face of the other. As shown in the photograph at right, the second kind of trim—called a down-corner tile—fills the square where vertical and horizontal courses of bullnose meet.

PLOTTING GUIDELINES

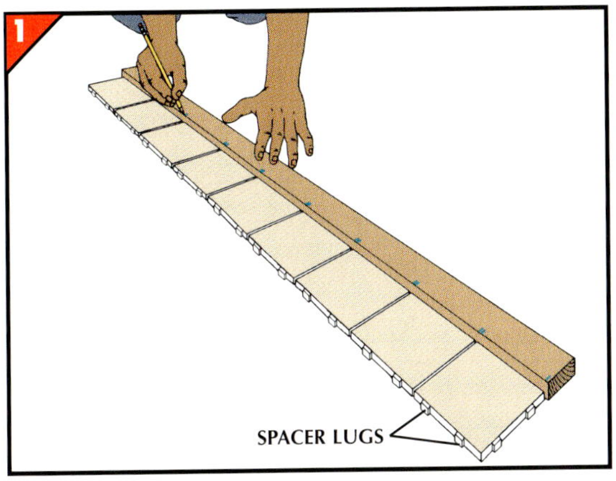

1. Making a layout stick.

◆ Cut a piece of straight 1-by-2 lumber to a length of between 36 and 42 inches.

◆ Working on a level surface, set out a row of tiles, lug to lug, and place the 1-by-2 alongside them, one end aligned with the lugs of the first tile.

◆ Mark the width of each tile on the stick *(left)*.

For wider grout lines or when working with tiles that have no lugs, take care to space the tiles evenly, then mark the layout stick accordingly.

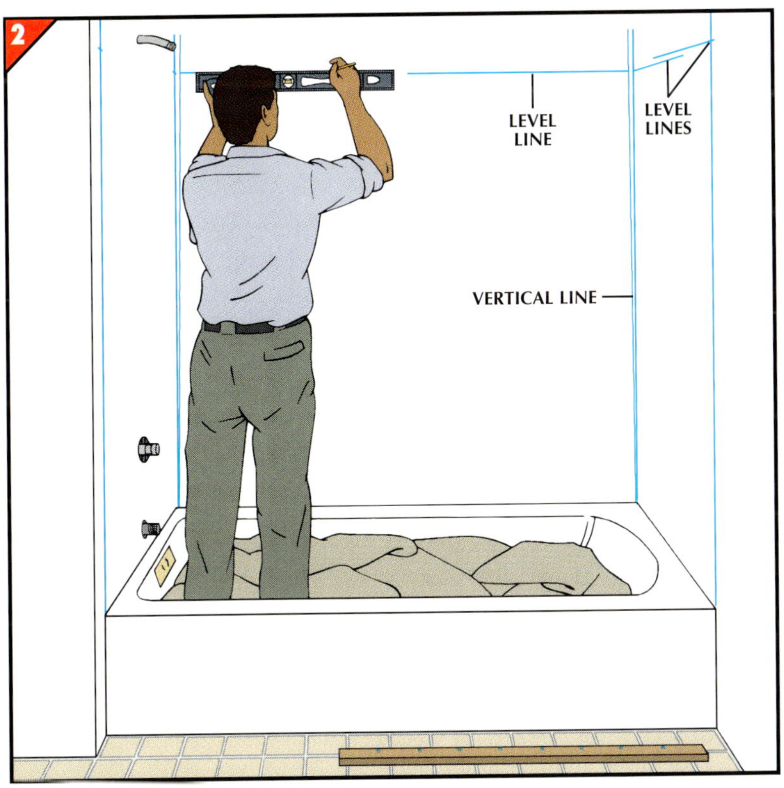

2. Checking the tub slope.

◆ Where each corner of the tub meets an end wall, draw a vertical line on the wall to the showerhead height, using a level to keep the lines plumb. Similarly draw vertical lines on the back wall from the inside tub corner. On each line, mark the planned height of the tiles, measured from the tub rim.

◆ On each tub wall, draw level lines inward from the marks on the two vertical lines. If the lines meet, the tub is level along that side.

◆ Where the lines do not meet, the higher line indicates the high side of the tub. Measure the distance between them.

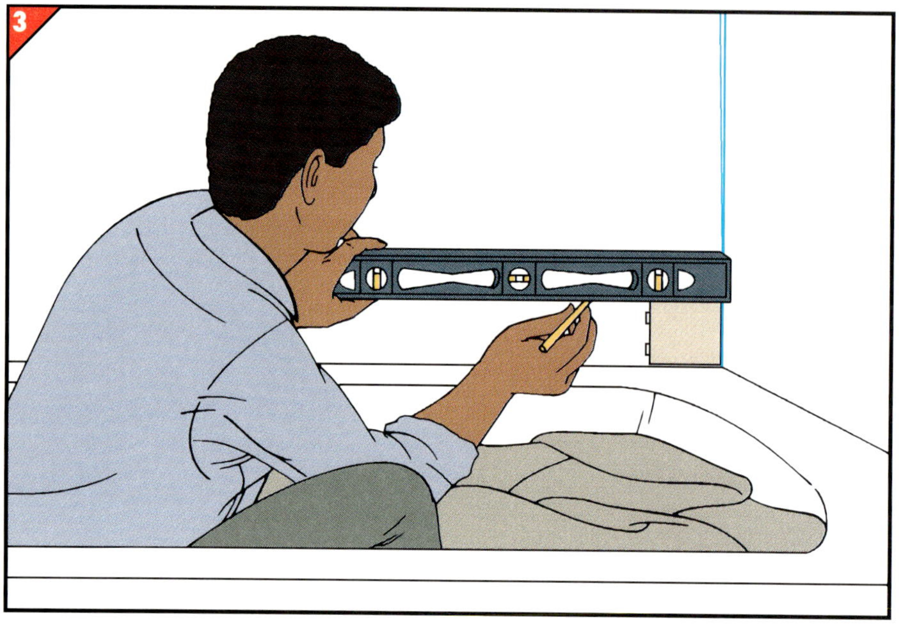

3. Marking a level starting line.

◆ If the distance between the level lines drawn on the back wall in Step 2 is less than $\frac{1}{8}$ inch, set a field tile at the high end of the bathtub's back rim. Otherwise, place the tile at the low end of the rim.

◆ In either case, place a level on top of the tile and draw a horizontal guideline across the wall *(left)*.

◆ If tub rim and guideline converge to less than a tile width, tiles must be trimmed to fit. When the distance between the tub rim and the guideline becomes slightly greater than the width of a tile, plan to fill the extra space with grout.

4. Selecting a center point.

◆ Mark the center of the guideline. Then hold the layout stick under the line so that it touches the end wall.

◆ If the center mark aligns with a joint space on the stick, the wall can be completed without cutting end tiles.

◆ If a tile would cover the center mark *(right)*, slide the stick to center a joint space on the mark. Measure the distance between the stick and the end wall.

◆ If the gap is 2 inches or more, draw a vertical guideline at the center mark. For a gap that is narrower than 2 inches, mark the wall half a tile width farther from the corner and draw the vertical line there.

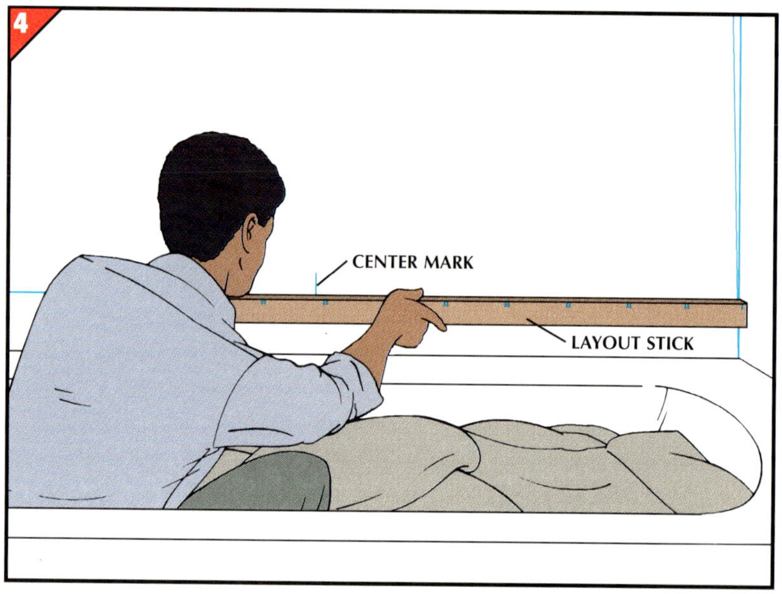

5. Guidelines for end walls.

◆ Mark a horizontal guideline on each end wall as in Step 3.

◆ At an outside corner, hold a tile against the guideline where it intersects the corner. If the tile edge and corner do not coincide, tack a chalk line at the inside corner, align the tile with the outside corner, and snap a new guideline along the bottom of the tile *(left)*. Mark a vertical guideline $2\frac{1}{8}$ inches from the corner.

◆ For an end wall with no corner nearby, extend the horizontal guideline one tile width past the tub and mark for a vertical guideline.

◆ In both cases, plan for uncut field tiles at the outer edge and check with the layout stick whether this layout will create tile slivers at the inside corner. If so, either lengthen the guideline half a tile width or set half-tiles at the outer edge.

SETTING TILES IN PLACE

1. Applying adhesive.

◆ Using dry-wall nails, tack a 1-by-2 board to the back wall with the top edge at the horizontal guideline; this batten will support tiles while the adhesive sets.

◆ With the straight edge of a serrated trowel, scoop up about a cupful of adhesive and smear it on the wall near the intersection of the horizontal and vertical guidelines.

◆ Hold the trowel's serrated edge at a 45-degree angle to the wall to spread a thin, even coat of mastic over about 3 square feet of wall space *(left)*.

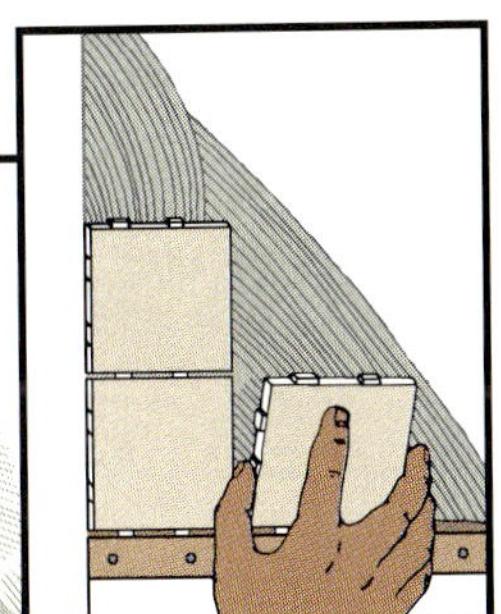

2. Placing the tiles.

◆ Set the first tile on the batten, side lugs against the vertical guideline. Press the tile against the adhesive with your fingertips, jiggling it slightly to help it stick.

◆ Add tiles according to the numbered sequence at left to form a pyramid. Continue the pattern upward and outward, coating the wall with adhesive as you go.

◆ Place tiles on the end walls in a half-pyramid *(inset)*, working from the outer edge toward the inside corner.

◆ Finish by removing the battens and filling in each bottom row. Allow the adhesive to cure for a few minutes before setting the tiles to keep them from sagging.

3. Accommodating the tub plumbing.

◆ If a pipe falls entirely within a tile, hold the tile below the pipe and mark its center on the edge of the tile. Cut the tile along the mark with a tile cutter *(page 72)*.

◆ Mark the width of the pipe on the cut edge of each piece *(above, left)*.

◆ Holding each piece glazed side up, use tile nippers to make a notch for the pipe *(above, right)*.

◆ For a pipe that falls at a joint, notch the edges of whole tiles to fit.

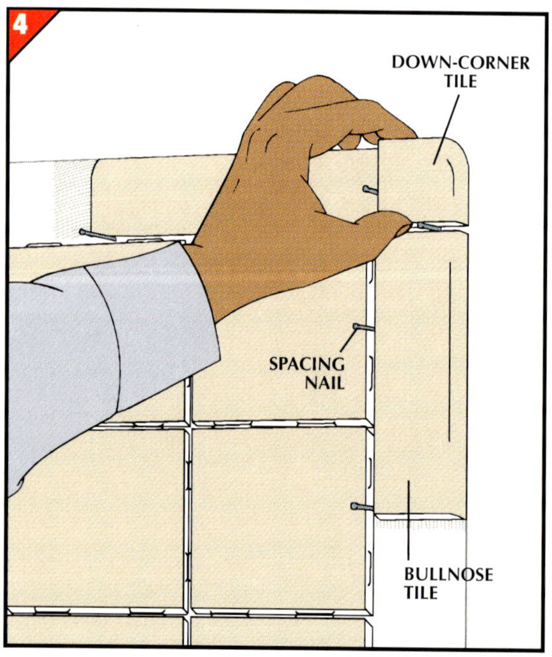

4. Adding the trim tiles.

◆ Measure the length in inches of the top row of tile on the back wall; divide by 6 to get a rough count of the number of bullnoses required. Allow $\frac{1}{8}$ inch more for each bullnose. Based on the result, plan to place the bullnoses along the top so that any partial bullnoses at the corners are about the same length.

◆ Spread enough adhesive for a few trim tiles at a time, then tap 2-inch finishing nails beside the field tiles between the spacer lugs to allow room for grout. Set the bullnoses in the adhesive.

◆ On each end wall, begin at the outside corner *(left)*. Set a bullnose above the top outermost field tile, flush with the edge and spaced away with a nail. Then set a bullnose vertically beside the field tile in the same way. Place a down-corner tile between the bullnoses. Extend the bullnose tile rows along both sides of the wall, cutting as needed at the inside corner.

FINISHING THE JOB

1. Applying grout.

◆ Let the adhesive cure for 24 hours, then remove the trim-spacing nails.

◆ Wearing rubber gloves and safety goggles, prepare a batch of grout according to the manufacturer's instructions.

◆ Trowel the mixture onto the tile surface with a rubber-faced grout float *(left)*, forcing the grout into the joints with crisscrossing diagonal strokes of the float edge. Be sure to fill the corner joints and the joint above the tub rim.

◆ Allow the grout to dry for 10 to 12 minutes. Then clean and polish the tiles as described on page 74.

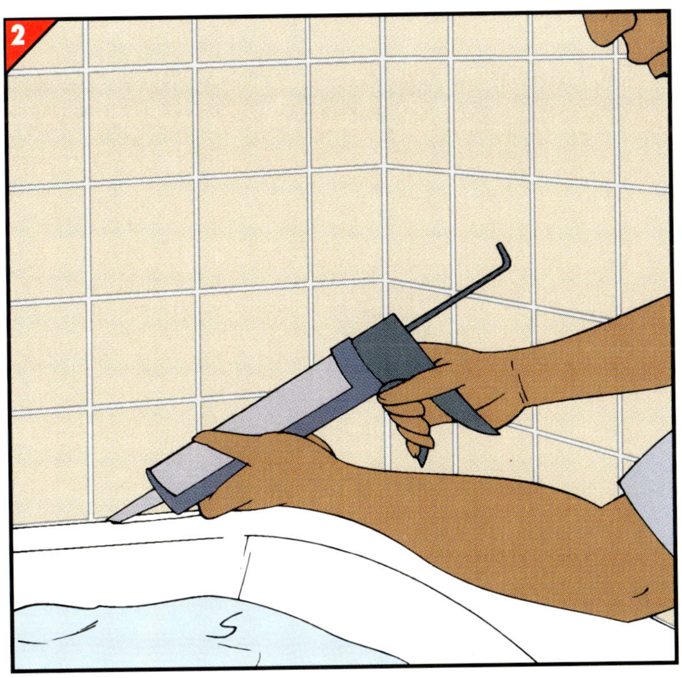

2. Caulking the tub.

◆ Wait 24 hours for the grout to cure; it will also shrink enough to form a shallow channel for a bead of caulk. Fill the bathtub with water to widen the tub-rim joint, which must be completely dry and free from dirt.

◆ Load a cartridge of silicone caulk, approved for bathtub use, into a caulking gun and cut the cartridge tip at a 45-degree angle.

◆ Place the tip at the joint and apply steady pressure on the trigger as you push the gun along the joint.

◆ To finish the bead, smooth it with a wet finger.

◆ Let the caulk cure for 24 hours before emptying the tub.

A few weeks later, apply sealant to the grout *(page 75)*.

4 Creating a New Bathroom

Whether you are adding a new bathroom or modernizing an old one, the details of the job will depend on a number of factors—among others, the structure of your house, the size of your budget, and your own tastes. The following pages explain the skills you are likely to need in any bathroom renovation, including planning, demolition, carpentry, laying new pipes, and installing fixtures.

A toilet flange →

Planning the Job

Remodeling a bathroom or adding a new one is a complex job that requires thorough planning. You must make basic decisions about the sizes and styles of fixtures and appliances, what floor and wall coverings to install, and how to provide or modify lighting, heating, and ventilation.

Preliminary Considerations: Unless you plan simply to remove the old fixtures *(pages 90-93)* and replace them with new ones, you will need to put in additional plumbing lines. The location of existing pipes and the distance they can be extended will often dictate the layout of a remodeled bathroom and may also limit your choice of locations for a new one. Especially critical is the location of the main stack for the house, which vents out of the roof and extends down to the house drain.

The additional fixtures required for a new bathroom can reduce water flow through the supply lines if your plumbing system already has low pressure or constricted pipes. Make solutions to such problems your first order of business.

To expand a bathroom, you will need to demolish old walls and you might have to build new ones *(pages 94-99 and 122-123)*. Avoid disturbing any bearing walls; you can recognize one by following the guidelines on page 48.

A Quartet of Codes: Learn the code requirements in your area as soon as possible in the planning stage to avoid wasted time and money. Four different codes may affect work on a bathroom: plumbing; electrical; mechanical, for heating and cooling systems; and building, for any structural changes to bearing walls, including exterior ones. Permits and specific plans are often required for each code. Your project will probably have to pass a rough-in inspection for each permit once the basic work is done, and a final inspection at the end of the job.

Pipe and Fixtures: For extending supply lines and drain lines, choose materials that are easy to work with. You do not need to match new pipe to old; adapters are available that will make the transition. For drains and vents, use polyvinyl chloride (PVC) plastic if local codes permit; most do. PVC is lightweight, readily cut with a saw, and easily assembled with special-purpose cement. Hot- and cold-water pipes may be any of several materials; in the examples shown here and on the pages that follow, the supply pipes are rigid copper, which remains a common choice for its durability.

Select your fixtures, usually including a toilet, washbasin, and tub or shower, early in the project so that you can take their dimensions and framing requirements into account. A sampling of basic options appears on pages 86-87.

Tips on Positioning Fixtures

- ✔ In a room with an existing stack, or in which a new stack must be located in a particular area, plan the placement of the toilet first—local codes normally dictate a maximum distance between the toilet and the stack.
- ✔ Because a full bathtub is very heavy, the best location for the tub is along a wall or in a corner, where it can be supported by proper framing. Provide extra floor bracing as shown on page 101.
- ✔ Position the foot of the tub against a wall that can be opened from the other side for plumbing repairs; whirlpool tubs must be installed so that there is also access to the motor.
- ✔ If possible, allow space around the washbasin for towel racks, hooks, and cabinets or shelves for storage.
- ✔ In a windowed bathroom, try to position the basin to take advantage of natural light for shaving and applying makeup.

Hiding Waste Lines: Drainpipes are large—the smallest drain from a bathroom fixture has a $1\frac{1}{2}$-inch inside diameter—and concealing them can be tricky. If the new bathroom is above a crawlspace or an unfinished basement, branch drainpipes can be run between or beneath the floor joists. For a new installation above a finished part of the house, you must cut away some of the ceiling below to install the pipes, and you may also have to drill through the joists to accommodate them *(page 103)*.

Vertical drainpipes and vent pipes are usually concealed inside a structure called a wet wall that is framed with 2-by-6 studs instead of the usual 2-by-4s in order to accommodate the pipes *(pages 96-99)*. Alternatively, supply lines and drain lines can be run alongside an existing wall and concealed—within cabinets, bookcases, closets, or specially made paneling.

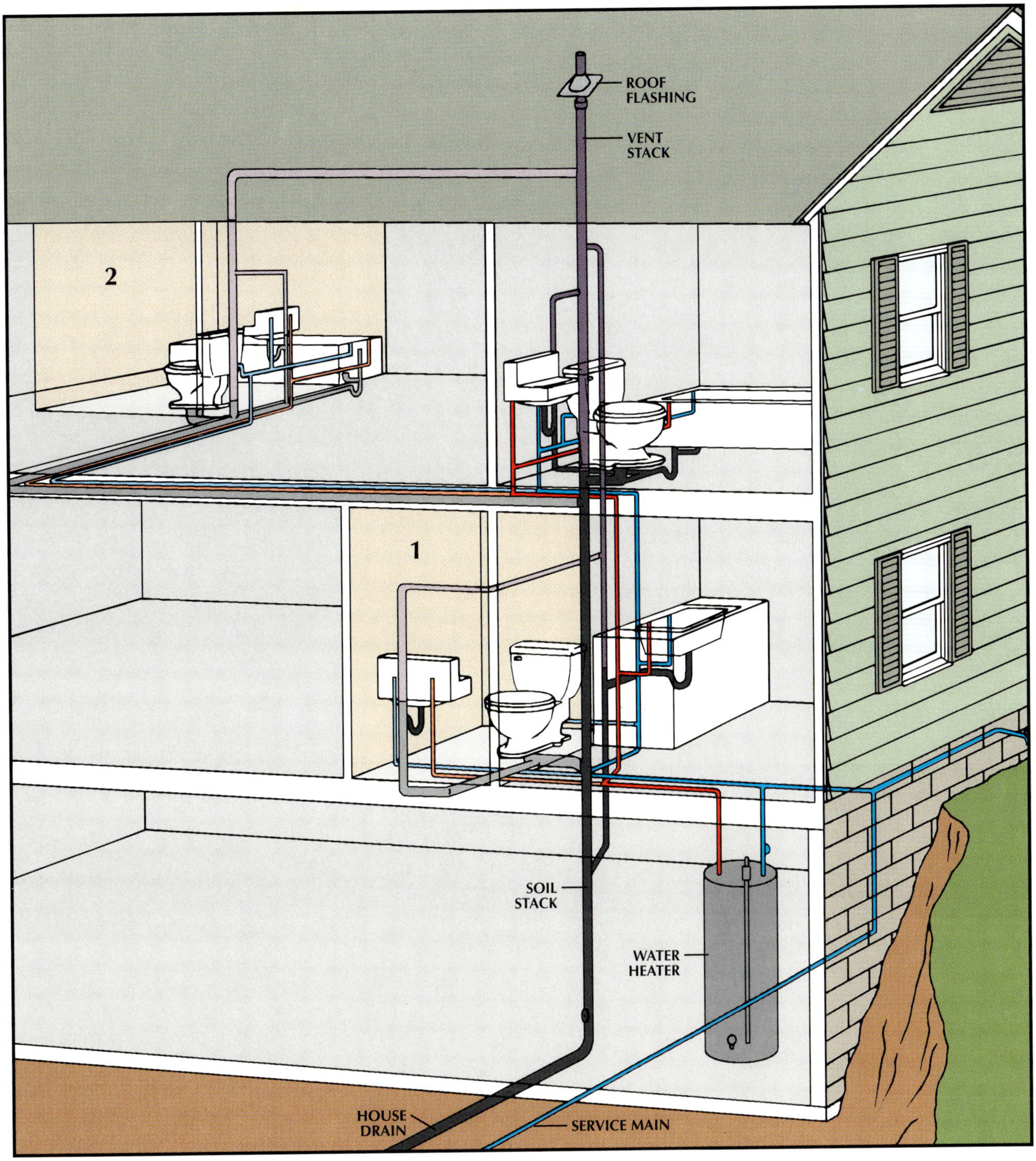

Paths for new pipes.
In this simplified diagram, the plumbing for a first-floor kitchen and a second-floor bathroom, both installed when the house was built, appears in dark colors. Pipes for a powder room *(1)* added next to the kitchen and for a second upstairs bathroom *(2)* have lighter tints.

The original plumbing core consists of pipes originating in the basement. Parallel supply pipes carry cold water *(blue)* from the service main and hot water *(red)* from the water heater. Drainpipes *(gray)* carry wastewater from the fixtures into the soil stack—the portion of the stack that leads down from the highest waste outlet to the house drain. Each fixture has a drain trap that prevents sewer gases from entering the house. Vent pipes *(purple)* linked to the vent portion of the stack exhaust waste gases through the roof.

Both the new powder room and the new second-floor bath illustrate ways new plumbing can be grafted to an existing system. The powder room contains a toilet and basin. It is close enough to the original plumbing core to be tied directly to it. The new drain runs across the unfinished basement ceiling below, and new vent pipes run parallel to the stack before connecting with it on the second floor. The supply lines are extensions of nearby hot and cold vertical lines, called risers.

The full-size upstairs bathroom requires a long run of piping across a first-floor ceiling. Fixtures are vented to a pipe that crosses the attic to connect with the existing vent stack.

AN ARRAY OF FIXTURES

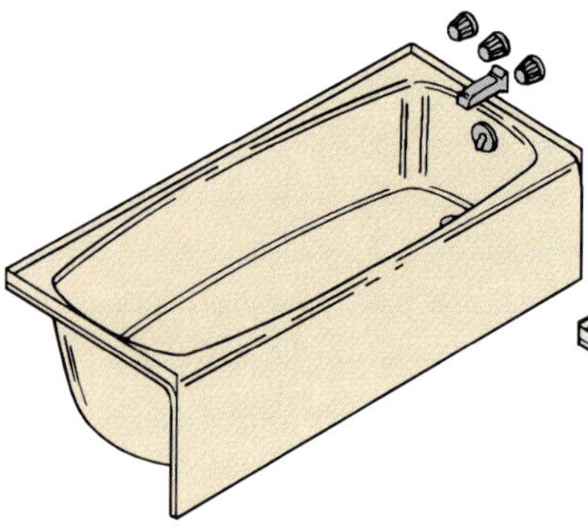

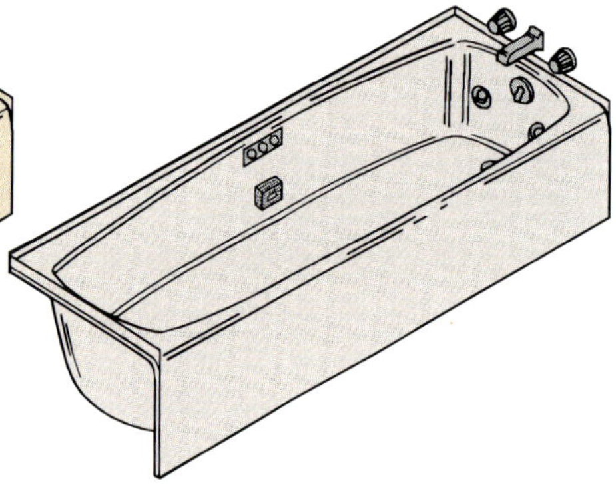

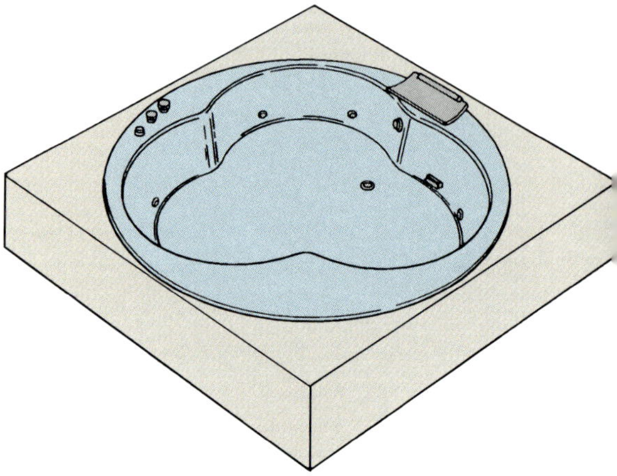

Standard tub.
This 60-inch by 30-inch tub is commonly available in fiberglass, cast iron, or steel. It may have one, two, or three skirted sides, depending on how many walls the tub will abut. You can also buy this style tub with all four sides unskirted and sink it into a floor or raised platform.

Whirlpool tub.
Equipped with a pump to circulate bathwater through nozzles in the sides, a whirlpool tub requires its own electric circuit. Modest units like this one resemble a standard bathtub and range up to 7 feet in length. A tub of this size usually fits through halls and doorways en route to the bathroom but may feel cramped to some.

Oversize whirlpool tub.
A unit wider than a standard tub offers luxurious comfort. However, it will not pass through a standard door or hall, so it is often practical only for a new bathroom near a sliding-glass door in an exterior wall. A large tub also may require extra floor reinforcement and two electrical circuits—one for the pump motor, another for a heater.

Multipiece tub surround.
Sold as a kit of separate panels, a tub surround like the one above can be carried through any doorway, then assembled as shown on pages 62-65. To prevent leaks,you must carefully maintain joints with caulk.

A seamless tub-and-wall unit.
Like a large whirlpool tub, a one-piece tub enclosure cannot fit through a standard hall or doorway, making it impractical for some renovations. This lightweight unit offers an advantage over surrounds built of separate panels: the corners remain watertight.

One-piece shower stall.
Some enclosures for showers come as a single unit like the one above; others must be assembled from panels *(pages 120-121)*. Select a shower that you can maneuver into the new bathroom, and allow room in your layout so the shower door can swing outward.

Two-piece toilet.
The traditional toilet consists of two major components, a tank and a bowl, which may be separated for certain repairs. Round bowls like the one shown here are standard, but elongated bowls are also available, at a higher price.

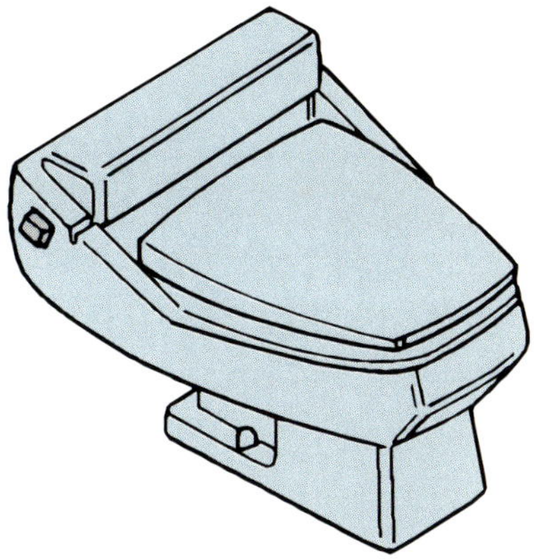

One-piece toilet.
A compact alternative to the two-piece version, this toilet frees wall space for shelves or cabinets. Because of their lower profile, one-piece toilets do not rely on gravity alone for flushing; instead, a special mechanism pressurizes the water that clears the bowl.

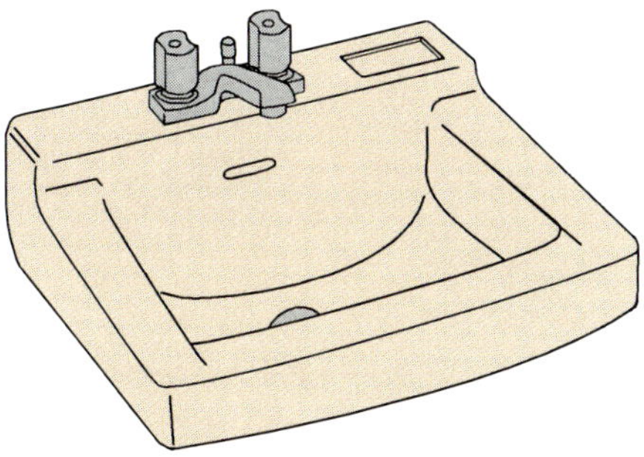

Wall-hung basin.
Requiring no cabinetry for support, a wall-hung basin occupies less space than many other kinds of sinks and so is well suited to small bathrooms. As its name suggests, this type of basin simply hangs from a mounting bracket attached securely to the wall.

Pedestal basin.
Most pedestal basins are supported by framing in the wall. The base, which is largely decorative, conceals the drain assembly while still leaving ample free space underneath.

Integral countertop basin.
Designed to be mounted onto a vanity, this type of basin is part of a small molded counter with a backsplash. The space between the basin and the backsplash may be ordered predrilled for any of the standard faucets shown on pages 19 to 22.

BASIC BATHROOM LAYOUTS

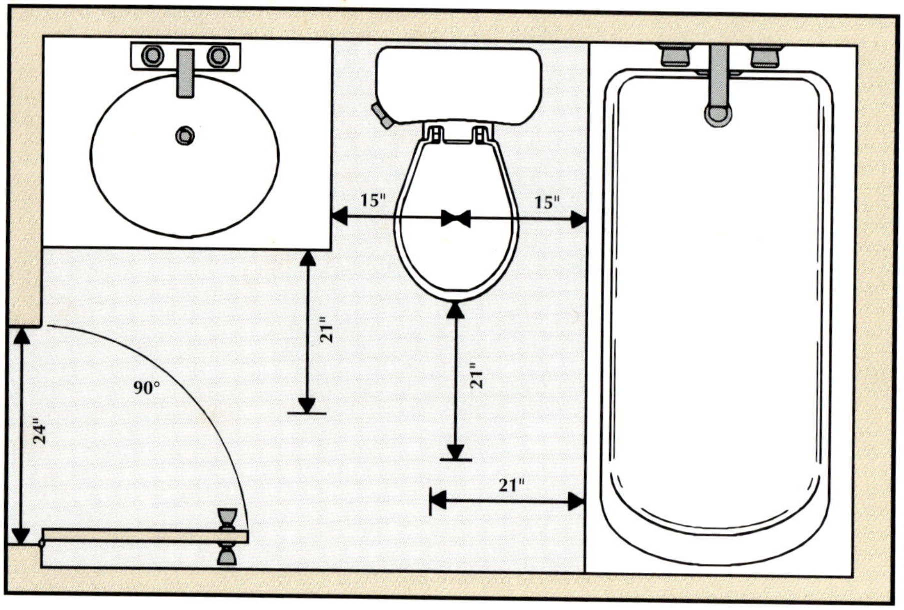

Standard clearances.
Most building codes specify minimum clearances to the front and sides of each bathroom fixture. The figures noted at left are common, but check your local code for specifics in your area. Code requirements set minimum clearances; for comfort, allow for more space if possible. Under most codes, fixtures must have a minimum of 21 inches of free space in front. Codes also commonly mandate 15 inches to each side of a toilet's centerline. A bathroom door is normally required to be at least 24 inches wide and to open through an arc of at least 90 degrees; see page 47 for the dimensions needed for wheelchair access.

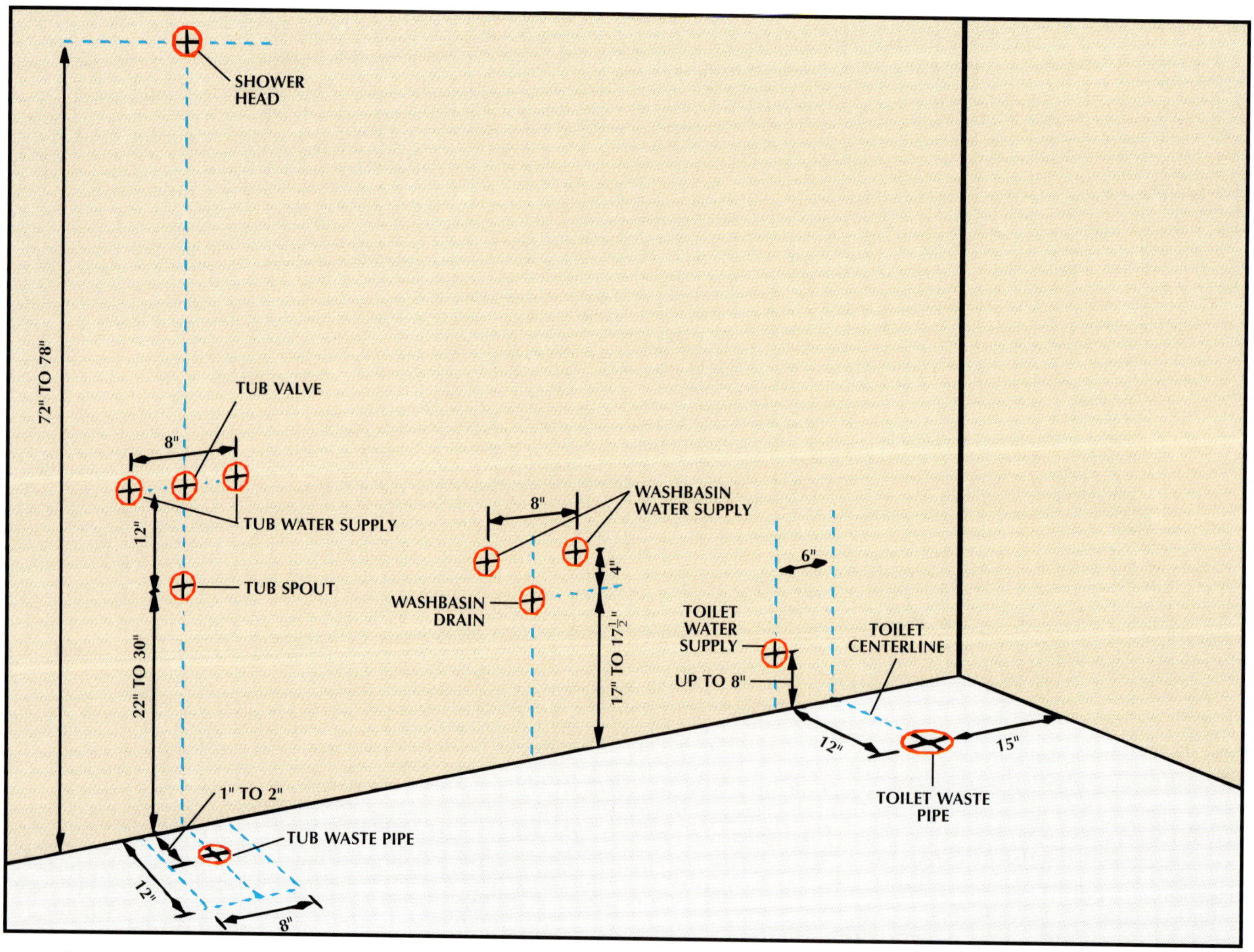

Rough-in dimensions.
After selecting fixtures and planning their placement, establish locations for pipes to enter the room. If you are using an old wall, mark the wall surface; otherwise, mark the framing members of the new wall. The measurements shown here along a single wall are typical for some common fixtures.

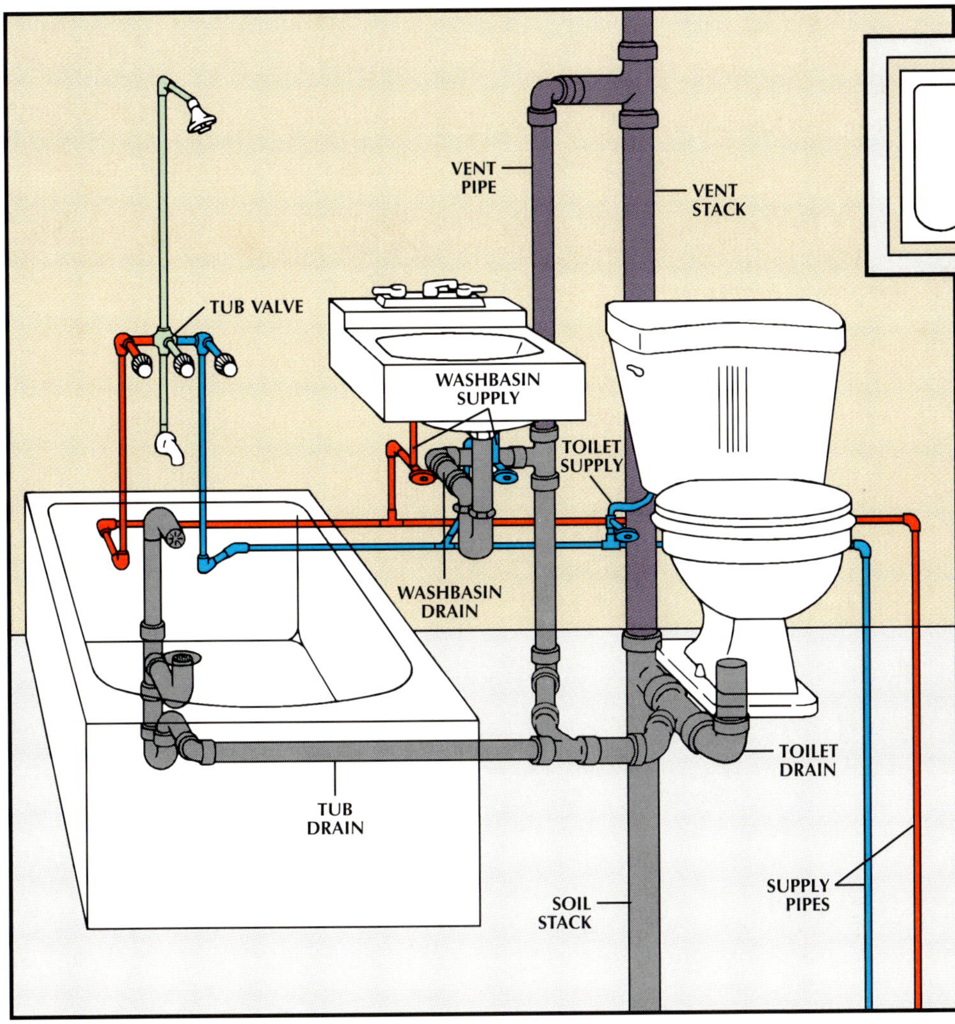

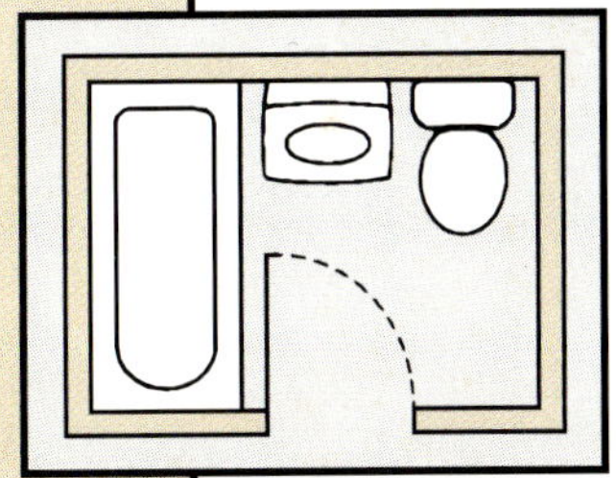

A one-wall plumbing pattern.
The simplest plan for a bathroom consolidates the plumbing along one wall, reducing the amount of cutting into the house structure and the amount of pipe installed. This arrangement may be the only choice for a small bathroom like that at left, which has rough-in dimensions identical to those in the illustration at the bottom of the preceding page.

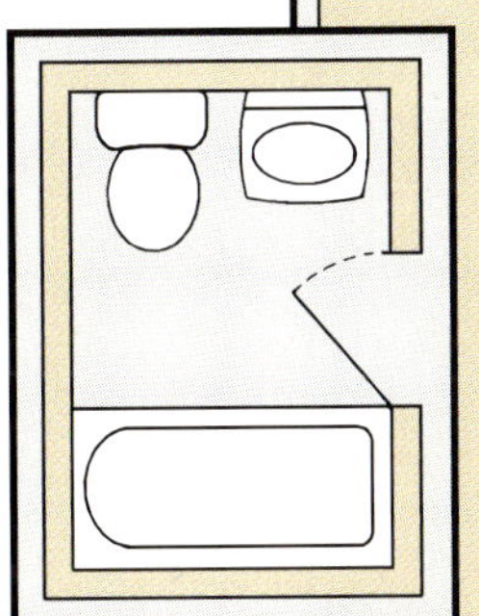

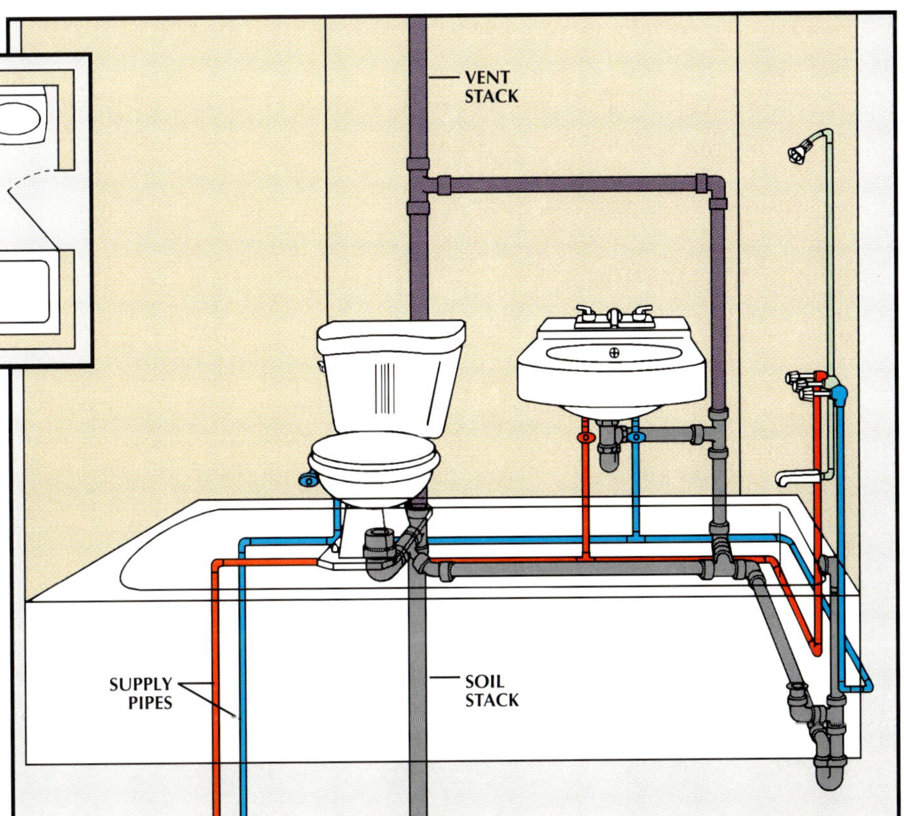

Plumbing in two walls.
Extending supply pipes and drainpipes to two adjoining walls provides more room around the basin than a one-wall room. (Three-wall plumbing patterns are less common, since they offer few advantages.) A bathroom with plumbing in two walls generally requires more cutting of studs and joists to accommodate the pipes. To minimize such work or to bridge a door *(inset),* try to run the supply pipes underneath or between the joists directly below.

Clearing the Way for a Major Renovation

Remodeling a bathroom usually requires that some or all of the old fixtures be removed. Enlarging a bathroom or creating space for a new one may also mean tearing down one or more walls.

Taking Out Fixtures: Always begin by cutting off water to the fixture, usually at the nearby shutoff valves in the supply lines. In the absence of such valves—or if they are stuck open—you may have to turn off the water supply to the entire house *(page 10)*. Removing most fixtures consists mainly of undoing nuts and bolts. A bathtub, however, can present a considerable challenge *(pages 92-93)*. Disposing of a plastic, fiberglass, or steel tub may be made easier with a reciprocating saw, which is available from tool-rental stores.

If you plan to reinstall your washbasin, bathtub, or toilet, handle the fixtures carefully; they are fragile and easily damaged when dropped or bumped.

Breaking Down an Interior Wall: If you plan to expand a bathroom, do not disturb a bearing wall *(page 48)*. Before starting demolition on a nonbearing wall, look for evidence of utilities—heating, air conditioning, or electricity—that may be housed within. Vents signal the presence of ducts, which can often be rerouted from the wall to the floor. Electrical switches or outlets indicate wiring that must be removed or relocated.

Supply pipes passing through a wall on the way to plumbing fixtures elsewhere may not be evident. If you find them during demolition, you will have to reroute them. Think twice about moving a plumbing wall. You can often redirect small branch drains, but large drains and stacks ordinarily must be left in place and concealed.

TOOLS

- Adjustable wrench
- Socket wrench
- Putty knife
- Large groove-joint pliers
- Small pliers
- Screwdriver
- Pry bars
- Cold chisel
- Dry-wall saw
- Reciprocating saw
- Sledgehammer
- 4-pound maul
- Tin snips
- Chalk line
- Utility knife
- 6-inch and 12-inch dry-wall knives
- Bucket
- Sponge

MATERIALS

- Pipe caps and plugs
- Rags
- Picture-hanging wire
- Fiberglass mesh tape
- Joint compound

Capping Pipes

Cover the open ends of all pipes to keep out construction debris and, in the case of drains, to prevent sewer gas from entering the house. Plug toilet flanges with rags, and cap the other drains and the supply lines. If a pipe is threaded, screw on a cap or insert a plug of the same material. Cement a plastic cap onto unthreaded plastic pipes (the capped end must be sawed off to reopen the pipe); unthreaded copper pipes require a soldered copper cap.

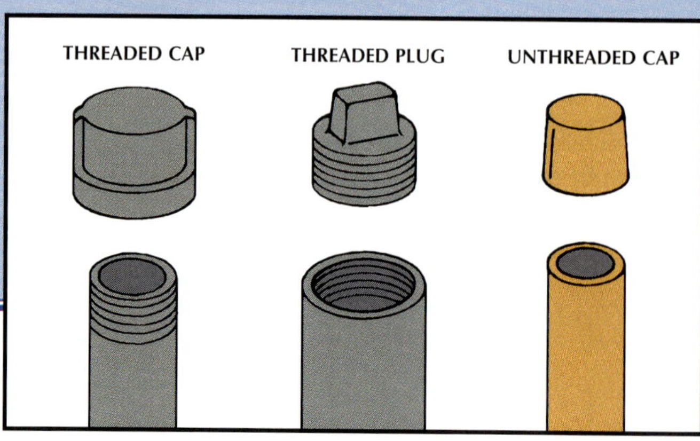

SAFETY TIPS

Demolition creates dust, flying splinters of wood and metal, and other potentially dangerous debris. Wear goggles, a dust mask, and leather work gloves. Long sleeves, sturdy long pants, and boots are also in order. A cap will keep the mess out of your hair.

REMOVING WASHBASINS

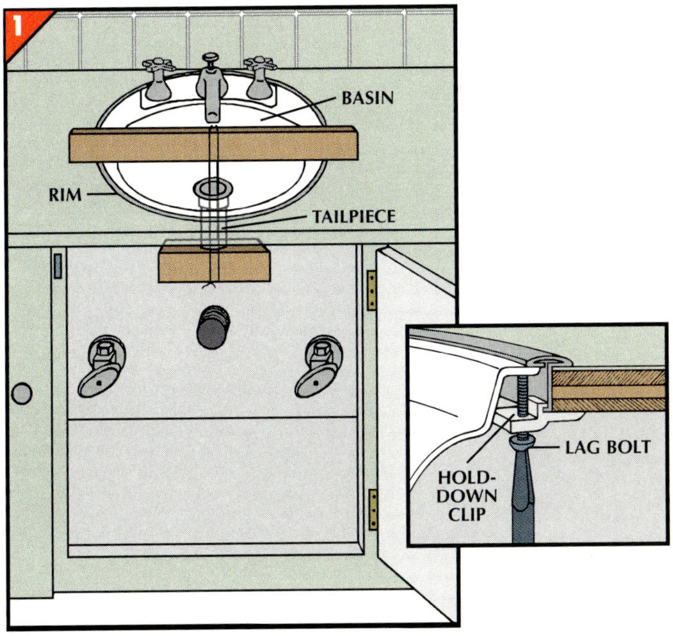

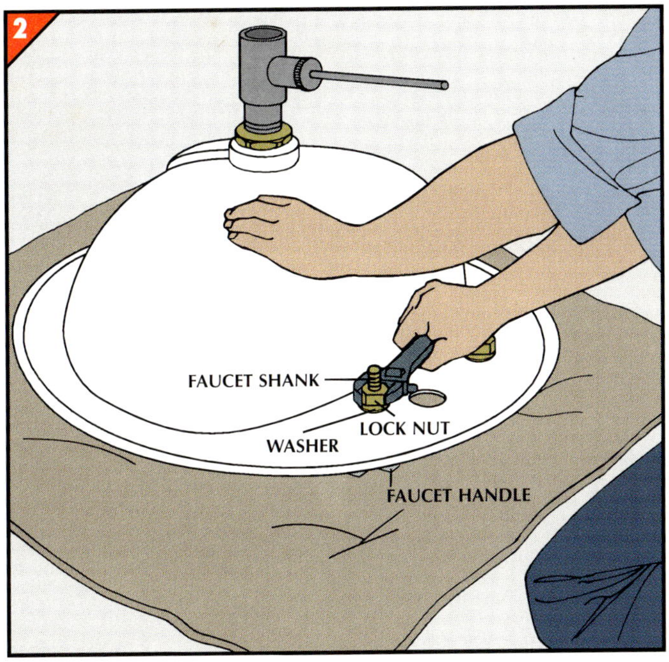

1. Freeing the fixture.

◆ Disconnect the supply lines, the pop-up linkage, and the trap *(pages 19 and 26)*. Remove a wall-hung or pedestal basin as shown on page 49. Lift out a basin with a lip that rests on a vanity top. For a basin that is part of a vanity top, unscrew and remove the top.

◆ To detach a sink secured by a metal rim *(above)*, lay a 2-by-4 across the basin. Bend a piece of picture-hanging wire over the 2-by-4, passing both ends through the drain hole. Twist the ends together below the tailpiece and insert a wood block between the doubled wire. Turn the block to draw it tightly against the tailpiece.

◆ Unfasten the lag bolts *(inset)* and hold-down clips and turn the block in the opposite direction to lower the basin.

2. Removing faucets.

◆ Place the basin facedown on the floor so that it is resting on the faucet handle. Pad the basin carefully if you intend to reuse it.

◆ With an adjustable wrench, unscrew the lock nuts from the faucet shanks. Lift off the washers.

◆ Turn the basin faceup and tap the faucet to break the seal of plumber's putty, if necessary, then lift out the faucet.

DISCONNECTING A TOILET

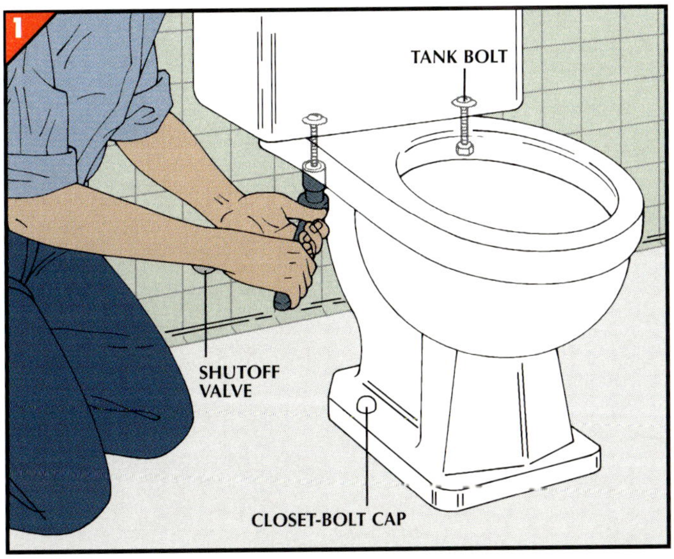

1. Disconnecting tank and bowl.

To remove a two-piece toilet, detach the tank, then unbolt and lift up the bowl. Take out a one-piece model as you would a bowl.

◆ Close the shutoff valve, flush the toilet, then bail and sponge the remaining water from the tank and bowl. Detach the supply tube as you would a sink line.

◆ For a bowl-mounted tank, unscrew the nuts under the bowl's rim with a socket wrench *(left)*. Use a screwdriver, if necessary, to keep the boltheads from turning.

◆ If the tank is hung on the wall, remove the L-shaped pipe connecting it to the bowl by loosening the slip nuts at each end. Then take out the screws or bolts that hold the tank to the wall.

◆ For any type of toilet, pry the caps from the closet bolts and remove the nuts.

◆ Rock the bowl to break the seal between toilet and flange. Lift the bowl free.

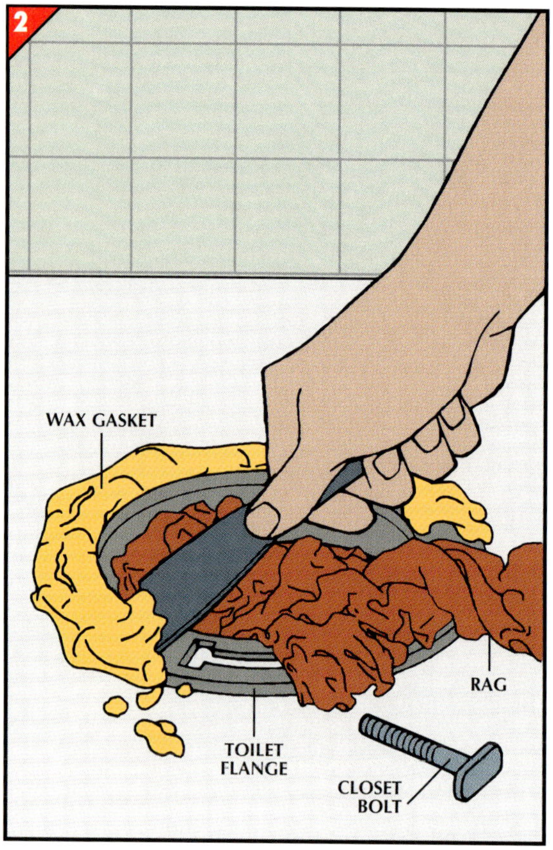

2. Scraping the toilet flange.

◆ Stuff an old rag into the toilet drain to block sewer gases.
◆ Slip the bolts out of the slots in the toilet flange and scrape away the wax gasket with a putty knife.
◆ Inspect the flange; if it is cracked, plan to replace it before seating the new toilet *(page 124)*.

TAKING OUT A TUB

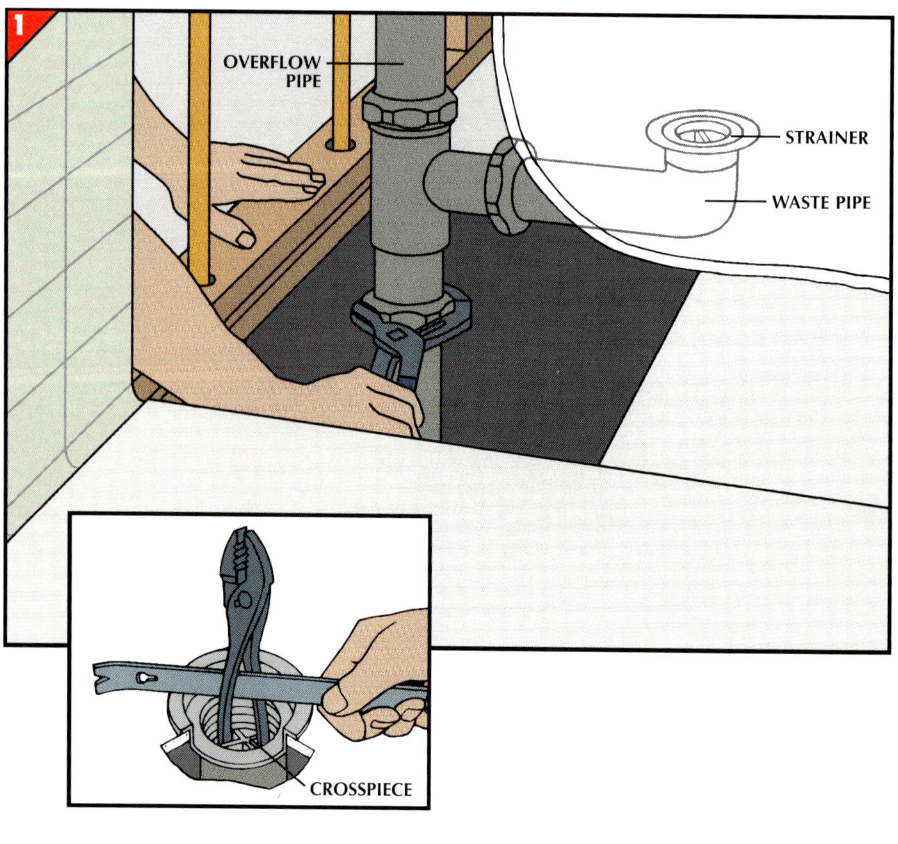

1. Disconnecting the tub.

◆ Remove the access panel in the wall behind the tub's plumbing fixtures. If there is no panel, cut a 14-inch-square hole, starting at floor level and taking care not to damage pipes in the wall.
◆ With large groove-joint pliers, loosen the slip nut connecting the waste and overflow pipes to the drainpipe outlet *(left)*.
◆ Returning to the tub, remove the overflow plate *(page 25)* and lift linkage, and take out the strainer by removing the strainer screw. If there is no screw, raise part of the edge of the strainer with an old screwdriver, then tap the screwdriver counterclockwise.
◆ Insert the handles of small pliers into the crosspiece. Use a pry bar along with the pliers to unscrew the crosspiece *(inset)*.

Remove the spout, faucets, and shower arm, following the procedures on pages 23-25.

2. Freeing tub flanges.

◆ Remove a foot-high section of finished wall above the tub. For a tile wall, such as the one shown here, use a cold chisel and hammer to chip away the tile. For molded panels, remove the entire surround.

◆ Cut the waterproof wallboard behind the tile with a dry-wall saw; demolish cement board or plaster with a hammer and chisel.

◆ Remove screws or nails anchoring the tub flange to the studs.

3. Removing the tub.

◆ If space allows, and you wish to save the tub, carry it out whole. Be sure to recruit enough helpers for the job. Even a lightweight fiberglass tub is hard to handle in a tight place.

◆ To demolish an unwanted tub for disposal, first examine an exposed edge to determine whether it is made of plastic, fiberglass, steel, or cast iron. Confirm your assessment by rapping the tub with your knuckles. Plastic or fiberglass tubs sound hollow. A steel tub emits a metallic ring. Cast-iron tubs respond with a dull tone.

◆ Cut up a fiberglass, a plastic, or a steel tub with a reciprocating saw *(above, left)*.

◆ Break up a cast-iron tub with a sledgehammer *(above, right)*. Wear safety goggles, long sleeves, and work gloves—and cover the tub with a drop cloth to trap flying shards.

TEARING DOWN AN OLD WALL

1. Tearing away the wall surface.
◆ Turn off electricity to any cables—and water to any supply pipes—before entering the wall.
◆ With a 4-pound maul, smash numerous large holes in the wall between studs. The holes prevent the surface from peeling off in one piece—a potential cause of injury.
◆ In a plaster wall, cut metal lath from the holes with tin snips; wood lath can be cut with a reciprocating saw.
◆ To strip the wall, grip the edges of the holes with both hands and pull outward sharply *(left)*. Doing so will break any wall material and will even tear metal lath.
◆ Use a pry bar to lever remaining bits of wallboard from the studs to which they are nailed.
◆ Remove any electrical cables, plumbing lines, or heating ducts that run through the wall, and reroute them if necessary.

CAUTION *If the wall you plan to demolish was built before 1978, check the surface for lead with a kit from a hardware store and have a piece tested for asbestos by your local government or a laboratory. If either substance is present, hire a contractor trained in dealing with hazardous materials to take out the wall.*

2. Removing the second wall surface.
◆ Loosen the other surface of the wall with a maul. For wallboard, hammer next to studs; once freed, entire wallboard panels can be pushed free of the studs into the next room. For plaster, knock all the material from the wall, then pry the lath from the studs.
◆ Saw all but the end studs in half and pull them free.

3. Dislodging the end studs and soleplate.
◆ Sever both end studs with a reciprocating saw and cold chisel to create a 2-inch gap in each board.
◆ Insert a pry bar into the gap and remove one stud section. A block of wood can serve as a fulcrum to lever off the second piece *(above)*.
◆ Remove the soleplate in the same way.

4. Removing the top plate.

◆ For joists parallel to the top plate, use a stud finder and a chalk line to mark the centers of the joists on either side of the plate. Score each line deeply with a utility knife.
◆ Use a hammer to break up the wallboard or plaster and lath between the ceiling cuts, then clean up the edges of the opening with the utility knife.
◆ Pry the top plate loose from the nailer blocks to which it is attached.
◆ For joists that cross the top plate, score the ceiling 12 inches to each side of the plate and pry both dry wall and top plate loose.

5. Patching the gaps.

◆ Cut dry wall to fit the ceiling gap. For an opening longer than 8 feet, trim sections of wallboard to end midway across either the joists or the nailer blocks.
◆ Where joists cross the gap, screw the patch to each one. Where joists parallel the gap *(above)*, drive the screws into the nailer blocks between the joists and into the edges of the joists, angling the screws slightly outward from the patch to anchor them solidly.

Fill the gap in the flooring left by the soleplate with a strip of plywood of the same thickness.

6. Finishing the ceiling patch.

◆ Apply a strip of self-adhesive, fiberglass mesh tape with a 6-inch dry-wall knife *(far left)*.
◆ Spread one coat of joint compound, holding the knife at a low angle *(left)*.
◆ Wait 24 hours to allow the compound to dry, then scrape off any ridges with the knife and apply a second coat of compound, diluting it for a smooth finish.
◆ After the second coat has dried, smooth the seam with a moist sponge. With a 12-inch dry-wall knife held at a steep angle, apply a final skim coat of compound diluted with water.

Framing for New Pipes

Before running new pipes, you must construct framing to support them—not only in the bathroom walls and floor, but along the course the pipes will follow through the house. Framing is also needed for most fixtures.

When attaching new framing, substitute $3\frac{1}{2}$-inch dry-wall screws for nails of the same length where hammering could jar a nearby finished wall or floor.

Thick Walls for Pipes: Drain and vent pipes in a bathroom range from $1\frac{1}{2}$ inches for a washbasin drain to 4 inches for a toilet; the small basin drain is most likely to be routed through a wall. For adequate support and concealment, an old wall of 2-by-4 studs can be made thicker with furring strips *(below)*. Or build a new wall for the plumbing, often called a wet wall *(pages 97-99)*.

Supporting Fixtures: Frame for fixtures as shown on pages 100 to 102. A washbasin set in a vanity requires no additional framing, but wall-hung and pedestal models are usually supported by a crosspiece between two studs. Tubs need framing in the floor and wall, as well as crosspieces for the faucet and shower assemblies.

Running Pipes: Route the bathroom's supply pipes and drainpipes horizontally toward the vertical plumbing core of the house *(page 85)*, either through the floor joists *(page 103)* or—preferably—just below the joists. Follow local codes for joists, which are part of the basic structure of your house. Never run a long section of drainpipe through joists, since the required pitch of $\frac{1}{4}$ inch per foot cannot be accommodated.

Drill holes for pipes, in studs or joists, $\frac{1}{8}$ inch larger than the pipe. Bore holes $\frac{1}{2}$ inch larger than the pipe if you must insert it at an angle, a technique permitted by the flexibility of copper and PVC. To reduce noise, you may opt for foam pipe insulation; this requires still bigger holes. In no case, however, should holes be larger than 60 percent of the depth of a stud or joist.

ADAPTING AN OLD WALL FOR PLUMBING

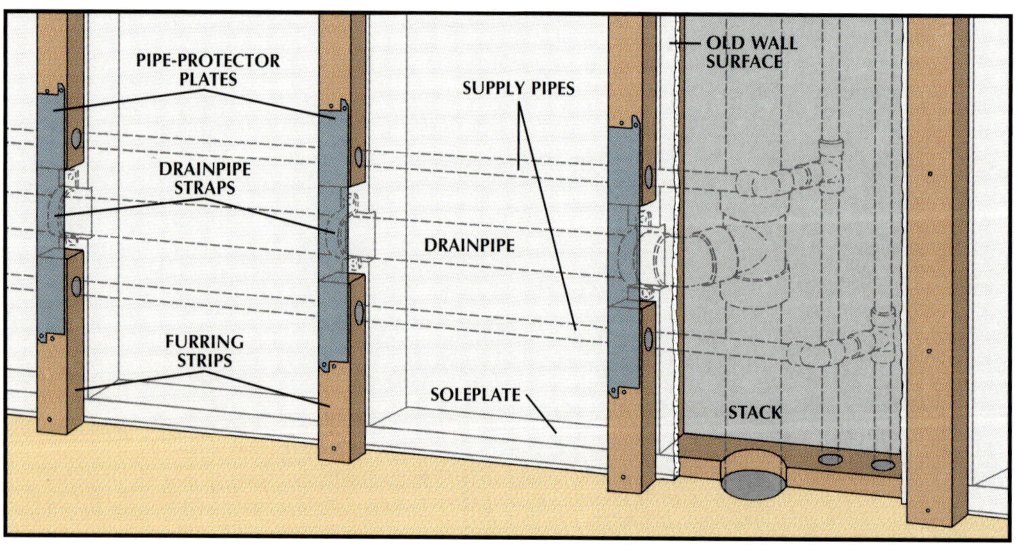

Fitting drain and supply lines.

◆ Remove the baseboard *(page 50)*.

◆ If you plan to install a stack, remove wallboard or plaster between the studs to each side. Drill a pilot hole through the soleplate and floor at the center of the stack. Expand the hole to full size with a hole saw; if necessary, drill first from above and then from below, tapping out any remaining wood with a hammer. With a spade bit, drill holes 4 to 6 inches apart for supply pipes.

◆ For studs that are not crossed by drains or vents, cut 2-by-2 furring strips the full length of the studs.

◆ Where studs will be crossed by washbasin drainpipes or vent pipes, mark the location of the pipe run on the wall. Cut 2-by-2 furring strips to fit above and below the pipe. Remove the wall surface as needed, and notch the original studs to recess pipes that exceed $1\frac{1}{2}$ inches in diameter.

◆ With an electric drill and a screwdriver bit, drive $3\frac{1}{2}$-inch dry-wall screws through the furring strips into the studs.

◆ Drill supply pipe holes in the furring strips, next to the old wall surface.

After drainpipes and vent pipes are in place *(pages 104-109)*, anchor them with drainpipe straps and shield them with metal pipe-protector plates, $\frac{1}{8}$ inch thick and long enough to extend past each supply pipe.

TOOLS

- Electric drill
- Hole saw, spade, and screwdriver bits
- Electronic stud finder
- Chalk line
- Plumb bob
- Utility knife
- Tape measure
- Carpenter's square
- Level
- Ball-peen hammer
- Small pry bar

MATERIALS

- 2-by-2 furring strips
- 1-by-2s, 2-by-4s, and 2-by-6s
- Larger framing lumber as needed
- $3\frac{1}{2}$-inch nails
- $3\frac{1}{2}$-inch dry-wall screws
- Hollow-wall anchors
- Cedar shims
- Joist hangers

SAFETY TIPS

Constructing walls and framing with nails produces loud banging and may cause nails and wood chips to fly. Use earplugs and goggles for ear and eye protection.

A NEW WALL DESIGNED FOR PIPING

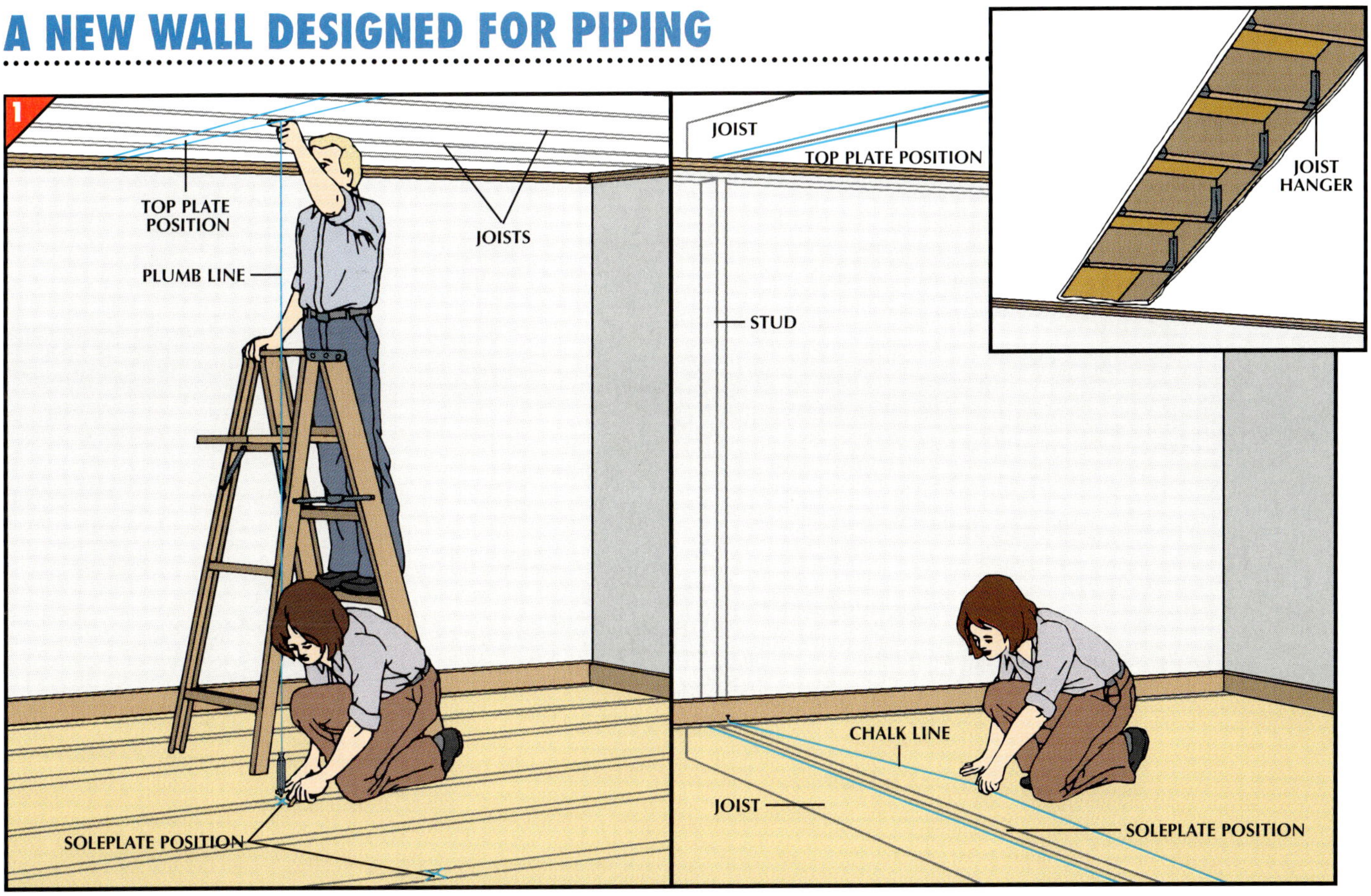

1. Planning the wall location.

◆ With an electronic stud finder, locate several ceiling joists.

◆ If the joists run perpendicular to the planned wall *(above, left)*, mark for a 2-by-6 top plate on the ceiling, snapping a chalk line along each edge. With a plumb bob, transfer the marks to the floor, then snap a chalk line along each edge of the soleplate.

◆ For joists parallel to the wall *(above, right)*, find the nearest joist. Snap chalk lines for the top plate so that it extends 4 inches into the new bathroom. Transfer the top plate location to the floor with a plumb bob, and mark the edges of the soleplate with a chalk line.

To place a wall between two joists *(inset)*, open the ceiling between them and use joist hangers *(page 100)* to install nailer blocks at 24-inch intervals. (No framing is needed under the wall, if the floor is at least $1\frac{1}{8}$ inches thick.)

2. Marking the top plate and soleplate.

◆ From 2-by-6 framing lumber, cut a soleplate and top plate the length of the new wall, and temporarily face-nail the boards together.

◆ Beginning at one end, mark the plates every 16 inches to indicate stud locations *(left).* Plan for studs at both ends of the wall, making the stud space at one end narrower than 16 inches if necessary. If you plan to place the drain of a tub or shower against the wall, adjust two stud positions to center the drain between them.

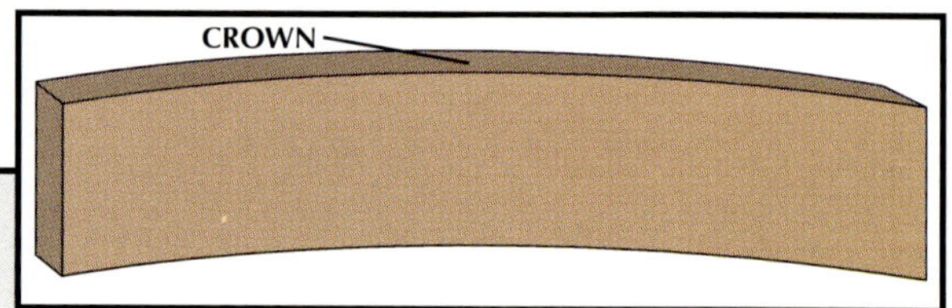

3. Assembling the frame.

In a tight space, you might have to nail the soleplate and the top plate to the floor and the ceiling, then toenail the studs to both of them. An easier method is to assemble the frame as shown here and raise it into position.

◆ Every 2 feet along a soleplate line, measure the distance from the ceiling to the floor. Cut 2-by-6 studs $3\frac{1}{4}$ inches shorter than the smallest measurement. Doing so assures a frame short enough to clear the ceiling when being raised from the floor.

◆ Fasten the studs to the top plate and soleplate with $3\frac{1}{2}$-inch nails *(above),* making sure that any crowns face up *(inset).*

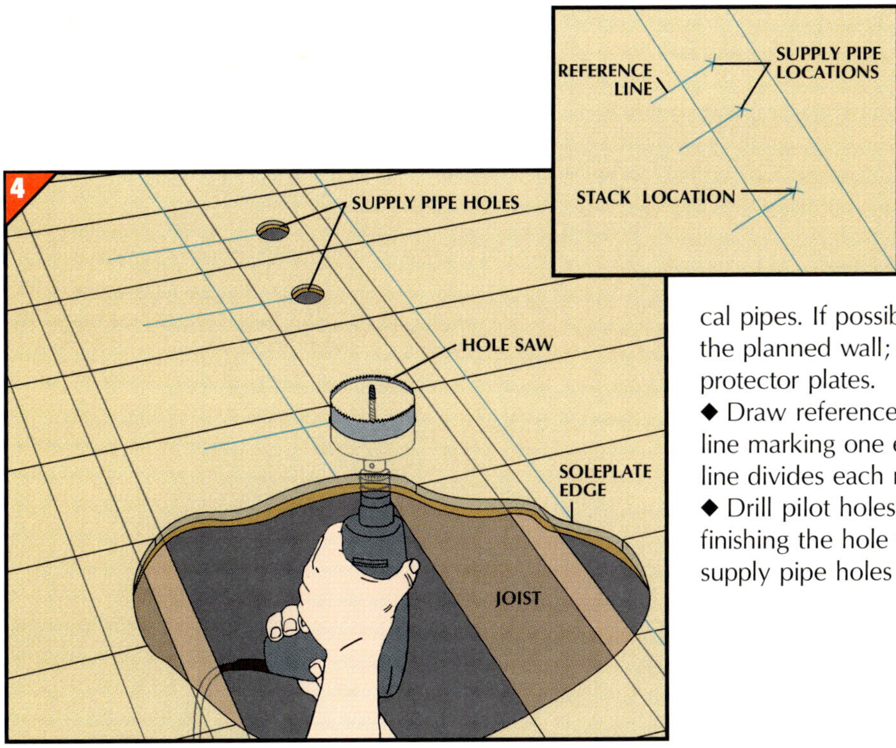

4. Cutting holes for vertical pipes.

◆ Before raising the new wall, mark the floor with the centers of holes for vertical pipes. If possible, keep holes at least $1\frac{1}{2}$ inches inside the planned wall; otherwise, you must later install pipe-protector plates.

◆ Draw reference lines from the centers across the chalked line marking one edge of the soleplate so that the chalked line divides each reference line into two equal parts *(inset)*.

◆ Drill pilot holes in the floor. Use a hole saw for the stack, finishing the hole from below if necessary *(left)*. Drill the supply pipe holes with appropriately sized spade bits.

5. Installing the wall frame.

◆ With a helper, raise the wall. If it lines up with studs inside the existing walls, attach the end studs with $3\frac{1}{2}$-inch dry-wall screws at 24-inch intervals *(above)*; otherwise secure the end studs with hollow-wall anchors.

◆ Push pairs of tapered cedar shims between the top plate and ceiling, one from each side. Put shims under perpendicular joists or nailer blocks; otherwise, 16 inches apart. Drive screws through the top plate and shims, into the framing. Score protruding shims with a utility knife; snap them off.

◆ If the joists run perpendicular to the soleplate, screw it to each joist.

◆ When a floor joist runs along the wall, screw the soleplate to it at 16-inch intervals, avoiding where the pipes will go. Between joists, screw the soleplate to the floor.

◆ Locate the reference lines for the pipe holes. Measure each line and extend it inward by the same amount, then drill through the soleplate *(inset)* to match the holes in the floor.

SUPPORTS FOR PIPE AND FIXTURES

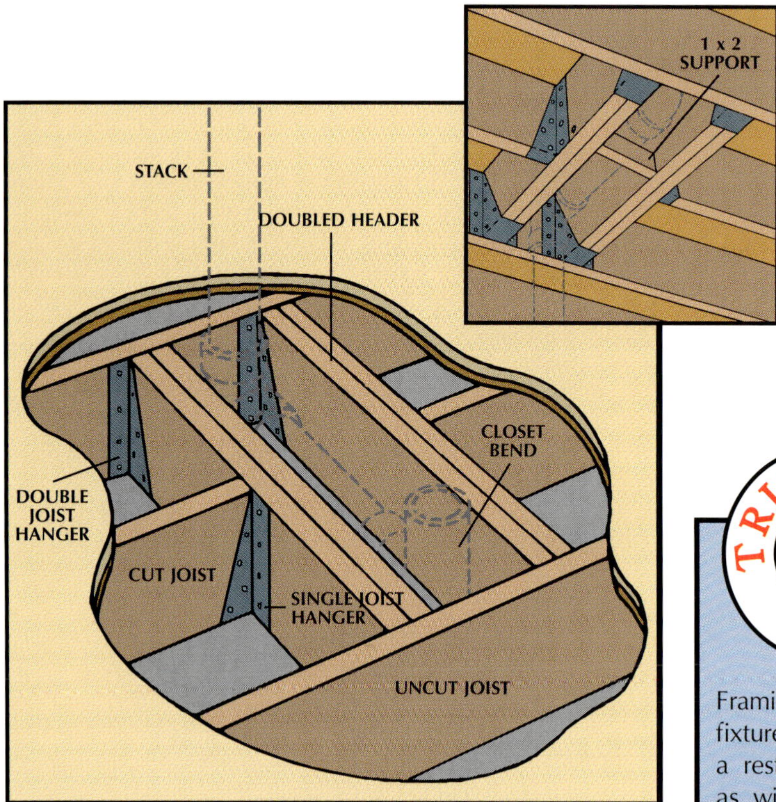

CAUTION

Procedures on these pages require cutting joists. If your house has wood I-beam or truss joists (page 103), *hire a structural engineer for those parts of the job.*

Framing for a closet bend.

◆ For a waste pipe that runs perpendicular to joists, you must cut a gap in the intervening joist. In the room below, remove a strip of ceiling, exposing the joist that blocks the planned path of the waste pipe and one joist to either side of it.

◆ Temporarily brace the middle joist with two vertical studs outside the opening, then cut out an 18-inch section of the center joist.

◆ From joist lumber, cut four boards to fit between the two uncut joists.

◆ Face-nail the boards together to make two doubled headers *(above)*, and nail double joist hangers to both ends of each. Nail the joist hangers to the joists, then secure the headers to the cut joist with single joist hangers. Remove the temporary support studs.

◆ Support the waste pipe at the correct slope with a 1-by-2 support between the headers *(inset)*.

The only framing necessary for a toilet waste pipe that parallels the floor joists is the 1-by-2 support.

TRICKS OF THE TRADE

Hammering Nails in Close Quarters

Framing for a fixture or pipe in a restricted space, as with the closet bend at left, can be extremely difficult. One solution is to start the nail, then place the end of a 2-foot pry bar against the nailhead. To drive the nail strike farther down on the pry bar with the flat face of a framing hammer (the hardened steel of a pry bar may chip an ordinary trim hammer).

Support for a washbasin.

◆ From a 2-by-6, cut a crosspiece to fit between the studs on either side of your washbasin.

◆ Level the crosspiece at the height specified by the basin manufacturer, and secure it with two $3\frac{1}{2}$-inch nails or screws through the studs *(left)*.

◆ Attach the basin mounting bracket to the crosspiece after the wall is closed and finished.

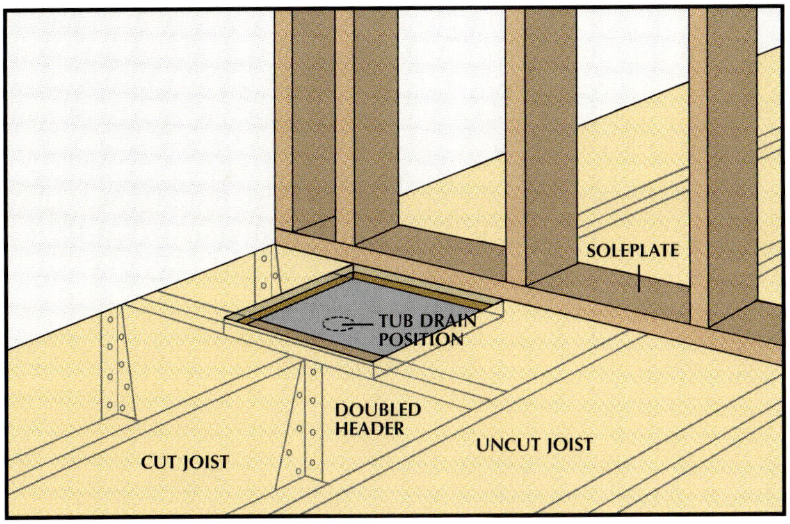

Underpinnings for a bathtub.

◆ In the floor, cut a 12-inch-square hole, one edge at the soleplate and centered side to side on the spot to be occupied by the tub drain; the tub overflow pipe and drainpipe will later connect to the drain system in this area *(page 117)*.

◆ If the opening exposes a joist and you cannot adjust the planned position of the tub, install headers as shown here. To do so, follow the procedure for a closet bend *(opposite)*.

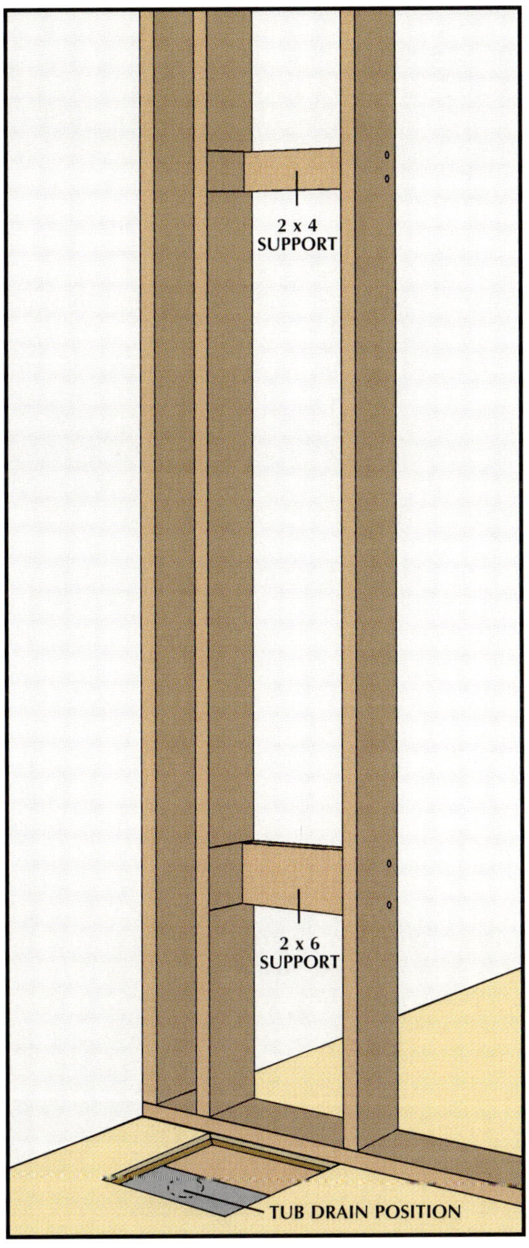

Bath and shower faucet framing.

◆ Mark the heights of the tub faucet assembly and the shower arm on the studs behind the drain end, or "head," of the tub.

◆ Cut a 2-by-6 faucet support to fit between the studs and nail it in place, recessing it into the wall according to the specification sheet provided by the faucet manufacturer.

◆ Attach a 2-by-4 support the same way for the supply pipe that will attach to the shower arm.

Supporting the tub.

◆ To provide the edge support needed by most bathtubs installed next to a wall, remove any wall surface to expose the studs, then cut a 2-by-4 support to extend from the planned location for the foot of the tub to the head of the tub.

◆ Level the support and nail it to studs at the height specified by the tub manufacturer. Use a vertical nailer block to attach the support at the head of the tub, as shown at left. If necessary, to anchor the other end of the support, toenail an additional stud at the end of the 2-by-4.

SAFE PASSAGE THROUGH STUDS AND JOISTS

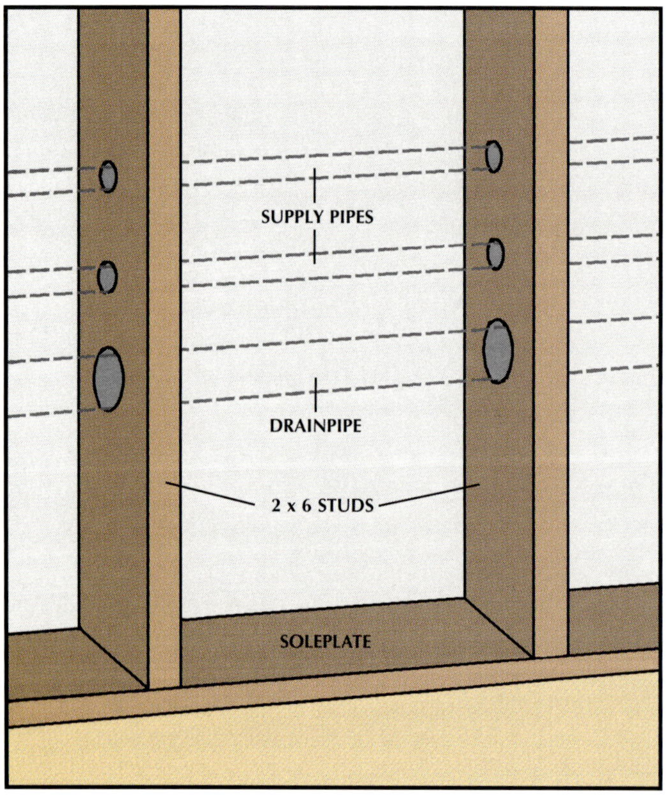

Pipes in a wet wall.

To run pipe inside a wall built for plumbing, drill holes through the studs with spade bits for the supply pipes and a hole saw for drainpipe or vent pipe. Align the holes for each pipe precisely, and try to keep them at least $1\frac{1}{2}$ inches from the edges of the studs; otherwise use pipe-protector plates *(page 96)*. The slope of supply pipes is unimportant, but drainpipes must slant downward toward the stack, $\frac{1}{4}$ inch per foot.

TRICKS OF THE TRADE

Drilling in Close Quarters

A drill and its bit may be more than a foot long—potentially awkward for working in the $14\frac{1}{2}$-inch space between joists and studs. A right-angle drill *(below)* offers a solution. Available at tool-rental stores, this tool also comes as an attachment for many standard drills and easily fits between framing members.

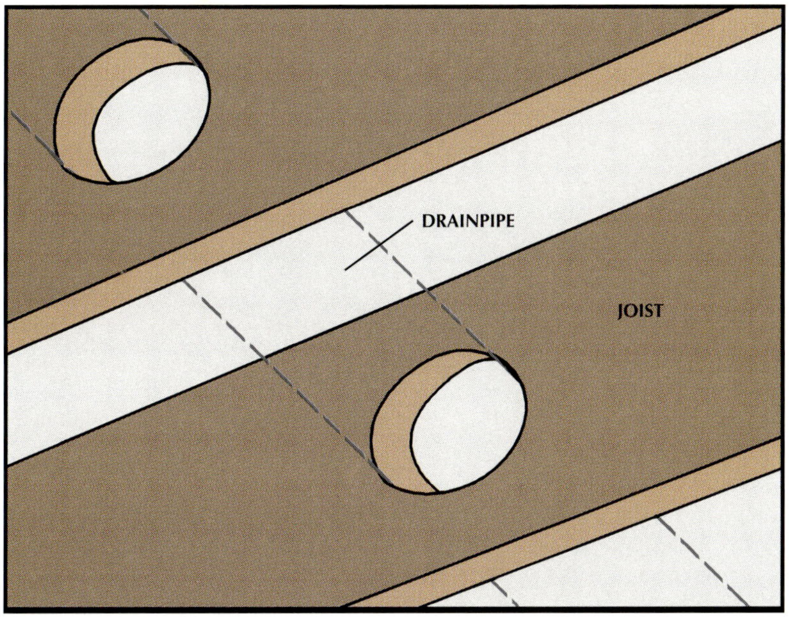

In standard joists.

Whenever possible, hang pipes under floor joists rather than cutting holes in the joists. If you must run pipes through joists, drill the holes to allow at least 2 inches between the hole and the top and bottom of the joist.

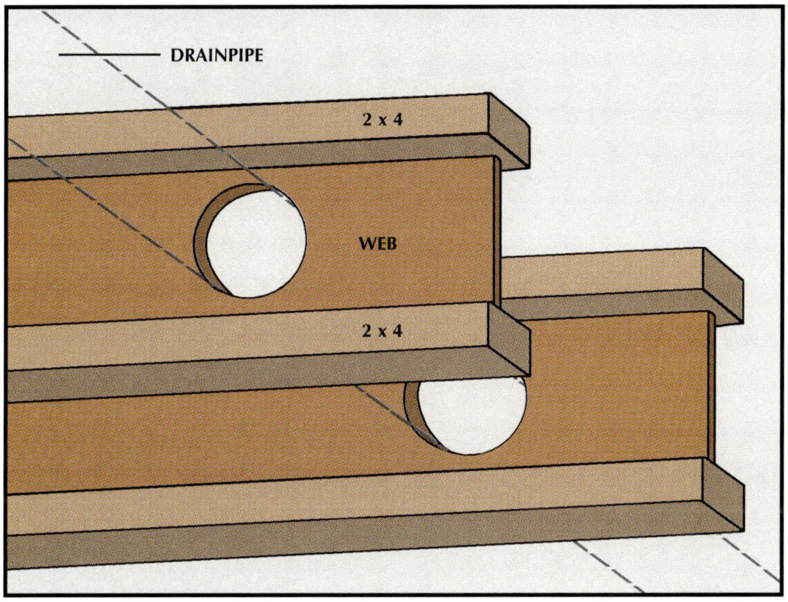

In I-beams.

Joists like those at left, consisting of a plywood web between two 2-by-4s, have become common in home construction. Do not cut the 2-by-4s, but cut pipe holes freely through the thin center piece; some I-beams come with knockout holes for the purpose.

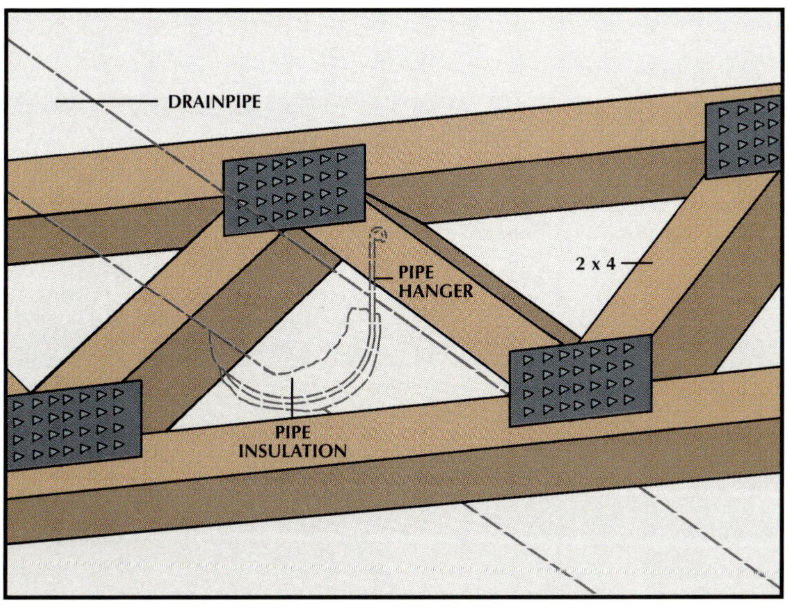

In truss joists.

Built like a bridge girder from 2-by-4s, a truss joist requires no hole drilling for pipes; when the time comes, pass them through the joists and suspend them with metal pipe hangers nailed to the cross members as shown at left. To minimize sound transferred in this particularly noisy arrangement from pipe hangers to joists, plan to fit foam pipe insulation around the pipe, as shown at left.

Getting Rid of Wastes: The DWV System

Drainpipes and vent pipes, collectively called the drain-waste-vent (DWV) system, are the most complicated part of a plumbing network. Work will go more smoothly if you install the DWV system before the supply lines.

Where to Start: Map your present DWV system and calculate where you will need to tie new drainpipes into the main stack. Remember that, because the pipes rely on gravity to carry the flow of wastes, they must slope downward. Plumbing codes require that a horizontal run have a pitch of $\frac{1}{4}$ inch for each foot of the run.

Check your plans against the local plumbing code before buying supplies or starting work. Most jobs that add new pipe must first be approved by building officials. Specify PVC plastic pipe: It is easily cut and joined, and along with its fittings, has smooth, continuous inner surfaces that do not obstruct waste flow. Get a plastic-pipe cutter or a backsaw and miter box to make the needed cuts, and use a utility knife or a file to remove rough burrs from cut pipe ends. To break into a cast-iron stack, rent a chain-type cutter *(page 106)*.

Venting the Drains: Vents release noxious gases outside the house and equalize air pressure so that waste and water can flow freely through the drains. A vent line runs from every fixture's trap to a vent stack.

The trap-to-vent connection can be made in two ways: by stack or self-venting, in which the fixture's drainpipe drains the trap and also vents it through the roof; or by individual or branch venting, in which a separate vent line links the trap to a central stack vent.

Testing the System: You must test new drains and vents by filling the system with water. Repair any leaks that are revealed, and have a plumbing inspector check and approve the installation before you use the drains.

TOOLS

- Plastic-pipe cutter, or backsaw and miter box
- Utility knife
- Sandpaper or emery cloth
- Level
- Hammer
- Electronic stud finder
- Dry-wall saw
- Soil-pipe cutter
- Hacksaw
- Soldering iron
- Electric drill with extension and hole saw bits
- Plumb bob
- Saber saw
- Screwdriver
- Pry bar
- Garden hose
- Awl or ice pick
- 50-gallon drum

MATERIALS

- PVC pipe and fittings
- PVC primer
- PVC cement
- Nails
- 1-by-2s and 2-by-4s
- Wood wedges
- Perforated plastic-pipe strapping
- Stack clamp
- Dry-wall screws
- Joint compound
- Pipe clamps
- Solder and flux
- Slip couplings
- Flashing plate with rubber collar
- Petroleum jelly
- Roofing nails
- Roofing cement
- Test caps

SAFETY TIPS

Wear gloves to protect your hands while cutting cast iron, and a hard hat while working overhead, especially in an attic, where roofing nails may be exposed.

When hammering or sawing, goggles help shield your eyes from flying chips.

ROUTING DRAINS TO THE STACK

1. Joining a closet bend and a sanitary T.

Typically, the heart of a new DWV installation is an assembly of three fittings: a closet bend, receiving toilet waste; a sanitary T, with a curved inlet for smooth flow; and a closet Y, joining both and providing another waste inlet.

◆ Dry fit these components to make an assembly long enough to center the closet bend under the toilet drain hole and the sanitary T under the stack hole. Add a piece of pipe to increase the assembly's length, if necessary.

◆ Make alignment marks across each joint, to quickly assemble and orient the pieces after applying cement.

◆ Take the assembly apart, cut or file away the burrs around cut ends, and smooth them with fine sandpaper.

◆ Apply PVC primer to all assembly surfaces, inside and out, that will receive cement.

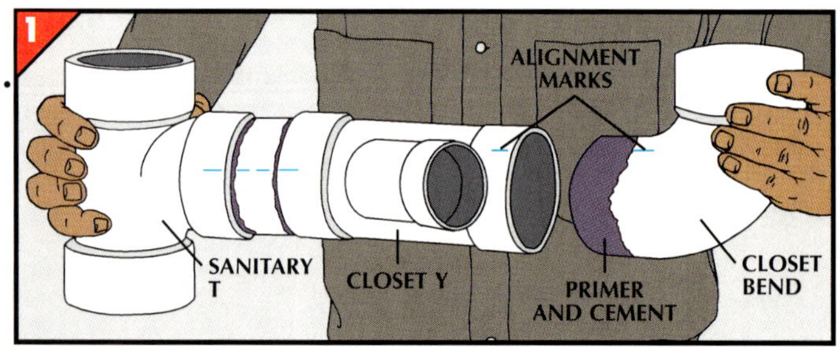

◆ Working one joint at a time, apply a thin layer of PVC cement to the inside end of the fitting and a thick layer to the outside of its matching piece.

◆ Push the parts together about 90 degrees out of line, then twist them until their alignment marks meet. Look for an unbroken bead of cement squeezing out all the way around the joint. If this bead is incomplete, quickly separate the parts, apply more cement, and rejoin. Hold the joint together for about 30 seconds.

2. Installing the closet-bend assembly.

◆ Dry fit lengths of pipe into the tops of the sanitary T and the closet bend that are long enough to reach above the floor when the closet-bend assembly is in place.

◆ Position the assembly, using a level to be sure that the sanitary T is exactly vertical.

◆ Nail a 1-by-2 across the joist space beneath the assembly to provide support. Recheck the assembly's position with a level *(right).*

◆ Use thin wood wedges to shim the pipes tightly into the floor openings.

3. Running pipe to the existing stack.

◆ To extend the assembly below the joists, dry fit a short piece of pipe and an elbow to the sanitary T bottom.

◆ Nail a perforated plastic strap to a joist on one side of the planned path of the new soil branch. If the pipe will parallel the joists, attach the strap to a 2-by-4 nailed across the joist space.

◆ On the other side of the branch path, drive a nail halfway into the same joist or 2-by-4. Use a nail with a head smaller than the strap holes.

◆ Fit a length of pipe into the elbow, loop the strap under the pipe, and hook the strap onto the second nail.

◆ Try hooking the strap by different holes until the pipe slopes down from the elbow at $\frac{1}{4}$ inch per foot. To check the slope *(above),* tape to one end of a level a strip of wood thick enough to center the bubble at the correct pitch *(inset).* For example, a 2-foot level requires a $\frac{1}{2}$-inch strip.

◆ Couple and suspend more pipe to extend the branch, and cut the end to just reach the existing soil stack. Hang additional straps every 3 feet while maintaining the slope.

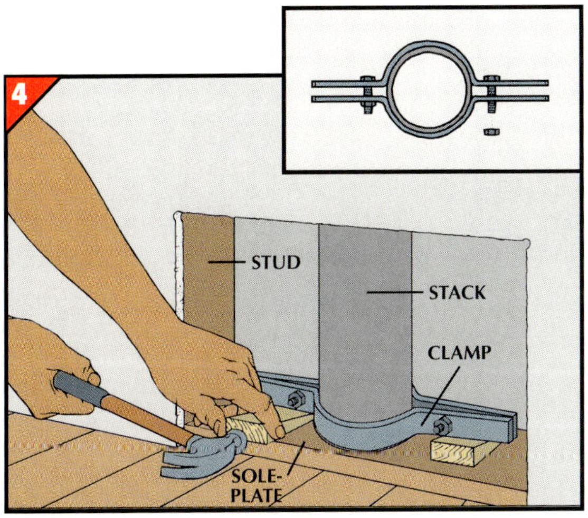

4. Bracing the stack for cutting.

To keep the top of the stack from dropping when you cut the bottom, add a brace where it enters the first floor.

◆ Find the point where the stack emerges from the basement. If it is behind a wall, locate the studs with an electronic stud finder; then, with a dry-wall saw, remove a 16- by 10-inch rectangle of wallboard between studs at floor level to reveal the stack.

◆ Position a stack clamp around the stack *(inset),* about $\frac{1}{2}$ inch above the soleplate or the floor; tighten the clamp bolts firmly.

◆ Drive wedges between the clamp and the soleplate or floor as shown at left.

◆ Attach 2-by-4 mounting blocks to the studs, and screw the wallboard over the hole. Patch the resulting seams *(page 95),* then repaint the wall.

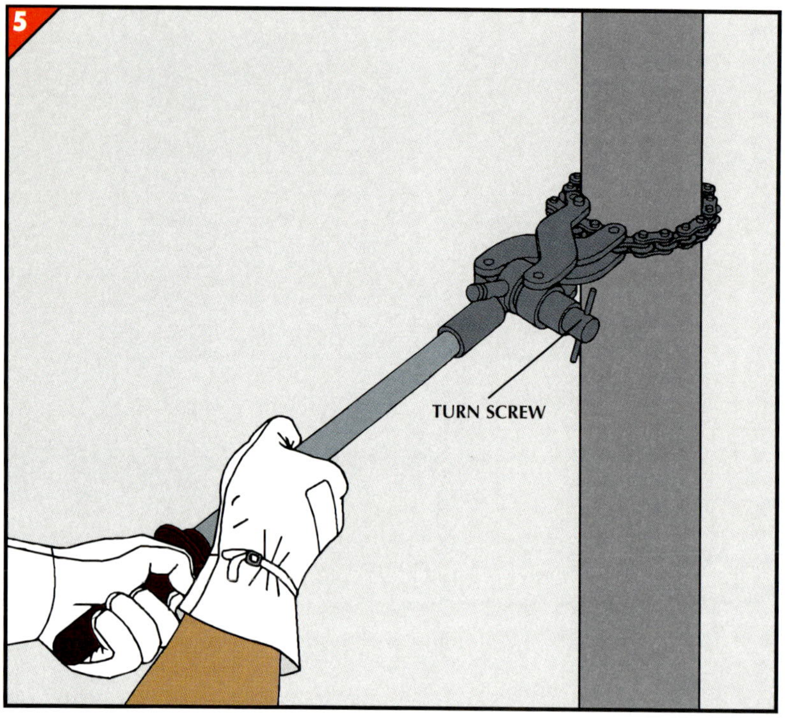

5. Opening the stack.

◆ Choose a sanitary T to fit the stack and the new soil branch, and hold it against the stack at the proper height to receive the branch. Mark the positions of the top and bottom of the T on the stack.

◆ Use a chain-type cutter on a cast-iron stack *(left)*. Wrap the cutting chain around the stack and slip it into the hooks on the other side of the tool head. Position the chain $\frac{1}{4}$ inch above the top mark on the stack, tighten the turn screw to compress the spring, and move the handle of the cutter up and down until the pipe separates. Make a second cut $\frac{1}{4}$ inch below the bottom mark. Discard the cut section and stuff toilet tissue loosely into both ends of the stack.

On a copper or plastic stack, use a hacksaw to cut the pipe 4 inches above the top mark and 4 inches below the bottom mark. Save the removed section.

6. Installing a T.

◆ On a cast-iron stack, slide a pipe clamp's stainless-steel ring onto the bottom of the cut stack.

◆ Fit the neoprene sleeve of the clamp halfway onto the pipe and roll the free end of the sleeve back so the upper half folds over the lower half.

◆ Repeat the process on the top part of the stack, folding the free end of the sleeve up.

◆ Place the sanitary T in the gap of the stack and unroll the sleeves over it *(right)*. Slide the stainless-steel rings over the sleeves; tighten the screws.

◆ On a copper or PVC stack, cut the removed section into two pieces, each as long as the depth of the collars on the T, plus $3\frac{7}{8}$ inches. Solder or cement these short lengths of pipe into the end collars of the T.

◆ Two slip couplings *(far right)* will be used to connect the T to the stack. Prepare the pieces of a copper assembly by burnishing all cut ends and the interior of the couplings, then applying flux to these surfaces. Rub the ends of PVC pipe with abrasive cloth.

◆ Slide a slip coupling over each stack end and place the T assembly in between. Position the lower coupling over the joint, and cement or solder it in place. Repeat with the upper coupling.

◆ Cement the dry-fitted parts of the soil branch.

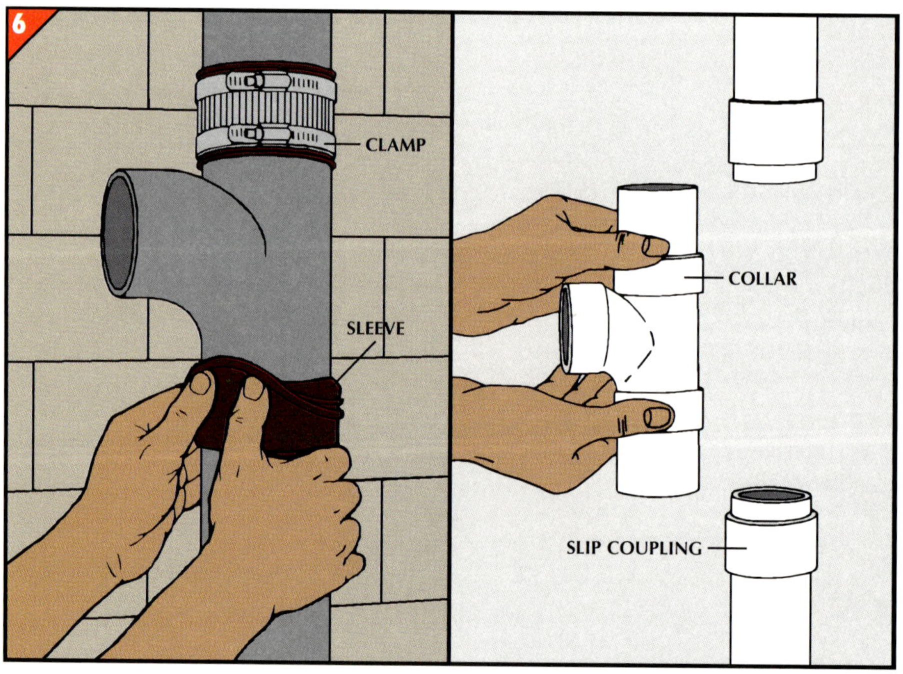

A DRAIN LINE FOR EACH FIXTURE

Bathtub or shower.

◆ Run pipe from the tub or shower drain to the closet-bend assembly through holes in the joists *(page 103)*, drilled at a slope of $\frac{1}{4}$ inch per foot.

◆ Install pipe in joist holes by cutting lengths that fit between the joists. Push the segments through the holes and join them with couplings.

◆ Many codes require individual vents for long drain runs. Typically a $1\frac{1}{2}$-inch pipe may be no longer than $4\frac{1}{2}$ feet from stack to fixture; a 2-inch pipe may run 5 feet. To create a separate vent, substitute a long-turn (offset) T for a coupling in the drain run *(right)*.

◆ At the closet-bend assembly, cement the pipe to the inlet in the closet Y. Do not add the trap at the other end of the run until the tub or shower is in place.

Toilet.

◆ Remove the guide pipes dry fitted earlier to both the closet bend and the sanitary T.

◆ Simulate the height of the finished floor by stacking a piece of the planned flooring atop a piece of the underlayment on each side of the closet bend. Set the rim of the toilet flange *(page 124)* on the flooring above the closet bend.

◆ Measure from the top of the flange's hub to the bottom of the closet bend's hub and cut a length of pipe to fit.

◆ While a helper braces the closet bend from below *(right)*, cement the pipe into the bend.

Washbasin.

The washbasin drain can be connected directly to the stack if no toilet on a floor above drains into the stack. (See page 109 for an alternative drainage route.)

◆ Cut a piece of pipe to join the below-floor sanitary T to a smaller one positioned at the height required by the rough-in specifications for the basin drain *(page 88)*.

◆ Dry fit the small T to the pipe, check its height, and make alignment marks. Cement the pipe and upper T to the lower T while a helper braces it from below.

◆ Inside the wall, dry fit pipe to slope upward from the inlet of the small T. End it with an elbow facing into the room at the rough-in location for the washbasin drain *(right)*. To the elbow, add a pipe extending 6 inches beyond the stud. Check the parts' positions, then cement them together.

ADDING THE VENT STACKS

A stack for self-venting.

◆ Drop a plumb line from the top plate at the center of the washbasin sanitary T, and mark the position of the string on the plate *(left)*.

◆ Mark a circle on the top plate, centered on the string position and slightly larger than the vent pipe. Cut out the circle with a drill with a hole saw bit.

◆ If the room above is floored, continue drilling through the flooring from below.

◆ Cut a length of pipe long enough to reach from the T to a point about a foot into the room above; angle the pipe into the hole, lower it to the T, and cement the joint.

Separate vent lines.

◆ To cut a vent from a tub or shower drain into the new stack, install a small sanitary T, bending upward, in the stack about 2 feet above the washbasin drain.

◆ From the long-turn T installed in the shower or tub drain line, route a vent pipe up through the soleplate and through the wall to the T fitting on the stack.

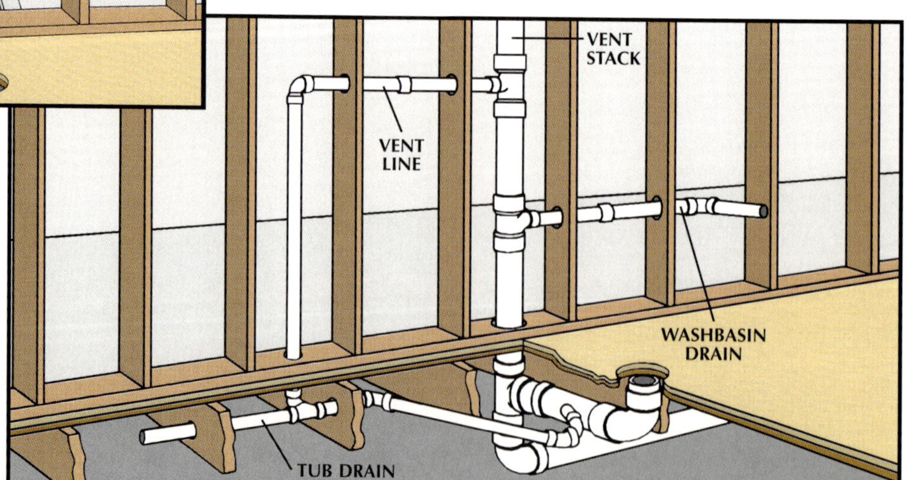

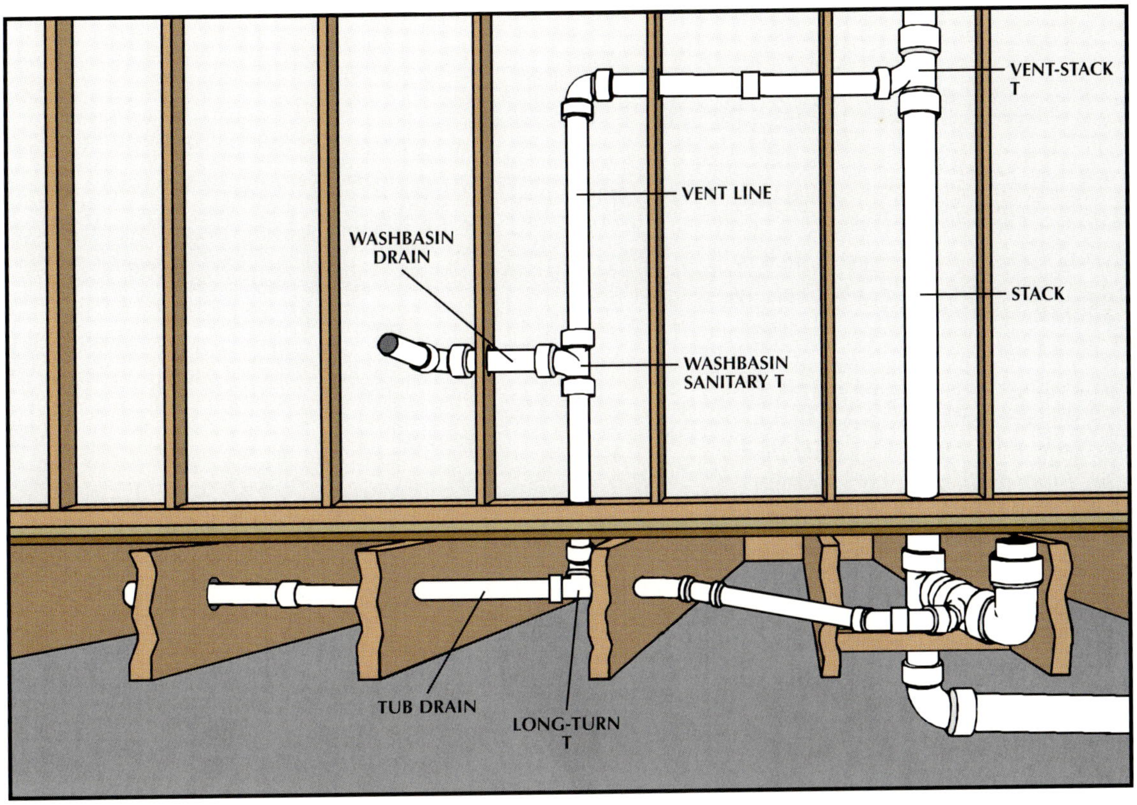

A shared vent line for two fixtures.

If your plumbing code lets you vent two traps with one line, you may be able to simplify your system *(above).*

◆ Extend the stack upward from the top of the below-floor sanitary T to a point at least 6 inches above the overflow drain of the washbasin.

◆ Run pipe vertically from the long-turn T in the shower or tub drainpipe, through the soleplate, to the level of the washbasin drain line. Install the washbasin drain sanitary T atop it.

◆ Complete the vent with a line from this T and through the wall to one installed in the vent stack. Extend the stack through the top plate *(opposite).*

◆ Connect the washbasin drain line to the washbasin sanitary T.

LINKING UP WITH THE MAIN STACK

A connection in the attic.

Before connecting to an existing stack, test the new system *(page 111),* but in the attic rather than on the roof.

◆ After testing, add an elbow to the pipe extending into the upper story.

◆ Install a sanitary T in the existing stack *(page 106),* making the top cut in the stack first. The upper section of the stack may come loose at the roof as you work; if it does, have a helper hold it in while you install the T.

◆ Cut a piece of pipe long enough to join the elbow and the T. Cement it in place.

◆ On the roof, reseal the stack with roofing cement if necessary.

A NEW VENT STACK THROUGH THE ROOF

1. Marking and cutting the hole.
◆ In the attic, drop a plumb line from the roof to the center of the stack vent. Mark the position of the string, and drive a nail into the roof through the mark. (If the stack rises directly under a rafter, alter its course with two 45-degree elbows.)
◆ Climb onto the roof and find the nail. Mark a circle around it slightly larger than the pipe. Use a utility knife to cut away shingles within the circle.
◆ Drill a starter hole inside the circle, then cut around the circumference with a saber saw.

2. Securing the flashing.
◆ To waterproof the exit hole of the stack, install a flashing plate that has a precut hole and a rubber collar.
◆ Lubricate the inside of the collar with petroleum jelly. Slip the edge of the flashing under the shingles above the hole and align the collar over the stack hole. (If any shingle nails get in the way, remove them with a pry bar.)
◆ Lift the shingles that cover the top edge of the flashing and fasten the flashing with roofing nails.
◆ Use roofing cement to caulk exposed nailheads and shingles you may have damaged.

3. Installing the pipe.
◆ Cut a length of stack pipe to reach the distance above the roof that is specified by your code.
◆ Have a helper angle the pipe up through the collar *(right)*. Hold the flashing in place from the outside.
◆ Permanently connect this uppermost segment to the stack pipe below.

TESTING THE NEW DRAINS ALL AT ONCE

1. Installing test caps.

When connecting a PVC soil branch to a cast-iron stack, prepare to test the system by applying cement to the inside of each open pipe. Press a test cap into place while twisting it.

For PVC or copper stacks, check your local plumbing code or with the plumbing inspector for regulations on testing the system.

2. Checking for leaks.

◆ With all drain openings blocked, pour water into the new vent on the roof to fill the drain system.
◆ If you find a leak, punch a small hole in the soil branch test cap with an awl or ice pick and drain the water into a large drum or divert it to a basement floor drain.
◆ Let the system dry overnight, then cut out the leaking joint and replace it.
◆ From the end of the run near the stack, cut off $\frac{1}{2}$ inch of pipe containing the old test cap. Cement a new test cap onto the end of the pipe.
◆ Retest the system.

◆ When the system has been inspected and approved by your local plumbing inspector, drain the water as described above.
◆ Connect the soil branch to the stack after removing its test cap. Use a sleeve and pipe clamp to join PVC to cast iron; a slip coupling and cement for PVC to PVC; and transition fittings for PVC to copper. Do not remove other test caps until you are ready to connect the fixtures.

Getting Water to the Fixtures: The Supply System

You must tap into your home's existing supply lines in order to bring water to your new bathroom. These pipes may be made of galvanized steel, plastic, or copper. Since galvanized steel is no longer in use and plastic is prohibited for supply lines by some local codes, copper is the material of choice.

To join copper pipe to steel, use a dielectric union—a five-piece transition fitting designed to prevent pipe corrosion. Copper can also be linked to plastic pipe with a two-piece adapter; a threaded copper coupling that is soldered to the copper pipe screws into a plastic collar, which has been cemented to the plastic pipe.

Pipe Sizes: Local codes dictate the diameter of a branch supply line, based on the number of fixtures that are attached to it. Most codes require $\frac{1}{2}$-inch pipe for one or two fixtures, $\frac{3}{4}$-inch for three or more.

In the system shown on pages 114 and 115, the cold-water line begins with $\frac{3}{4}$-inch tubing because it feeds three fixtures—toilet, washbasin, and tub. The hot-water line is $\frac{1}{2}$-inch; it supplies only the last two.

Installation: Choose the shortest, straightest route from existing lines to the bathroom, using angled fittings to join lengths of pipe at turns. When measuring and cutting pipe, be sure to include the distance each segment will extend into the fittings at either end. Solder all the joints in the same manner as described for the T fitting that is shown on the opposite page.

Once you reach the bathroom, bring the branch lines up through predrilled holes in the soleplate *(page 97)*, and attach 90-degree joints to extend them horizontally to the fixtures. Pages 114 and 115 show how to do this for the layout that is shown on page 88. Your sequence may vary, depending on where the branch lines enter the bathroom and where you install your fixtures.

CAUTION *Use lead-free solder on copper pipes and a flameproof pad to protect nearby wooden surfaces. Use a striker to light your propane torch to reduce the risk of fire. Do not stand directly under a joint when soldering. Keep a fire extinguisher nearby, and turn off the torch before setting it down.*

TOOLS

- Tube cutter with built-in reamer
- Flux brush
- Wire fitting brush
- Clean cloth
- Striker
- Propane torch
- Hacksaw
- Pipe wrenches
- Plumber's abrasive sandcloth
- Flameproof pad

MATERIALS

- $\frac{1}{2}$- and $\frac{3}{4}$-inch copper pipe
- Fittings (T, L, wing L, coupling)
- Paste flux
- Lead-free solder
- Penetrating oil
- Dielectric unions
- Pipe joint tape
- Test cap

SAFETY TIPS

Wear goggles, gloves, and long sleeves when soldering.

TAPPING INTO COPPER SUPPLY LINES

1. Cutting the supply line.

◆ Close and drain the system *(page 10)*.
◆ Fit the jaws of a tube cutter around the section of pipe where the new line will begin. Turn the knob clockwise until the cutting disk bites into the pipe and the rollers grip the pipe *(right)*.
◆ Rotate the cutter around the pipe, tightening the knob as necessary until the pipe is severed. For $\frac{3}{4}$-inch pipe, cut the pipe again $1\frac{1}{2}$ inches away from the first cut to accommodate a T fitting (for $\frac{1}{2}$-inch pipe, 1 inch away).
◆ Remove any burrs from the cut ends with the cutter's built-in reamer.

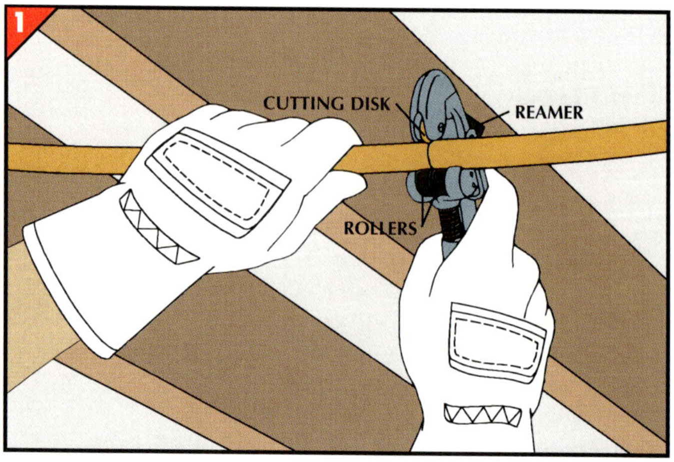

2. Installing a T fitting.

◆ Clean the inside ends of the T with a wire fitting brush. Then clean the last $\frac{3}{4}$ inch of the outside surface of the cut pipe with plumber's abrasive sandcloth until it is uniformly shiny. Do not touch this area, as oil from your hands can interfere with the bond of the solder.

◆ Brush a thin, even coat of flux on the cleaned area and fit the T over both ends of cut pipe *(right)*.

◆ Proceed immediately to Step 3, before the flux dries.

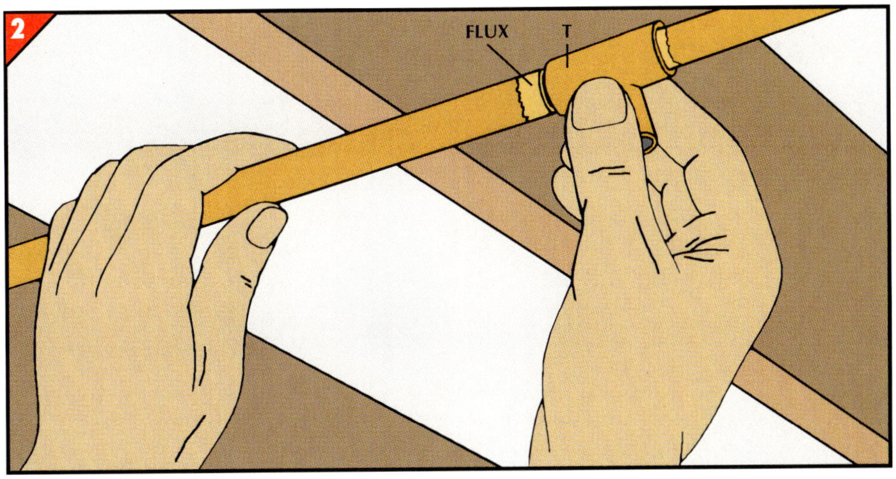

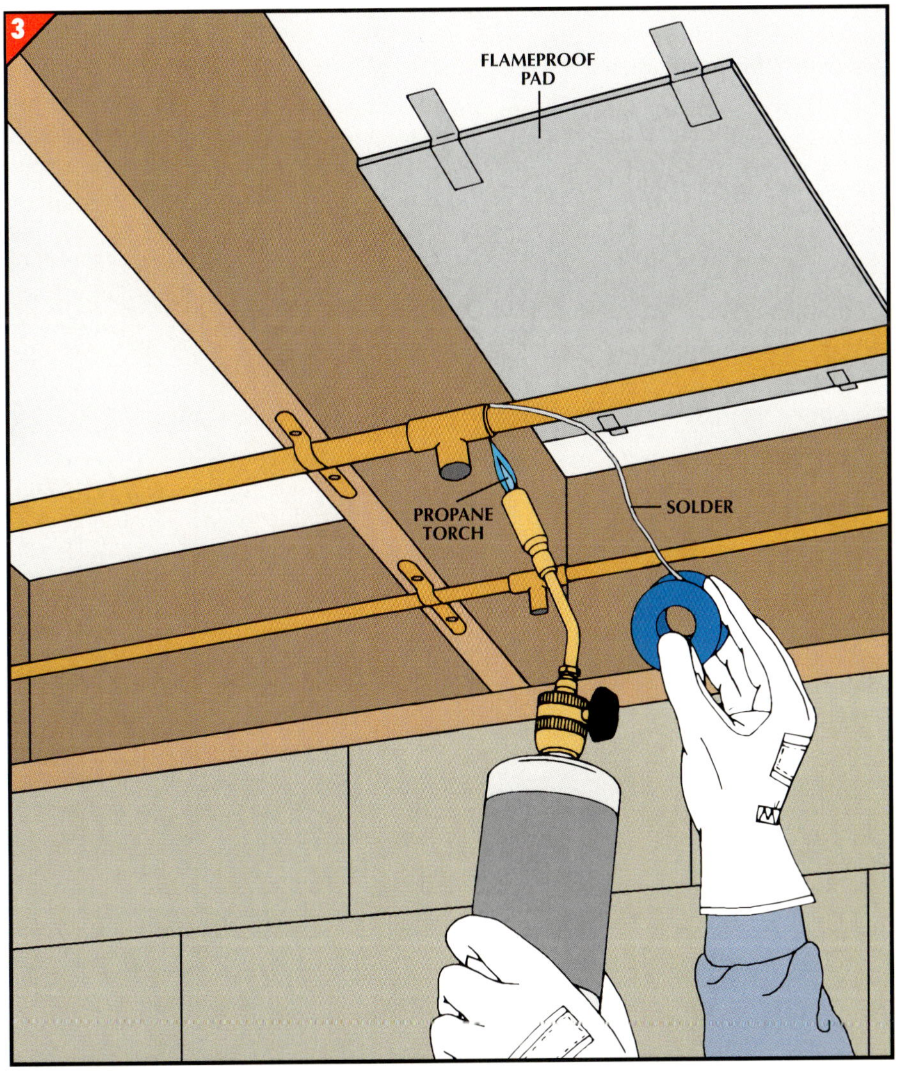

3. Soldering a T fitting.

◆ Light a propane torch with a striker and hold it with the tip of the flame touching the underside of the joint between the T and the pipe until the flux starts to bubble.

◆ Hold the tip of the solder against the top of the joint *(right)*. When the solder starts to melt, remove the torch. The solder will flow into the joint and seal the connection; examine it closely to make sure that the solder has filled the entire circumference of the joint. If there are gaps in the solder, reheat the joint and apply more.

◆ Repeat the process for the other joint. Remove excess flux and solder with a wet cloth after about 5 minutes.

DEALING WITH GALVANIZED STEEL WATER PIPES

1. Cutting and removing the pipe.

◆ Close and drain the system *(page 10)*.

◆ With a hacksaw, remove a 2-inch section of steel pipe between two joints.

◆ Unscrew the resulting pipe stubs from the nearest joint collars by fitting pipe wrenches to the collar and stub as shown above. Holding the collar stationary with one wrench, turn the other to remove the stub. If the joint is corroded, squirt penetrating oil on it.

◆ Next, unscrew each collar with one wrench while holding the pipe stationary with the other.

2. Attaching dielectric unions.

To join steel and copper pipe, use a dielectric union, which consists of a steel spigot and a brass shoulder separated by a rubber washer and attached with a nut and collar.

◆ Screw the spigots of two unions onto the ends of the steel pipe, and measure the gap between the spigots.

◆ Solder a copper T between two copper pipes to make an assembly 1 inch shorter than the distance.

◆ Install the copper section by assembling a union on each end as shown above and tightening the ring nuts on the spigots. Use a pipe wrench to keep the steel pipe from turning. Mark the copper pipe at each brass shoulder, then take down the copper section.

◆ Slide a ring nut and plastic collar back to the T; then clean inside a brass shoulder and outside the copper pipe. Apply flux and solder the shoulder at the mark. Repeat at the other end of the pipe.

◆ When the work is cool, wrap the spigot threads with pipe joint tape. Tighten the ring nuts on the spigots.

LINES FOR EVERY FIXTURE

1. The toilet.

◆ Run the $\frac{3}{4}$-inch cold-water line horizontally to the toilet location.

◆ Attach a $\frac{3}{4}$- by $\frac{1}{2}$- by $\frac{1}{2}$-inch reducing T at the rough-in height of the toilet inlet.

◆ Cut a 6-inch length of $\frac{1}{2}$-inch pipe to extend into the bathroom, and solder it to the T. Solder a test cap on the end.

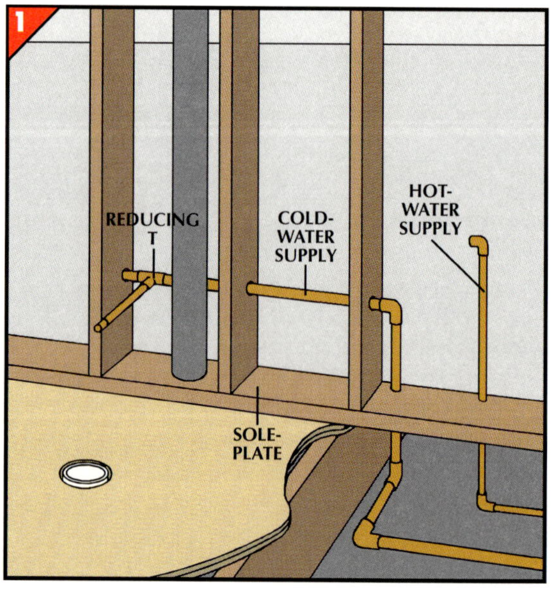

2. The washbasin.

◆ Extend a $\frac{1}{2}$-inch hot-water line below the hot-water rough-in point for the basin and install a $\frac{1}{2}$-inch T.

◆ Install a $\frac{1}{2}$-inch cold-water supply line from the toilet T under the cold-water rough-in point of the washbasin.

◆ Attach a T to the cold-water line at 45 degrees and add enough $\frac{1}{2}$-inch pipe to clear the hot-water line by 4 to 6 inches, then attach a 45-degree $\frac{1}{2}$-inch elbow—or L—so that it is pointing up.

◆ Fit the hot-water T and the cold-water L with $\frac{1}{2}$-inch vertical pipes—called risers—that extend to the height of the fixture. Attach a 90-degree L to each riser, then add a 6-inch length of pipe to each of them.

◆ Seal the ends with test caps.

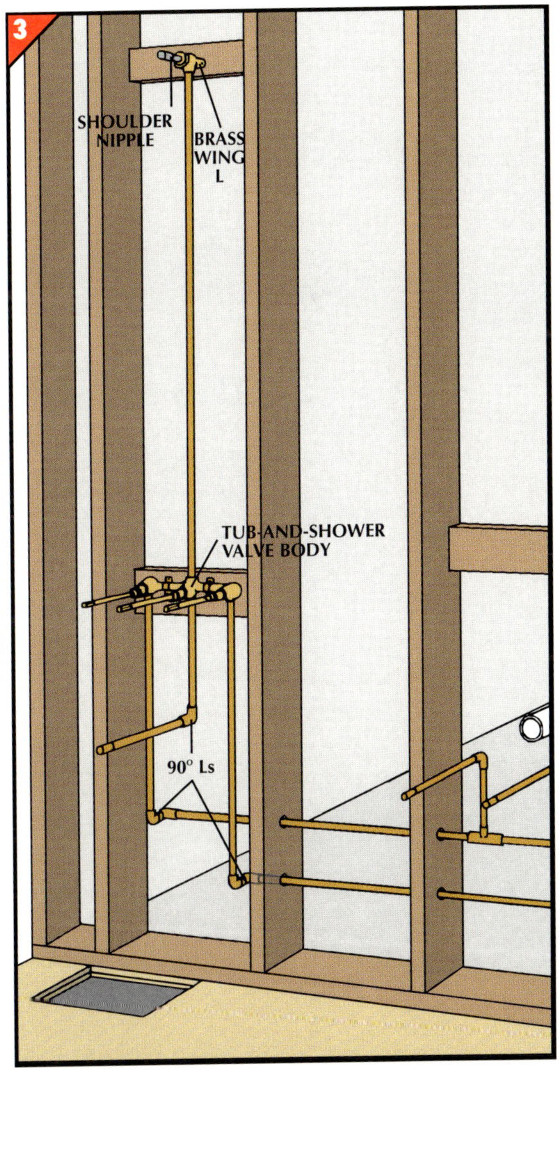

3. The tub and shower.

◆ With pipe clamps, secure a tub-and-shower valve body to the support installed earlier *(page 101)*. Then screw the three valve stems into the valve body.

◆ Run $\frac{1}{2}$-inch hot- and cold-water supply lines horizontally through the studs and up to the valve body, using 90-degree Ls.

◆ Run a $\frac{1}{2}$-inch pipe from the shower outlet of the valve body up to the height of the showerhead. Solder a $\frac{1}{2}$-inch brass wing L to the top of the pipe and screw the sides, or wings, to the wood support. Screw a $\frac{1}{2}$-inch capped shoulder nipple into the threaded opening of the wing L.

◆ Install $\frac{1}{2}$-inch pipe from the tub-filler outlet of the valve body to the level of the tub filler. Add an L and a 6-inch-long piece of pipe and seal with a test cap.

◆ Test the entire supply system by turning on the water and checking carefully for leaks. Wait at least 24 hours before concealing the pipes or mounting fixtures.

Installing a Tub or Shower

The first fixture to install in a new or renovated bathroom is the bulkiest—the tub or shower. As noted on page 86, planning how to get the fixture from outside the house into the bathroom is essential; for example, in many homes a molded tub-and-wall unit can be brought in only through a patio door from which the sliding-glass panels have been removed. To simplify tub and shower installation, do the work before fully enclosing the bathroom.

Three Bath Options: Made of heavy cast iron or of lighter-weight fiberglass, plastic, or steel, a standard 5-foot bathtub like the one shown on these pages remains a popular choice. Instructions begin on page 118 for installing two common alternatives: a tub-and-wall unit *(pages 118-119)*, which offers finished walls and the least chance of leakage, and a shower stall of prefabricated panels *(pages 120-121)*, which is compact and easy to clean.

Framing to Match the Fixture: Tubs and shower pans alike can rest on either the subfloor or the underlayment. Select whichever is convenient; if you are installing new subfloor in the bath area, you do not need to add underlayment, but if you are preparing an old floor, you can leave the underlayment in place.

When you are installing a standard tub, strip the wall beside it to the bare studs and add a horizontal support *(page 102)*. For a tub-and-wall unit or for a shower stall, construct a separate three-wall enclosure against a bathroom wall as shown on pages 118 and 120.

Protecting the Finish: Avoid standing in the new fixture. If you must step inside, pad the bottom with cardboard and blankets.

MATERIALS

- 2-by-4s
- $1\frac{1}{4}$-inch roofing nails
- Tub waste and overflow kit
- Plumber's putty
- PVC drainpipe and trap
- Supply pipe
- Fiberglass insulation with vapor barrier
- Mortar mix
- Construction adhesive
- Shims
- Silicone caulk
- Flameproof pad
- Moisture-resistant wallboard
- Solder
- J bead
- Sealant
- Corner bead
- Shower and bath fittings

TOOLS

- Hammer
- Screwdriver
- Pliers
- Electric drill with $\frac{1}{8}$-inch bit
- Pry bar
- $1\frac{1}{4}$-inch hole saw
- Trowel
- 2-foot level
- Caulking gun

SAFETY TIPS

Wear work gloves, a face mask, and safety goggles when working with fiberglass insulation. Also wear safety goggles when you hammer nails.

EASING A BATHTUB INTO POSITION

1. Placing the tub.

◆ For a cast-iron tub—which can weigh 300 pounds or more—lay 2-by-4 runners on the floor *(left)*. Enlist three helpers to get the tub onto the runners. Two people can push the tub into place. Rest the tub rim on the horizontal support installed earlier *(page 102)*.

Handling a fiberglass, plastic, or steel bathtub requires at least one helper.

◆ For a fiberglass or plastic tub, lay a supporting bed of mortar before setting the fixture in place *(page 119)*.

◆ With all three materials, drive a $1\frac{1}{4}$-inch roofing nail into each stud, overlapping the flange with the nailhead; use a nail set to avoid hitting the tub.

2. Adding waste pipes and overflow pipes.

◆ Place a slip nut and washer on the overflow pipe and the waste pipe of a waste and overflow kit, then loosely connect both pipes to the waste T. Slide the pipes in the T to fit them to the tub's drain and overflow openings. Tighten the slip nuts.

◆ While a helper holds the assembly in place, attach the overflow plate to the lift linkage for the stopper *(page 25)*. With the trip lever in the up position, hold the linkage against the overflow pipe at the center of the flange; adjust the length of the linkage so that the stopper is at the right height to block the waste pipe *(inset)*.

◆ Have your helper place a large rubber washer, supplied with the waste kit, between the overflow pipe flange and the outside of the tub. While the helper holds the pipe in place on the washer, lower the lift linkage into the pipe and set the overflow plate against the inside tub wall. Connect the plate to the overflow pipe flange with screws supplied in the kit.

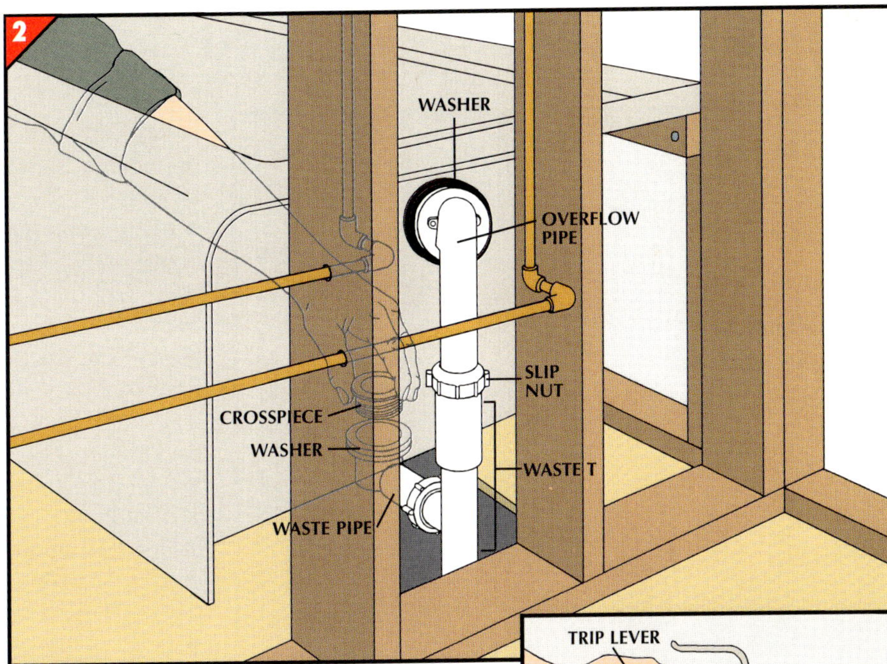

◆ Next, ask your helper to place a washer on the waste pipe flange and then hold the assembly firmly against the underside of the tub at the drain opening. Press plumber's putty under the flange of the crosspiece, and screw the crosspiece into the drainpipe by hand *(above)*.

◆ Tighten the crosspiece by inserting pliers as shown on page 92 and turning clockwise with a pry bar.

◆ Attach the strainer to the crosspiece.

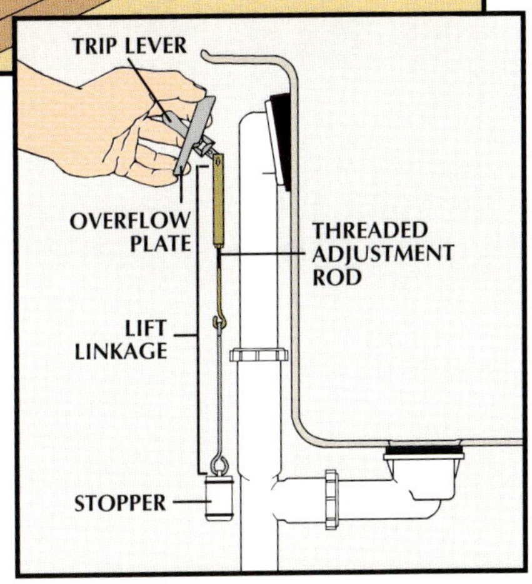

3. Connecting the trap.

◆ Working under the bathroom floor, add a tub trap to the end of the horizontal tub drainpipe *(page 107)*, trimming the pipe so the inlet of the trap is directly beneath the tub waste T. If necessary, use an elbow and a short piece of pipe to center the trap.

◆ Measure and cut a pipe to serve as a tailpiece between the trap and the waste T.

◆ Join the waste T, the pipe, and the trap with slip nuts and washers *(left)*; avoid cementing the trap so it can be removed if necessary for service.

SETTING UP A TUB-AND-WALL UNIT

1. Framing and insulating.
Before you frame for a tub-and-wall unit, check the manufacturer's instructions for special support requirements.

◆ Construct a three-wall enclosure of 2-by-4s against a bathroom wall to fit the tub-and-wall unit; locate the enclosure's plumbing wall so that you will be able to access it from behind after the unit is in place. Build the enclosure to the ceiling, doubling the studs at the end of each side wall. Provide for nailing surfaces in both the side wall and back wall where they meet. If the unit has a grab bar, add 2-by-4 backing for it.

◆ Frame for the tub's drainpipe and supply pipes *(pages 101-102),* then run the pipes *(pages 107 and 115).* After testing the supply pipes, desolder and remove the tub spout pipe stub. Wait to install it, as well as the shower arm and faucet stems, until the unit is in place.

◆ To muffle the drum of shower water on the unit's walls, staple fiberglass insulation between the studs with the vapor barrier (covered side) in *(left).* Do not insulate the stud space containing the supply lines.

2. Measuring for openings.

◆ Dry fit the tub-and-wall unit into the enclosure, and mark the back with locations for the shower, spout, and faucets. Lift the unit out and transfer the marks to the inner face by drilling a $\frac{1}{8}$-inch hole at each one; have a helper press a block of wood against the inside of the unit to keep the fiberglass from cracking as you drill.

◆ Without standing in the tub, drill $1\frac{1}{4}$-inch holes through the inner face with a hole saw, using the smaller holes as guides *(left).*

3. Setting the tub-and-wall unit.

◆ To support the bottom of the tub, spread a bed of mortar, mixed to the consistency of damp sand, about $1\frac{1}{2}$ inch deep *(right)*.

◆ If the unit includes a grab bar, apply construction adhesive to the back of the unit behind the bar before setting the unit in place.

◆ Tilt the tub-and-wall unit and push it into the enclosure *(inset)*, then lower it onto the mortar. If the unit sits too high, quickly remove it and adjust the mortar bed.

◆ Add the waste pipe, overflow pipe, and trap as for a standard tub *(page 117)*, then attach the shower arm and showerhead and faucet stems and handles *(pages 24-25)*. Working behind the unit with a flameproof pad, solder the stub for the tub spout, then attach the spout.

4. Nailing and finishing.

◆ Shim between studs and the flanges on the top and sides to fill any gaps.

◆ Fasten the tub-and-wall unit to the studs with $1\frac{1}{4}$-inch roofing nails driven through predrilled holes in the flanges; drill additional nail holes if necessary. While hammering, use a shield of cardboard or thin plywood to protect adjacent fiberglass surfaces *(far left)*.

◆ Finish the walls above and beside the tub-and-wall unit with wallboard that is moisture resistant. Before installing each wallboard piece, push a length of J bead onto the edge bordering the unit, mitering the metal channel to a 45-degree angle at corners.

◆ Lay a bead of sealant along the inside corner of the flange. Set the wallboard J bead in place, into the sealant, and screw the wallboard to the studs.

◆ Cover other exposed studs with moisture-resistant wallboard, finishing corners with metal corner bead *(near left)*. Hide seams with wallboard tape and joint compound *(page 95)*.

ASSEMBLING A SHOWER STALL

1. Marking for the shower pan.

◆ To allow for the back wall of the shower-stall enclosure, place a length of 2-by-4 against the wall in the planned shower location.

◆ Turn the shower floor, or pan, upside down and set it against the 2-by-4 spacer. With a pencil, outline the pan on the floor *(left)*.

◆ Stand a short length of pipe that is 2 inches in diameter in the drain hole. Steady the pipe as a helper lifts the pan and sets it aside, then use the pipe as a guide to draw a circle on the floor showing where the shower drain will go.

2. Installing the shower pan.

◆ Frame and insulate a three-sided shower enclosure as for a tub-and-wall unit *(page 118)*, establishing the side walls $\frac{1}{16}$ inch outside the penciled outline of the pan.

◆ Add supports for a showerhead and faucets *(page 101)*. Draw a large X through the planned center of the drain, then cut a 5-inch-square hole around that point, leaving the ends of the X as reference. Run supply pipes and drainpipes *(pages 107 and 115)*, leaving the shower arm and faucet stems until after the panels are in place. For a shower, the trap may be located either under the pan drain or at the end of a drainpipe leading to a wall beside the enclosure.

◆ Some shower pans—but not all—are meant to be supported on a mortar bed. Check the manufacturer's instructions and lay the mortar *(page 119)* if it is called for.

◆ Set the shower pan securely on the floor inside the enclosure, and level it with shims if necessary *(above)*.

◆ Fasten the shower pan flanges to the enclosure studs with roofing nails.

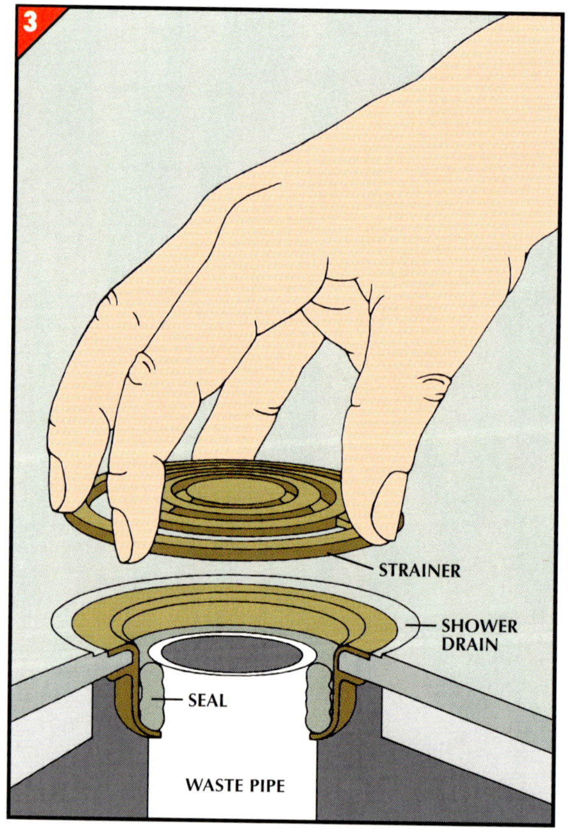

3. Connecting the drain.

Shower pans may be connected to a drainpipe by any of several systems. In the example shown here, a rubber, doughnut-shaped seal from the shower kit fits tightly between the pan's drain hardware and the drainpipe. After pressing the seal in place, screw on the strainer *(above)*.

4. Cutting holes for plumbing.

◆ Dry fit the side panel that will house the plumbing connections, seating it on the pan flange below. Mark the panel from behind with the positions of the faucet and shower arm connections as with a tub-and-wall unit *(page 118)* if access permits. Otherwise, measure the location of each pipe from the end stud and transfer those measurements to the panel.

◆ With a $1\frac{1}{4}$-inch hole saw, cut openings in the panel for the shower arm and faucet stems *(left)*.

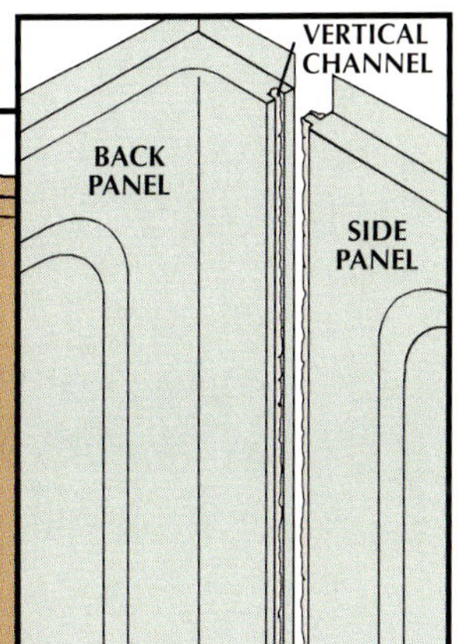

5. Assembling the shower stall.

Since sealant dries quickly, try for a speedy installation. Avoid smearing sealant on shower stall panels; it can be hard to remove.

◆ Run a bead of sealant in the back flange of the shower pan. Set the back panel in the flange, temporarily holding the panel in place with a roofing nail just above its top flange.

◆ Apply sealant to the channel on the right edge of the panel *(left)* and to the right flange of the pan; add sealant to the right side panel's edge.

◆ Put the side panel on the pan flange and interlock the edges of the back and side panels *(inset)*. Lightly anchor the side panel with a nail above the flange.

◆ Install the left panel the same way.

◆ Check that the panels meet snugly and remain square and plumb to the pan; if necessary, shim under the flanges. Then secure all three with nails just outside the flanges, using a punch or nail set to avoid scarring the finish.

◆ Finish the walls above and beside the panels as with a tub-and-wall unit *(page 119)*. Add the shower arm and showerhead, faucet stems and handles, and a shower curtain and rod.

Completing the Room

Depending on the extent of your bathroom project, you may need to add new walls—a step best performed after installing the bathtub and any other large items. An ordinary partition wall resembles the wet wall that is described on pages 97-98, but with one difference. The studs and soleplates and top plates of a partition wall are 2-by-4s rather than 2-by-6s, because no plumbing must be concealed inside the wall.

Installing a door in such a wall is a simple matter of nailing a factory-made, prehung door to the sides and top of a rough doorframe built as part of the partition. Buy the door assembly ahead of time, and use its measurements as starting points for the built-in doorway.

A Sequence of Final Steps: Before hanging the door, you probably need to arrange for a rough-in inspection for each permit. In most areas, these inspections take place after the walls are framed but not closed and the ducts, wiring, and pipes are in place but not connected to any fixtures.

Once these inspections have been completed, close the walls with moisture-resistant wallboard or, where it is needed, cement board *(box, opposite)*. Then paint the ceiling, finish the walls, and put in the finished floor. See Chapter 3 for floor- and wall-surfacing techniques. Hook up the lighting and the appliances, and then complete the job by adding a door, a sink, and—as depicted on pages 124-125—a toilet.

Hanging a Door: A prehung door assembly *(below)* consists of two halves that are pushed into the rough doorframe from opposite sides of the wall. The door itself comes hinged to the inside of one of the sections, with the casing and doorstop already attached to the top and side jambs.

Many doors come with predrilled doorknob holes and bolt channels. To install a doorknob-bolt assembly—using a lever knob *(page 47)* for greater accessibility—drill a hole into the jamb for the bolt; chisel mortises on the door and jamb for the bolt and strike plates.

MATERIALS

- 2-by-4 studs
- Nails
- Wood shims
- Spacing blocks
- Prehung door
- Doorknob assembly

SAFETY TIPS

When hammering, wear safety goggles to protect your eyes from flying debris or loose nails.

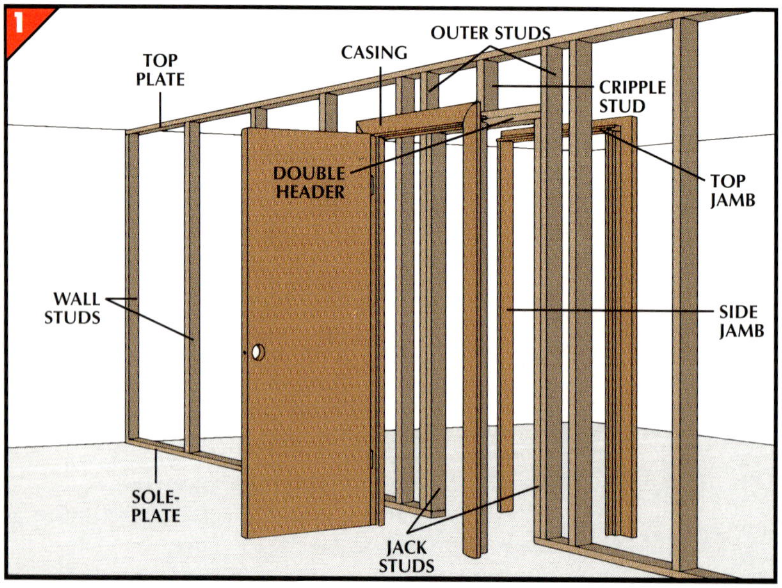

1. Building the wall and doorframe.

Construct a partition wall of 2-by-4s using the methods on pages 97-98, but avoid nailing the soleplate near the area that must later be cut for the doorway.

◆ At the planned door location, install two outer studs, spacing them $3\frac{1}{2}$ inches farther apart than the width of the prehung door's top jamb.

◆ Cut two jack studs $1\frac{1}{4}$ inches shorter than the top of the top jamb. Nail them to the outer studs flush with the bottoms of the studs.

◆ Place two headers, one atop the other, across the tops of the jack studs and nail them in place.

◆ Attach a cripple stud between the double header and the top plate.

◆ Cut away the soleplate between the jack studs where the doorway will be.

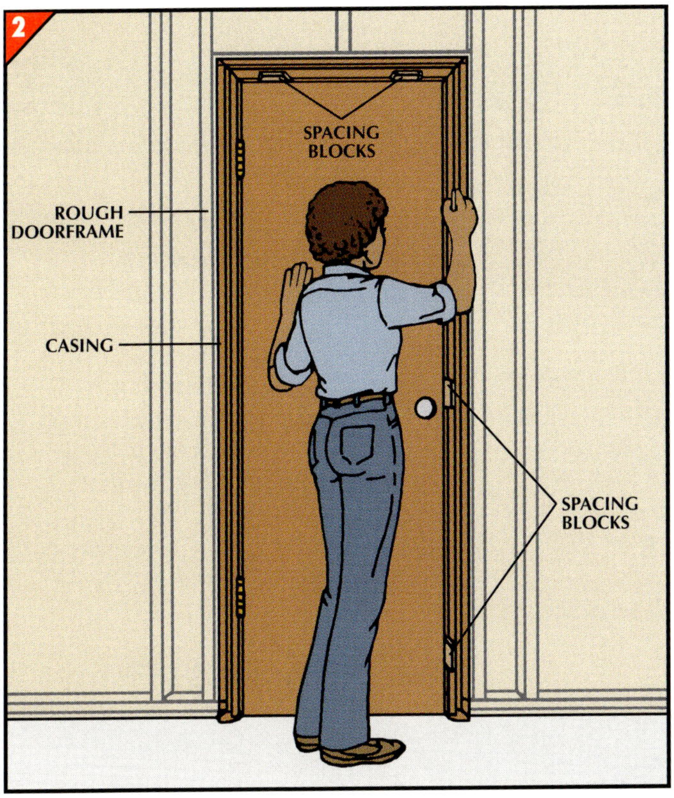

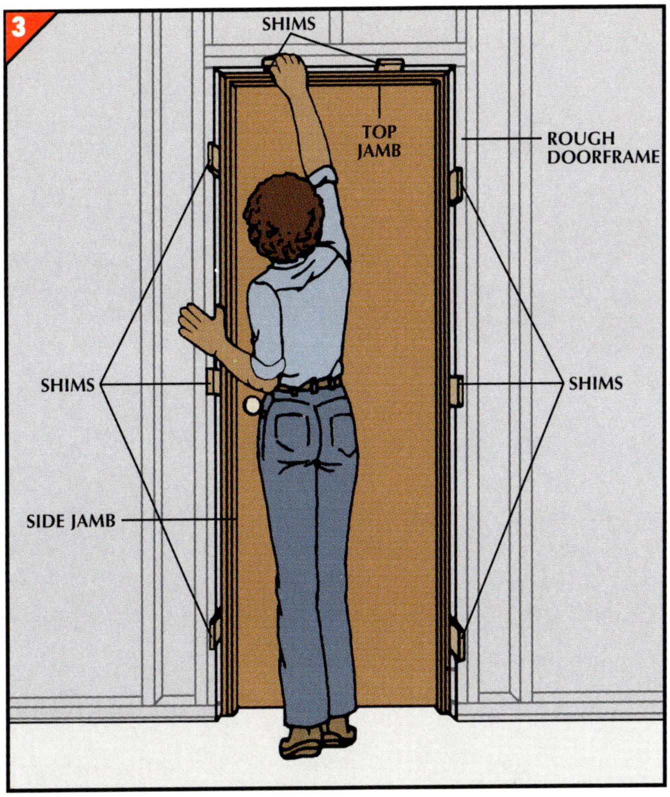

2. Installing the prehung door.

After closing the wall and applying a finished surface, install the prehung door.

◆ Remove the shipping braces holding the door assembly together. Prehung doors are often nailed closed for shipping; free the door before installing the assembly.

◆ Plan to attach the section containing the door first; if the second section will be installed from inside the bathroom, place it there before beginning.

◆ Slide the first section into the opening in the wall.

◆ Insert three $\frac{1}{8}$-inch spacing blocks between the strike side of the door and the side jamb, and two blocks between the top of the door and the top jamb *(above)*.

◆ Nail the casing to the rough doorframe.

◆ Remove the blocks, open the door, and walk through.

3. Completing the job.

◆ From the other side of the wall, insert two $\frac{1}{4}$-inch tapered shims between the top jamb and the rough frame, and three between each side jamb and the frame *(above)*.

◆ Break off the excess portion of each shim. With the door open, secure the shims in place by driving nails into the jambs, through the shims, and into the frame.

◆ Slide the other half of the door assembly into position so that it fits snugly into the first section; the two attach with a hidden tongue-and-groove joint.

◆ Nail the casing to the wall.

◆ Nail the jambs to the frame at 1-foot intervals.

Special Forms of Wallboard for a Bathroom

Ordinary wallboard becomes soft and spongy in a damp setting, so its use should be avoided for bathroom walls. Instead, close the walls with moisture-resistant wallboard, or with cement board for areas you intend to tile.

Moisture-resistant wallboard, called "greenboard" for its green, water-resistant face paper, has a core saturated with asphalt to resist absorption and softening. Cut and install greenboard as you would any wallboard, but do not employ it on ceilings, where it has a tendency to sag; ceilings are the only bathroom surface for which ordinary wallboard is often used.

Cement board, commonly available under the trade name Durock, consists of an aggregated Portland cement held together by fiberglass mesh. To cut it, score through the surface skin of cement and the mesh below with a utility knife, making several passes and substituting new blades as necessary. Then snap the board along the cut, and plane the edge with a rasp. Alternatively, cut cement board with a circular saw and a carbide-tipped blade; wear safety goggles and a dust mask. Make any necessary holes by scoring the desired shape onto the cement board, then smashing out the marked area with a hammer. Cement board should be secured in place with $1\frac{1}{2}$-inch hot-dip galvanized roofing nails or with special screws called wafer-head fasteners. Space the nails or screws no more than 8 inches apart.

Hooking Up a Toilet

Begin toilet hookup by installing a shutoff valve and a plastic toilet flange *(below)* if you moved a toilet drain or added one during a bathroom renovation. Before cementing the flange in place, remove the rag that was stuffed into the drain earlier, then replace the rag until you are ready to set the toilet. If you are installing a new toilet on an old drain, you usually can use the existing flange and valve; start with Step 3 on the facing page.

In either case, the new toilet's dimensions must match the wall-to-drain distance in your bathroom. Furthermore, water-conserving toilets, which have been mandated by federal law since 1994, require the use of a $\frac{3}{8}$-inch supply tube between the shutoff valve and the toilet tank.

To conceal the bolts anchoring the toilet to the floor, there are plastic caps available that snap in place and there are porcelain caps that are secured with putty.

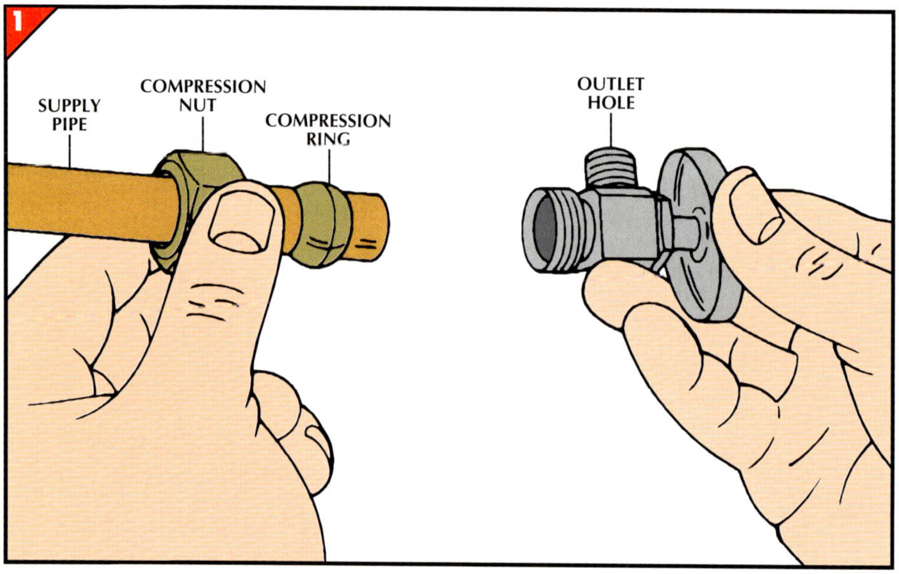

MATERIALS

- Shutoff valve
- Toilet flange
- PVC cement
- Toilet flange screws
- Wax gasket
- Plumber's putty
- Closet bolts and caps
- Toilet supply tube

1. Attaching a shutoff valve.

◆ Cut the supply pipe 2 inches from the wall, then slide an escutcheon over the stub and press it against the wall.
◆ Slip the compression nut and compression ring that came with the valve over the pipe.
◆ Position the valve on the pipe with the outlet hole pointing up. Tighten the nut one turn past finger tight.

2. Seating the flange.

◆ Apply PVC cement to the inside of the flange stem and the outside of the waste pipe. Push the flange onto the pipe so that a line drawn between the bolt slots is perpendicular to the wall, as shown at left, then immediately rotate the flange a quarter-turn, positioning the slots an equal distance from the wall.
◆ Drill through the screw holes into the subfloor (on a tile floor, use a masonry bit). Secure the flange with toilet flange screws.

CAUTION *Work quickly when you are setting a toilet flange; PVC cement dries permanently within 30 seconds.*

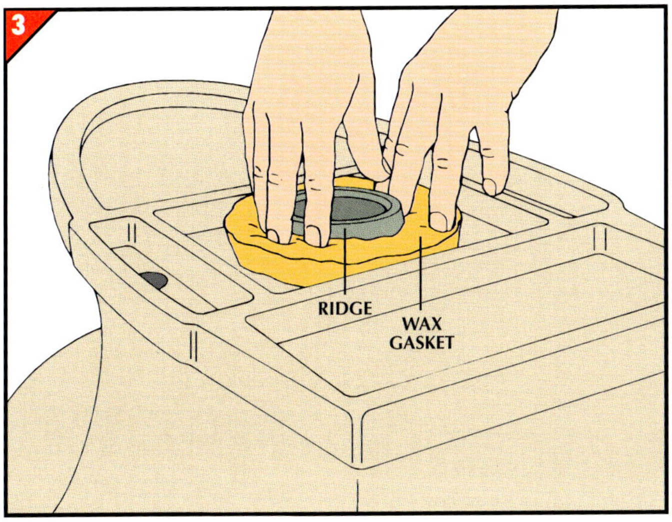

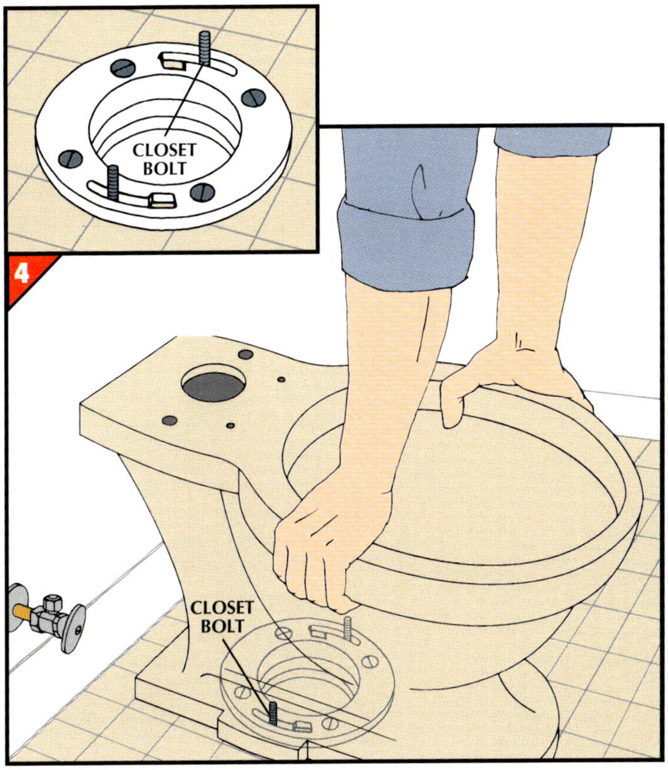

3. Attaching the wax gasket.

◆ Turn the toilet bowl upside down and set it on padding.

◆ Slip a wax gasket over the ridge around the waste hole. With your fingers, press the gasket firmly against the bowl bottom *(above).*

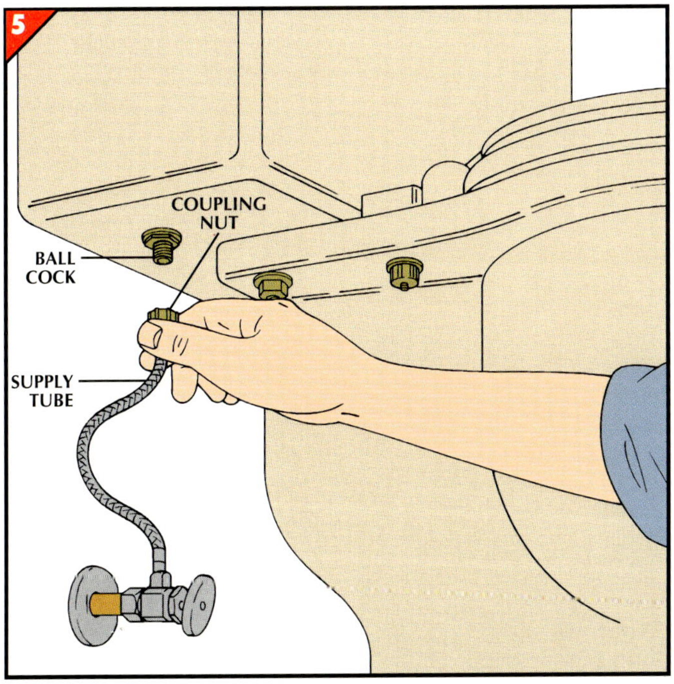

4. Setting the bowl.

◆ Insert a closet bolt head downward into each bolt slot *(inset),* positioning them equidistant from the wall.

◆ Lower the bowl onto the bolts *(above).* Press down firmly on the bowl, rocking it slightly. Do not raise it from the floor; doing so will break the seal between toilet and drain.

◆ Level the bowl from side to side and front to back. If necessary, shim with copper or brass washers without lifting the bowl up.

◆ If using plastic bolt caps, slip a cap base onto each bolt, followed by a metal washer and a nut. Tighten the nuts finger tight, then a quarter-turn more with a wrench. Trim the bolts with a hacksaw as needed and snap the bolt caps in place.

◆ For porcelain caps, secure each bolt with a washer and nut, then attach the caps with putty.

5. Connecting the water supply.

◆ Attach the toilet tank as shown on page 34, and bolt on the seat and cover.

◆ Wrap plumbing-sealant tape onto the threads on the shutoff valve and on the base of the ball cock, which protrudes under the tank.

◆ Screw the compression nut on one end of a toilet supply tube to the outlet hole on the shutoff valve; fasten the coupling nut on the other end to the ball cock *(left).*

◆ Open the valve, flush the toilet, and check for leaks. If necessary, tighten the nuts a fraction of a turn at a time until the leaks stop.

INDEX

Time-Life Books is a division of Time Life Inc.

PRESIDENT and CEO: John M. Fahey Jr.

TIME-LIFE BOOKS

MANAGING EDITOR: Roberta Conlan

Director of Design: Michael Hentges
Editorial Production Manager: Ellen Robling
Director of Operations: Eileen Bradley
Director of Photography and Research: John Conrad Weiser
Senior Editors: Russell B. Adams Jr., Janet Cave, Lee Hassig, Robert Somerville, Henry Woodhead
Library: Louise D. Forstall

PRESIDENT: John D. Hall

Vice President, Director of New Product Development: Neil Kagan
Associate Director, New Product Development: Quentin S. McAndrew
Marketing Director: James Gillespie
Vice President, Book Production: Marjann Caldwell
Production Manager: Marlene Zack
Quality Assurance Manager: James King

HOME REPAIR AND IMPROVEMENT

SERIES EDITOR: Lee Hassig
Administrative Editor: Barbara Levitt

Editorial Staff for *Bathrooms*
Senior Art Director: Cynthia Richardson
Art Directors: Kathleen D. Mallow, Barbara Sheppard
Picture Editor: Catherine Chase Tyson
Text Editor: Esther Ferington
Associate Editors/Research-Writing: Denise Dersin, Annette Scarpitta
Technical Art Assistant: Angela Johnson
Senior Copyeditor: Juli Duncan
Copyeditor: Judith Klein
Picture Coordinator: Paige Henke
Editorial Assistant: Amy Crutchfield

Special Contributors: John Drummond (illustration); William Graves, Craig Hower, Eileen Wentland (digital illustration); Susan Butler, George Constable, Brian McGinn, Peter Pocock, Glen B. Ruh, John Sullivan, Karen Sweet, Luba Vangelova, Eric Weissman (text); Mel Ingber (index).

Correspondents: Christine Hinze (London), Christina Lieberman (New York), Maria Vincenza Aloisi (Paris).

PICTURE CREDITS

Cover and Frontispieces: **Cover:** Photograph, Jody Boozel; Art, Tyrone Taylor and Patrick Wilson/Totally Incorporated. **7:** Sheldon Cotler Associates, Inc., and Tyrone Taylor/Totally Incorporated. **37:** Photograph, Jody Boozel; Art, Tyrone Taylor and Patrick Wilson/Totally Incorporated. **61:** Photograph, Courtesy Laufen Tiles; Art, Tyrone Taylor and Patrick Wilson/Totally Incorporated. **83:** Photograph, Jody Boozel, location courtesy Beautiful Baths, Bethesda, Md.; Art, Tyrone Taylor and Patrick Wilson/Totally Incorporated.

Illustrators: James Anderson, Jack Arthur, Terry Atkinson, George Bell, Frederic Bigio, Laszlo Bodrogi, Charles Forsythe, Gerry Gallagher, William J. Hennessy, Elsie J. Hennig, Walter Hilmers Jr., Fred Holz, John James, Al Kettler, Dick Lee, John Martinez, John Massey, Joan McGurren, Eduino J. Pereira, Daniel Rodriguez, Michael Secrist, Tyrone Taylor and Patrick Wilson/Totally Incorporated, Anthony Woolridge.

Photographers: **End papers:** Renée Comet. **11, 21, 28:** Renée Comet. **47:** Renée Comet, prop courtesy Stanley Hardware. **73, 77, 100:** Renée Comet. **102:** Courtesy Porter-Cable Power Tools.

ACKNOWLEDGMENTS

John Bryan, Fairfax Tile Co., Fairfax, Va.; Petro Exis, Gaithersburg, Md.; Hope Herring, Rockville, Md.; Melvin and Ken Keller, Bethesda Plumbing and Heating, Rockville, Md.; Robert L. Kreutzer, Tatro Plumbing Co., Inc., Garden City, Kans.; Jim Kuhnhenn, Silver Spring, Md.; Mary Levine, Tile Promotion Board, Jupiter, Fla.; Ron Lips, Metropolitan Bath and Tile, Wheaton, Md.; Bob Marcotte, Stanley Hardware, New Britain, Conn.; Sue McHugh, Silver Spring, Md.; John Owens, Owens Electric, Inc., Springfield, Va.; Louise Reynolds, Silver Spring, Md.; Michael Sydorko, Crescent Plumbing, Alexandria, Va.; James Teasley, Falls Church Supply, Falls Church, Va.; George W. Thornton, Thornton Plumbing and Maintenance, Alexandria, Va.; J. Paul Trueblood, Falls Church, Va.; Marvin Walker, Falls Church Supply, Falls Church, Va.

Third printing. Printed in U.S.A.
Published simultaneously in Canada.
School and library distribution by Time-Life Education, P.O. Box 85026, Richmond, Virginia 23285-5026.

Library of Congress Cataloging-in-Publication Data
Bathrooms / by the editors of Time-Life Books.
p. cm. — (Home repair and improvement)
Includes index.
ISBN 0-7835-3858-8.
1. Bathrooms—Remodeling—Amateurs' manuals. 2. Plumbing—Maintenance and repair—Amateurs' manuals.
I. Time-Life Books. II. Series.
TH4816.3.B37B5 1994
643'.52—dc20 94-30217